T0301697

SNIPER TRADING

WILEY TRADING

SNIPER TRADING

Essential Short-Term Money-Making
Secrets for Trading Stocks, Options, and Futures

George Angell

JOHN WILEY & SONS, INC.

Published by John Wiley & Sons, Inc., New York.
Published simultaneously in Canada.

This publication is designed to provide accurate and authoritative information in regard to the subject matter covered. It is sold with the understanding that the publisher is not engaged in rendering professional services. If professional advice or other expert assistance is required, the services of a competent professional person should be sought.

Library of Congress Cataloging-in-Publication Data:

Angell, George.
   Sniper trading : essential short-term money-making secrets for trading stocks, options, and futures / by George Angell.
      p. cm.—(Wiley trading)
   Includes index.
   ISBN 0-471-39422-X (cloth : alk. paper)
   1. Speculation.   2. Stocks.   3. Investments.   I. Title.   II. Series.

HG6041 .A54 2002
332.63'228—dc21   2001045395

Transferred to Digital Printing in 2007

10 9 8 7 6 5 4 3

Also by George Angell

Winning in the Futures Market
Agricultural Options
West of Wall Street
Profitable Day-Trading with Precision
Sure-thing Options Trading
How to Triple Your Money Every Year with Stock Index Futures
Real-Time Proven Commodity Spreads
Inside the Day-Trading Game

To Joel Harris

Contents

Acknowledgments

This book was based on the almost thirty years of experience I've had trading the futures, options, and stock markets. Over the course of those years, I've had the opportunity to meet many fine people who have taught me important lessons. I am especially indebted to the loyal readers of my previous eight books who kept asking for more.

I would like to thank Pamela van Giessen, my editor at John Wiley & Sons, who was patient when circumstances might have dictated another approach. Pam saw the potential in this book when just a few thousand words were on paper. My friend Joel Harris, to whom this book is dedicated, also deserves more than a word of thanks. Joel was one of those people who became a shining star in my life both for his unremitting generosity and for his boundless knowledge of the futures business which he so willingly shared with me. Joel was a member of the Chicago Mercantile Exchange back when it was still known as an eggs and butter exchange. He knew all the players on LaSalle Street and he wasn't above calling in a favor for a friend. One time the president of a major brokerage firm called me up, shouting; he had mistakenly targeted me as posing a liability for his firm. I immediately called Joel. The next day, the offender called back and apologized. We had many enjoyable dinners over big steaks and wine. Joel never let me pick up the check. He was absolutely crazy about his family and spoke of them often. I will miss him.

I would also like to thank Duane Davis, who did all the research for the statistics and systems that are included here. Without Duane, I never would have learned why selling on Thursday proved such a good idea. In addition, I would like to include the following people whose presence exists in these pages: Clarkson Jones, Joe Strickland, Peter McKay, John Deeb, John Parce, Greg Protano, Todd Axelrod, Bill Sobolewski, and Tom and Sandy Melchior. All of these people have made my life infinitely richer.

Lastly, I would like to thank Brad Janssen of CQG, Inc. in Glenwood Springs, Colorado, and Bill Cruz of Omega Research, Inc. in Miami, Florida. Both of these gentlemen have provided me with an excellent software program that truly brings the market alive. I highly recommend their products to anyone wanting to get into the trading game.

Preface

The Fastest Game in Town

Learning to trade is an arduous task. A skill that few possess naturally, but one that definitely can be taught and learned, trading is the high-wire act of the investment world. It is a world of excitement and wonder, but also one of tragic consequences if one slips and falls. Perhaps this is an apt metaphor, since the successful trader must possess a balance of courage and discipline while rigorously analyzing rapidly changing events. It is the ultimate left- and right-brained activity. On the one hand, it helps to be a dreamer and poet; on the other, you need the analytical brain of a NASA scientist. It also helps to be able to enjoy risking large sums of money on uncertain outcomes—and not worrying when the results are not satisfactory. For its successful practitioners, trading is the ultimate liberating experience. After all, the happiest people are those who have found a way to do what they love and get paid for it.

Think of the conventional wisdom that prevails in today's workplace. Wednesday is "hump" day, with only two workdays remaining until the weekend, presumably when you can start having fun and enjoy your life. "Take This Job and Shove It" did not become a popular song by accident. Most people don't enjoy working for a living. For the trader, though, all this angst is turned on its head. He actually enjoys looking forward to Monday morning when he can again match wits with the market—and, in the process, get paid handsomely for his efforts. If anything, it might be the long holiday weekend when he finds himself out of sorts. When you are trading, the time flies and your mind is engaged. There is nothing boring about mapping out a winning market strategy and putting it into action. Learn to trade and you won't feel like going back to your old job anymore. And it is not just the money. It is the freedom to do what you like.

Chances are, if you are very lucky, you have already discovered the joys of making a living on your own terms. Perhaps you have already started trading and you are looking for a few good rules or strategies to improve your success. You might be a successful entrepreneur, a self-made man or woman who is looking for another world to conquer. No matter what your background, you will need all your talents to master this challenging investment strategy. This is no substitute for immersing yourself in this high-stress, high-reward activity. Trading demands a lot, but it is immediately gratifying. There is no better feeling than exiting a trade having executed your game plan with precision. There are even ways to fine-tune your trading to the point where you know exactly where the market will go and when it will get there—to the very minute! I call this "time and price" trading, and it is immensely gratifying to see the market behave in an understandable fashion. I use the word "understandable" with caution since so much that occurs in the market seems random and nonsensical. I won't deny that a steady diet of bewilderment challenges every new trader. But after awhile, one learns to embrace the uncertainty, which is in itself a liberating experience. To win, we need to learn to let go. That's when the money really starts to pile up.

So many would-be traders fail because they simply don't know what they are doing. Despite the abundance of commentators, pundits, and gurus, there is comparatively little good information about how to trade successfully. But why should learning to trade be any easier than learning to become a good chef, or fly a plane, or become a police officer? You have to lay the groundwork. You have to understand the basics. Once you've mastered the basics, you have to learn what works. Some of the concepts are easy. Some are more difficult, but they can be learned.

Traders are made, not born. While there are some who have an intuitive gift for this challenging activity, most learn the old-fashioned way—through hard work. Trading offers unlimited potential. To tap that potential, you have to uncover your own hidden abilities and sharpen your senses. A good trader needs to understand what is going on; this has nothing to do with following tips, guessing, watching CNBC, or indulging one's opinions. Hopefully, this book will show you how to become a better trader. Drawing on extensive research, I've tried to introduce the most important concepts—the essential elements—from the opening bell when the uncertainty is often the highest, but the profit opportunities the best, to the closing bell when the market is being set up for tomorrow's session. There is a rhyme and reason for everything that happens in the market. The sooner you gain an appreciation for this interconnectedness of events, the sooner you will be on the road to profits.

The material presented here is based on exhaustive research. This is not one man's opinion, but proven techniques that should help you discover an exhilarating new way to trade. These step-by-step strategies are designed to help you overcome the inevitable pitfalls and successfully master the learning curve.

When I first got started in the market, some 28 years ago, there were no books available on trading. Then, as now, a neophyte trader's primary training ground was the proverbial school of hard knocks. And who hasn't paid a steep price for matriculating in that particular institution?

As the years passed, and my tuition costs rose, my fascination with the markets grew. Then, in the early 1980s, I met Duane Davis, who was to become my researcher and programmer. Duane's full-time specialty was the burgeoning futures markets. I asked him if he would test some of my ideas and tell me whether they worked. He agreed, and we established a long-term relationship that exists to this day. My goal was to create methodologies that would stand the test of time. I explained that I wanted to find short-term strategies that would work under a variety of conditions: in bull markets and bear markets and markets that traded sideways. I wanted this information for my own use. But I realized I had no problem sharing the information. After all, experience has taught me, bread cast upon the waters comes back a thousandfold.

Years later, we hit upon the notion of "Trade for a Living." What would a person have to know in order to survive as a full-time trader? There were many approaches to winning profits in the markets, short-term trading being just one of them. One could trade stocks or options, futures or options on futures; one could place spreads or seasonal trades; there were many ways to trade. We knew that a lot of investors treated their market activities much like a weekend gambler on a Las Vegas junket. Roll the dice and perhaps make a score. We wanted consistency, though, something you could take to the bank—not a reckless gamble. What are the essentials to making money on a consistent basis? What are the secrets of market professionals? What works?

This was not an assignment I took lightly. My students and readers have depended upon me for good information for a number of years. If we couldn't come up with a breakthrough—namely, new ideas that hadn't been recycled by others before—why go to the trouble? I knew I had a loyal group of followers. I didn't want to let them down. Moreover, as always, I wanted the material to work in my own trading—which is why I got started testing trading systems in the first place! Finding a way to trade for a living that would provide a roadmap to profits for the nonprofessional trader was a tall order.

Despite my lifelong fascination with trading, I knew I had my work cut out for me. Over the years, we had already developed some good information that continued to work, but there were always exceptions. Why, for instance, were we sometimes buying the high of the day late in the afternoon? While I knew some of the formulas we used were good, they occasionally disappointed us. There had to be a way to filter out the less-promising trades. And what about day-of-the-week trading? As an inveterate short-seller, I've always been partial to Thursdays. But I never knew why. Today, I can confidently say that Thursday is the weakest day of the week—if you are in a bull market. If the market goes into a sustained bear market, you'll find that Thursdays are the countertrend days, the days of the week when the market will rally. There is a lot more I can say about day-of-the-week trading . . . but I am getting ahead of myself.

The question is: Can you really learn to trade like a professional?

Clearly, not everyone can. For most, however, the lessons of the professionals who trade these markets everyday can be assimilated. We live in a world of unprecedented opportunity. One way to tap into that opportunity is to successfully play the fastest game in town: trading. This is a guidebook that should help you on that journey.

George Angell
March 2001

Introduction

The Trade That Got Away

I'd been waiting for this one all week. It was a Friday morning in late January. The market had been up for two straight days, and today's open, given the surge in the overnight Globex trading, was almost certain to be higher. I was trading that day with my friend, Tom Melchior, an attorney and CEO of a couple of banks in Colorado. When I got to the office, Tom was already there, excited about the prospects for a strong opening. I grabbed the phone and told them to sell five S&P's market on open.

"This is the third day up," I explained to Tom. "We are almost certain to get a strong break off of a higher opening."

No sooner did the market open, tried to go higher and failed, than I knew I had the right trade. My five-lot was profitable right away, but not by much. It was a question now of simply waiting and seeing if the break would materialize. Tom joined me in the trade, selling a couple of contracts.

It was now 9:37 A.M. East Coast time. The market was dead in the water, unable to rise or fall. I knew the timing was critical and we needed a break for this trade to work—but when? I decided to give the trade another five minutes.

Although the trade was only modestly profitable at that point, I knew the risk; we could get a powerful rally that would leave the short-sellers, me among them, grasping for a seller should I have to bail out at higher prices.

Time was running out.

Then it happened. Prices edged higher. Sensing trouble, I grabbed the phone, hit the speed dialer, and told them to buy back my five contracts at the market. Following my example, Tom covered his positions as well. We were both now out of the market.

Why had I abandoned the position? Too much time had passed and I knew I didn't want to join a crowd of buyers in new high ground. We might be in for a blow-off top. The loss on the position was minimal. But my real question remained: Where is this market going? Everything says down, but, contrary to reason, here we are at the high of the day. What was going on?

The market started to slip. First, back into the consolidation, where it had been churning for the past 15 minutes. Then it broke out the bottom and never looked back. I had frozen at the switch. Watching it plummet, I knew I didn't want to be a hero and try to pick a bottom (and a good thing, too!). I sure wasn't going to sell it in the hole. An hour later that five-lot I'd sold at the top was worth $18,000—and I didn't have it!

I told Tom that the party was over. We'd seen—and missed—the trend of the morning. There was nothing to do now but wait several hours until the afternoon trend emerged, probably well after three o'clock. It was a nice January day. We decided to take a swim and go to lunch.

Returning from lunch, we noticed that the market was choppy. Trading near its lows, a couple of thousand points away from the morning's top where I'd originally sold and subsequently covered my opening position, the market was churning sideways. I regretted what had happened that morning. But that was history. We had to find the late afternoon trend, and rather quickly, since there was less than an hour left in the trading day. The loss of the potential huge gain still bothered me. But I had calmed down enough to put it out of my mind. The one-minute bar chart was showing nothing, just a lot of choppy price action.

"Let's look at the five-minute chart," I suggested, clicking the computer mouse. And then I saw it. "Of course," I said, as if it were the most obvious thing in the world. "It's going higher."

What the five-minute chart revealed was a classic failure swing to the downside. Three attempts to break lower all failed. And the third attempt was met with aggressive buying since the prior lows held. It was already well off the lows. There was no time to waste.

"Buy me three S&P's market!" I yelled into the phone.

By the time they gave me the fill—about 20 seconds later—the market was already higher. About two minutes later they were raiding the stops at the prior afternoon highs. The trade was looking good.

"I'm buying more," I announced, realizing this was the real thing and it was about to surge higher. Tom, who was already long from down below, joined me. The market began to run.

We had them. But there was one critical challenge still facing us: where to get out. Knowing that late-Friday-afternoon rallies can be powerful, I was also well aware that nothing goes up forever. In time, there would be profit-taking and that would drive the market lower—at least temporarily. I wanted to sell into strength, not into a crowd of like-minded sellers who would only butcher themselves in an emotional frenzy to exit.

Doing some quick time and price calculations, I realized we were approximately seven or eight minutes away from a near-term top, if not the actual high for the afternoon. We held on and waited. And cheered.

Tom's enthusiasm was an important clue we were getting near the top. One is always the most bullish right at the top. It is human nature.

"It is almost time to get out," I announced. "Give it another 60 seconds."

The seconds seemed like hours. We both held the phones in our hand. I hit the speed dialer. "Sell 'em market!" I heard myself yell into the phone. We were both out right near the top. The market traded lower on profit-taking after that, churning sideways into the close.

The profit was a few hundred dollars shy of 10,000. Not the $18,000 I'd left on the table in the trade that got away, but an excellent way to end a profitable week.

We booked reservations on the 7:30 P.M. ferry to have dinner out on Sunset Key, a private island off of Key West.

Later that evening, dining out on the sand surrounded by flaming torches, I explained to Tom that we'd encountered a well-known pattern—Friday's late-afternoon rally into the close. We've researched 577 Fridays over the past ten years. And that one we'd just witnessed was stereotypical of the pattern. The early-morning break, the sideways pattern into the lunch hour, the registering of new daily lows in the early afternoon, and, significantly, the late-afternoon rally, in which we had participated so handsomely, and were at that very moment enjoying out there on the tropical night sand; all were part and parcel of the composite pattern we had developed. In other words, it was a percentage play, one that the knowledgeable trader can take to the bank again and again.

A LESSON LEARNED

Looking back, I suppose there's no substitute for stepping up to the plate. You cannot let trading mistakes get you down. But you do need to know when to be cautious and when to be bold. Trying to make a good trade out of a bad one doesn't work. Once the opportunity is missed—as it was so decidedly that morning in January—you must exercise the discipline to wait until the timing is right.

Opportunity is elusive in the futures market. Trying to seize it can be like trying to capture running water. While elusive, it can be omnipotent, a paradox that confounds the average trader. How do you know when the timing is right? How do top traders take risks in the market while others only want certainty? What works? What doesn't? How does one master the learning curve? How does one learn to win—and keep on winning?

The answers to these, and to similar questions, is what this book is about. Certainly, the journey is difficult and the knowledge hard-won. My friend, Joel Harris, who had first become a member of the Chicago Mercantile Exchange back in the early sixties when the exchange was best known for trading eggs and butter, once commented to me that "futures trading is the hardest easy dollar I ever made." Truer words have seldom been spoken. Yet I cannot tell you the number of times that I've received phone calls from someone explaining to me that he or she would really like to make a living as a trader. Wouldn't we all! Everyone wants to grab the brass ring. In the past 24 hours, no less than five people told me they are considering taking up trading. One was the contractor building my new house, one was the husband of the woman selling me kitchen cabinets for the house, another was a security guard working at the residential community where I live, and the other two were people who had read one of my books.

SHORT-TERM TRADING IS NOT FOR EVERYONE

What each of these people had in common was the wish to be a trader. I doubt that all had an appreciation for the difficulties involved. The pitfalls of short-term trading are many. Not everyone understands that there can be a sizable downside risk. No one enjoys losing money. Yet, all traders lose money at some time or another. Managing risk is at the heart of trading.

Not long ago, the television show *60 Minutes* ran an episode on the pitfalls of trading. Somehow these novice traders, who sought to extract money from market professionals, decided they had been set up. Their money was gone and they were looking for someone to sue. Citing the addictive nature of short-term trading, they continued on in their losing ways long after most reasonable people would have called it quits. The sad and simple truth is that most people get what they want from the market.

For those of us who have been around for a while, trading is a bit more like rock climbing. Just learning to grab the first toehold is a major accomplishment. In time, after many starts and stops, one can occasionally look down from the heights, marvel at the sight, and wonder, "How did I get up here?"

There are definite rules that you have to follow to succeed at short-term trading. All the cliches are true. You have to manage risk, exercise discipline, and walk a fine line between fear and greed.

But there are other, less tangible qualities that separate the winners from the losers.

YOU HAVE TO KEEP TRYING

As a former Chicago floor trader, I've had my share of scraps trying to survive in the market. Indeed, looking back at my years on the floor, I'd say this was one of the most valuable experiences that a new trader can have. On the one hand, you had to continually fight your fellow traders lest they attempt to take advantage of you. And, more importantly, the day-to-day market experience was a continuous battle between oneself and one's emotions.

There is an old-boy network that exists to this day down on the floor. Essentially, the veterans, or guys who have been around for a while, aren't receptive to sharing with newcomers—nor, when you think about it, should they be. This means the newcomer, like the outside public trader, isn't going to get the edge—the difference between the bid and the asked—on any trades. The new trader is going to have to give up this advantage. Understandably, the veterans want to buy and sell with their friends, people they trade with day in and day out. They know that these fellow professionals will "card" the trade properly and there will be no mistakes resulting in "out-trades" or mistakes that don't clear properly the next morning. Since a miscarded trade, or out-trade, can result in thousands of dollars in losses, it is entirely understandable that professional floor traders are wary of the guy in the new jacket in the trading pit. Yet there is another side to floor etiquette that every new trader must learn. You have to stand your ground and not let your fellow floor traders intimidate you. This intimidation can take many forms, but once your fellow traders see that you are still standing after six months, your credibility is established, and you are pretty much accepted.

While there is a propensity to blame a host of villains for one's difficulties in the market, the real struggle, at bottom, comes down to you against yourself. As in life, unless you are willing to take responsibility for what happens to you, you are pretty much setting yourself up to become a perpetual victim. In the market, what you do—and don't do—matters. The problem is that the lessons you learn in the market often prove to be so expensive.

My own introduction to futures is probably not unlike the experience of most readers of this book. Some 28 years ago, I'd taken a reckless plunge in the copper futures market. Due to inordinate luck, I purchased the red metal just prior to devaluation. This led to a handsome paper profit and, like most new traders, I figured I could continue my winning streak indefinitely. After I made several hundred percent gains in a week's time by pyramiding my profits, I purchased more contracts at "limit up," the maximum price at which the market could trade that day. Soon the market plummeted lower and "locked limit" against me—meaning there were only sellers, no buyers. If I hadn't been so lucky in getting into the position, I'd still be paying the losses. I had no idea what leveraged risk could do to my modest bankroll. But I'd learned an important lesson: Perhaps I'd better learn what I was doing before risking more money in the market.

At the time, I had little appreciation for what lay ahead. After many abortive starts and stops, however, I began to gain a small toehold on how to win in the futures market. There were definite dos and don'ts that you had to follow to remain solvent. Once again, all the cliches were true. You had to manage risk, exercise discipline, and take reasonable risks—all while walking a fine line between fear and greed. Despite one's tendency to try to romanticize the life of a high-stakes trader, there was nothing romantic about it. It was all hard work, but in time I began to see progress and began to fashion myself as a futures trader. I was on my way.

By the mid-eighties, my long-held fantasy turned into a reality. The first thing they tell you down on the floor is, "If you can just break even after six months down here, you can make a lot of money." This wasn't exactly what

I'd wanted to hear—really, I was hoping to get rich overnight—but it proved to be good advice. I'd survived some rough, day-in and day-out ups and downs and I was still solvent. In my determination to survive, I'd learned some valuable lessons, the most important being that you had to keep trying. Trading was a battle, going to war, hand-to-hand combat. It took everything you had to give—and more.

As a trader, you could be on top of the world one minute and down in the gutter the next. The daily adrenaline rush was incredible. You could fight and get knocked down and then get up and fight some more. The constant emotional turmoil of this kind of life reminded me of a well-known quote from Vince Lombardi: "It is not whether you get knocked down," said Lombardi, "it's whether you get up."

By then, trading was in my blood. Being a trader was like being a cop in the sense that only another trader would understand the constant turmoil and risk. You couldn't really talk about what you did every day with someone who wasn't "in the business." Either they saw only the upside and thought you'd found El Dorado, or they would dwell on the losing side and think you were a fool for throwing away thousands on a risky speculation. You felt that no one who didn't risk that kind of money every day could understand. It wasn't, however, like being a cop in the sense that you knew no one would look out for you. "They hate you if you win," a friend said to me one day about our fellow traders. "And they despise you if you lose."

EMBRACE THE RISK

I'd been paying my tuition in the futures market for a number of years. I had made all the stupid mistakes that traders inevitably make and learned to survive them, though sometimes I wondered how. I had been knocked down many times, really clobbered, but I'd learned to live with the risk. I'd struggled with the mistakes I'd made out of fear, which is, after all, one of the primary motivating factors, along with greed. Examining these mistakes proved an eye-opener. How many times had I given up in the market due to fear? I was simply afraid. Rather than lose money out of fear, I reasoned that I might as well embrace the risk—really go for the brass ring. At least, then I would know that I'd given my best. Wasn't a sense of fearlessness a hallmark of winning trades? What were the qualities that enabled you to win? I had hit upon a trading benchmark: Embrace the risk.

WINNING QUALITIES

Over the next few years I continued to observe the qualities of those who were really able to win at the trading game. First, they were masters of themselves. The reckless cowboys occasionally had good days and won bragging rights around the Chicago pits—the stories were legendary—but their tenure was definitely limited. The attrition rate on the floor was something like one percent per week! Floor traders, especially the hotshots, were always blowing out. The survivors, on the other hand, respected risk. When the market turned, they turned with it.

Years later, one of my brokers was explaining why she wasn't going to let a new client go directly to the floor. The client wanted the right to call the pit directly and place the order. "You let George go to the floor," the client protested in frustration.

"George knows when to get out," she replied.

The old deer-in-the-headlights syndrome had ruined many of her previous clients, and, understandably, she was not about to be responsible for another blowout, especially since any losses on an account that had gone debit would come out of her pocket. Later, I learned that I was her only client who was allowed to call the floor directly. She knew I kept six figures in my account and that I would never do something stupid that would jeopardize that equity.

Second, the traders who win consistently in the market know how to trade. They understand the basic rules and they have the discipline to follow them. I'm sure you know these rules as well—they are all cliches—but do you have the discipline to follow them? Managing the risk is an important one. I'm convinced that if you successfully manage the risk, you can make a lot of money in the futures market. Yet this is the first rule that most novice traders violate. They let small losses grow large. And when they have profits, they are quick to take them on the mistaken notion that you won't go broke taking a profit. Unfortunately, given the leverage in the futures market, you will most certainly go broke taking large losses and small profits. Indeed, this is a virtual prescription for failure.

Whenever someone asks me where I think the market is going, I know that he doesn't understand trading. The truth is, no one "knows" where the market is going. The professional does know, however, how to trade. This knowledgeable insider knows that winning is a percentage game, nothing more. Understanding these percentages is the key to generating profits. For most of us, short-term trading is simply hard work that requires that you master a learning curve. The task is to speed up the process.

I've mentioned that trading is the ultimate right- and left-brained activity. Learning the mechanics is one thing, implementing the trades is another. On the one hand, you might want to start out paper trading. This means there is no money at risk. You simply pretend to trace and track your results. On the other hand, even a modest commitment will heighten your senses and emotions in a way that paper trading never can. Moreover, the degree of that commitment, as measured by the number of contracts, will certainly have an impact on your ability to think straight and trade properly.

There is no substitute for the real thing—real dollars-in-the-market money. You can try to simulate trading, but sooner or later you are going to have to take the plunge into real trading. The challenge is to make this transition as painless as possible.

I knew a fellow who traded S&P's at the Chicago Mercantile Exchange. He wanted to teach his girlfriend to trade, so he purchased an exchange membership for her and she joined him in the pit. He made her take a trade the very first day, explaining that watching the market wasn't going to help her. She made over $100,000 her first year. It wasn't beginner's luck. He was an accomplished trader and he told her when to buy and sell. Nevertheless, his insistence that she trade helped her clear the first obstacle that every new trader encounters—the fear of loss.

When I started trading back in the early seventies, there weren't more than a handful of books on the futures market. Today, there are dozens. Perhaps like many readers of this book, I started out with determination but very little money. Once I arrived in Chicago, with a very modest stake, I realized that, despite whatever courtesies fellow floor traders would extend to you before the open, once the bell rang you were entirely on your own. There was a real sink-or-swim mentality.

In time, I began to earn a modest living trading futures. By taking note of my mistakes and making efforts to correct them, I learned to take reasonable risks. I studied what the winning traders did (the same people won every day without exception), and tried to emulate their behavior. Frankly, what the winners often did was beyond my emotional capabilities at the beginning. But, in time, I realized I had only two options: Trade like an amateur and lose, or learn to trade like a professional and win. I was determined to succeed.

TECHNOLOGY BOOM LEVELS THE PLAYING FIELD

Today, the new trader finds him- or herself in an enviable position vis-à-vis the novice trader just 10 or 15 years ago. With the advent of all the on-line data services and electronic trading, the playing field has been leveled between professional floor traders and novice off-floor traders using a personal computer for quotes and relaying orders. Witness the sharp break in trading seat prices in recent years. This is an important clue that the off-floor trader is no longer at the severe disadvantage that he was several years ago. Indeed, you could even make the case that computer-assisted trading has benefits not accorded to pit traders. For instance, I can often see a divergence, suggesting an important reversal, between S&P futures prices and the slow stochastics running at the bottom of my chart. I can count one-minute bars both in terms of time and price on my screen. My charting program gives me more than 100 indicators I can call up in an instant. Today's technology simply gives the short-term trader an edge she didn't have years ago.

Even still, while undoubtedly helpful, technology is nothing more than a tool—albeit an important one—for today's trader. I am reminded of a student of mine who blamed the lack of multiple monitors for his trading losses. He had *seven* monitors. The bottom line is, the technology cannot save you from yourself if you make classic trading mistakes. Nor, for that matter, is the answer in the technology. The key is not just having the correct indicator, but knowing how to correctly interpret that indicator. This, by the way, is why formulas are so alluring for the novice trader. She thinks the answer is in the numbers, when in fact her personal psychology has much more to do with her success or failure in the market.

Sometimes, you can have everything at your disposal—a fully funded trading account, first-rate computer software, a good clearing firm, even a winning trading system—and still endure losses. This is the time to step back and take a good look at your trading style. How are you contributing to your losses? What mistakes are you making? One way to formulate an intelligent strategy is to emulate those who have succeeded at this challenging game.

LEARN TO BE A SPECIALIST

One observation I've made over the years, which is especially notable on the trading floor, is that everyone who truly succeeds is a specialist. Unlike the novice trader, who may dabble in as many as a dozen different futures contracts, the professional floor trader is identified with just one kind of futures and one specific type of trading. So you may learn that so-and-so is a bean trader or a bond trader or an S&P trader or a lumber or currency trader. But you won't find the professional running from pit to pit to find a trade. Moreover, the professional is identified by his specialty—scalper, short-term trader, spread trader, or whatever. He does the same thing every day. He stands in the same exact spot in the pit every day. He trades with the same people every day. Significantly, he is the ultimate expert within that narrow field that he occupies. Every market has its own rhythm. By doing the same thing every day, the professional floor trader understands that rhythm to a degree that is not discernible to the casual participant.

You'd be surprised what a trading edge this knowledge can give you. This is why I only trade the S&P 500. By doing the same thing every day, I have a grasp on the market which can alert me if something is wrong. Moreover, my specialty is aggressive, short-term trading of the S&P. I know how it traded yesterday and the day before. You can bet every pit trader knows yesterday's highs and lows, not to mention today's intraday highs and lows, essential to knowing where the stops are, as well as the key breakout points. Throw the same people into another market and they won't have a clue. These experts are the same people you are competing against when you enter a market as a newcomer. Do you have any doubt that, given their expertise in a particular market, you are operating at a disadvantage? Would you prefer to fight them with one hand tied behind your back—or with all your resources?

In my "Trade for a Living" seminars, I cover a number of legitimate technical approaches. Yet, I am not asking you to try all of them. Rather, learn to be a specialist and become the best short-term trader or spread trader or seasonal trader you can be. You'd be surprised how many people are shocked—as if I were limiting myself—when they hear I just trade the S&P 500. Over the years, of course, like most traders I've tried trading a lot of markets and a lot of different strategies. Some worked better than others. About ten years ago, I was having some success positioning the currencies during the day. By trading eight-lots, the tick value was $100 a point and I was picking up 10 to 50 points—$1,000 to $5,000—on a fairly consistent basis. But then strange things started to happen. I'd be ahead 10 or 20 points going into the close and it would disappear in an instant. I didn't like what I was experiencing. And I finally gave up on currency trading and began concentrating on the S&P's.

FIND A MENTOR

One of the best ways to learn to become a better trader is to find someone who can offer you guidance and support, a mentor. Over the years, I've been fortunate in that I've had mentors who appeared in my life at just the right moment. Usually they were older men who perhaps saw in me some of the potential they had when they were younger. They would often offer sound advice. I remember asking one of these gentlemen once, "How could I possibly repay you?" He dismissed the offer with a wave of the hand. "I have all the money I'll ever need. You don't owe me a thing." There must have been at least a half dozen of these gentlemen who helped me over the years and I've tried to repay their generosity whenever possible. As luck would have it, one younger version of these mentors materialized at the moment when I was having serious doubts about my ability to make a living trading. Realizing I was struggling, he offered guidance over a cup of coffee one afternoon across the street from the exchange.

"Look," he said to me after a particularly tumultuous day in the pit. "I see you in there buying the highs and selling the lows. You are not going to last long down here doing that." Then he took out a trading card and placed it on the counter. "Here's the only way I can lose," he explained, drawing a volatile market that whipsawed back and forth. It was the classic search-and-destroy day pattern with rising tops and lower bottoms. "Fortunately, this doesn't happen every day. Instead, you usually get some sort of trend off the open—either up or down. If I'm wrong, I double-up and reverse. Even if you lose ten ticks on one, you only need five ticks on the reversal to get even."

"But what about the money?" I asked.

"Don't think about the money," he said. "Just do it."

The first time I had to double-up and reverse, I was terrified. But it worked. After that, we became good friends and I often sought his advice.

"How do you know the direction?" I asked him one day when we were having one of our end-of-day coffee sessions.

"You don't. That's why you see me standing there at the open watching all the confusion. I wait until the market tells me a direction and then I wait for a pullback and load the boat."

"And then—getting out?" I asked.

"If I get a pop or a break," he said, "I take profits. You have to take those profits." He said this as if it were the most natural thing in the world.

QUANTIFYING THE INTUITIVE TRADE

This was especially telling to me since I was earning paper profits only to see them disappear because I was hoping for more. It was only years later that I realized my mentor was doing on an intuitive basis what I'd been able to quantify through my time and price Sniper Trading Program. There was a symmetry in the market and he'd found a way to mine the riches of the market by capitalizing on that symmetry. I see that symmetry every day without exception. Just this afternoon there was a 10-minute, 400-point rally in the S&P's followed by the inevitable pullback. What was to follow? Another 400-point rally—to the exact tick—but this rally took 11 minutes, not 10. The timing required another 60 seconds. But who cares, when you are making money?

By knowing what *should* happen in the market, you have a valuable piece of information if it fails to materialize. You know you have had a failure in time and/or price; this is often the clue you need to spot a market reversal. It takes some training to be able to identify the two legs of a trend developing. But I've been able to teach students of mine within a week's time to pinpoint the key trends with a high degree of accuracy. The problem is, most novice traders don't have the patience to wait for a profitable trade to develop. "You taught me patience," one of my more successful students told me after a week's training. I considered it a high compliment. But I knew there's a lot more the new trader needs to learn before she can truly trade like a professional.

In recent years, we've been able to do lots of research in the markets on what works and what doesn't work. The more you qualify a trade, the greater the number of parameters that a trade meets, the better the likely outcome. We have done studies by isolating days of the week and comparing them with how the market traded on the prior day and the prior five days. The results are encouraging because they identify statistical probabilities that are proven by past results. We've looked, for example, at 577 Mondays in the S&P 500 market and identified the prior-day patterns that suggest higher prices on any given Monday. For years, I've greatly enjoyed trading on Thursdays but never knew the reason why. Now I know. We have conclusive evidence that, over time, Thursday has proven to be the weakest day of the week—and I'm an inveterate short-seller! Today I can demonstrate that what was once just an intuitive feeling is a proven fact. Believe me, this adds confidence to your trading.

STEPPING UP TO THE PLATE

I understand that all the research in the world is meaningless unless you can pick up the phone and put your money at risk. Not everyone is suited to this task; indeed, I suspect most people are not. But when you can successfully combine the two, the analytical researcher and trader of action, you have a winning combination. I can teach you the patterns and formulas, what to look for in the market to help your timing, but you have to supply what W.D. Gann once called *nerve*—the courage to trade. This, I'm afraid, is the hard part. It has been my experience that the best traders can suspend both their fearfulness and their greediness. It is this middle course that inevitably works best.

Part of being able to step up to the plate, to cultivate nerve, is to know that patterns, like human nature, persist. When I first began research on George Douglas Taylor's "Book Method"—what later evolved into the LSS 3-Day Cycle Method (defined later in the Introduction)—I found a unique perspective on the market that is as true today as it was almost 50 years ago when Taylor first released his work. The market, said Taylor, is engineered from within. It is taken down to generate buying among the insiders. Then, as the market inevitably rises, it is engineered higher on the third day up and the smart money sells. Then the process begins all over again.

When I first started applying these principles to the futures market, I was amazed how accurate this premise proved to be: down to go up, up to go down. In the world of pit trading, one observed this engineering again and again. The public would buy all morning and the floor locals would sell to them. Finally, often late in the afternoon, the market would break and the public buying turned to panic selling; the locals bought everything in sight, covering their short positions and earning handsome profits. This struggle between the locals and public traders went on every day, usually to the benefit of the floor traders. Or, at least, to the benefit of some of the more intuitive floor locals who knew enough to jump on a good thing.

I remember one Friday afternoon when we were trading bonds. The locals, who are often edge traders who attempt to buy at the bid and sell at the offer, were engaged in their usual late-day activity—namely, trying to nickel-and-dime the public orders. You have to remember that a substantial number of floor traders make a living scalping the market, simply buying at the bid and selling at the asked price, or offer. They do this routinely whether the market is going up, down, or sideways. Indeed, among the locals it is considered foolish to ever give the edge to a fellow trader and certainly not to the *paper,* or public orders. So imagine my surprise when my friend and mentor started hitting the bids that Friday afternoon.

"Sold! Sold! Sold!" he yelled out.

He hit every bid he could find. The edge traders couldn't believe their good fortune. Here's this hotshot floor trader giving away money. Among the ranks of floor traders, this was unheard of; a local doesn't give an inch to another local. They would rather fight like cats and dogs over every tick. That willingness to jump aboard the move should have been the clue that something big was about to happen. Why was this trader who commanded the respect of the pit suddenly giving up the edge?

The hapless edge buyers soon found out. The market broke like a rock and the panic selling, which was now driven by the scalpers who'd just bought, was causing the market to free-fall.

"What's your bid? What's your bid?" the frenzied sellers yelled at my friend.

With arms folded, he looked at them and smiled. "Ain't got no bid!" he yelled back. "It's going lower!"

The panicked sellers butchered themselves in a bloodbath as the market plummeted.

Later, across the street in the greasy coffee shop, we did a postmortem on the day.

"How did you know," I asked him, "that the market was going lower?" His answer was a revelation. "These edge traders," he said, "think all you have to do is buy the bid and sell the offer and you'll make money. And they'll do that for nineteen out of twenty trading days a month and win. And then you'll have an afternoon like this today when they lose an entire month's trading profits. It is better to have never made the money at all than to lose it on one panic break like we saw today."

Better to have a point of view. Better to understand the market so that you'll see the trends developing. Here was a specialist who understood that you could *fade*—or trade against—the entire pit and be proven correct. Talk about contrary opinion. He knew on an intuitive level what others failed to see. He would judge the market according to his own subjective opinions. There were enough mini-panics each week—perhaps four or five—when the pit got caught unawares and would themselves have to give up the edge, even to the point of sharply driving the market higher or lower, that my friend soon found himself making excellent money. "That's the time," he said, referring to these panic situations, "when you have to load the boat."

Much to my surprise, I was starting to get a sound education on what it took to become a professional trader. Here was a person from a modest background who had found a niche that he was good at and had become an extraordinarily successful trader by recognizing his talents and capitalizing on them. Meanwhile, I was still making stupid mistakes and giving up too easily when the market all too readily relieved me of my trading capital. Indeed, I was still too fixated on the money. I really was undercapitalized and didn't have the funds to lose. Like most new traders, I began my career looking for an easy formula that would enable me to take the trade, place a stop, and hope for the best. Typically, you would earn some paper profits, but then the market would reverse and your stop would be hit—and you'd be demoralized again. Another bad trade. Moreover, I was asking for too much. I wanted to buy at the exact low and sell at the exact high, an almost impossible task. Sometimes, I'd buy the open and only get out at the close. Hours of running ten steps forward only to see the market reverse and run ten steps backward. There had to be some magical formula. Sound familiar?

Fortunately, it didn't take too many months of getting hammered, seeing all sorts of high-flying pit traders crash and burn, before I realized that there is nothing wrong with making steady profits by being focused and patient. I decided that after a period of time, when I was charting my equity. Sure, there were some dramatic rises in the chart when I hit a series of big winners, but inevitably the losing cycle would kick in and I'd be back where I started from. Better to have a steady, albeit less dramatic, growth in the equity than to work for weeks, only to lose it in a couple of careless trades. I couldn't forget the lesson of the scalpers who would profit on nineteen days a month, only to lose it all in one panicked market late on a Friday afternoon.

After taking inventory of my strengths and weaknesses, I decided I wanted to learn to identify trends and jump aboard the trend just long enough to capture the bulk of the move. Experience had taught me that hanging onto a position usually meant giving back a portion or all of my profits. Why not emulate my winning mentor in the pit who seemed to have the knack to jump aboard a move, ride it to its conclusion, and get out? I didn't have to buy the bottom tick, nor did I have to sell it at the high. My only goal was a simple one: I wanted to make money. What's the difference if I buy the high tick of the afternoon if the market is going higher? Or if I sell the low tick when the market is breaking? Embracing these ideas was a liberating experience. I was now free to buy new highs or sell new lows, or even quit trading for the day at ten o'clock in the morning if I'd made good money.

A BREAKTHROUGH

The real breakthrough came after I discovered a way to quantify what can only be adequately described as intuitive trading. The master intuitive trader will tell you she knows before she knows where the market will go. She's the one who buys when the market is still in the consolidation or showing nothing. She understands that the market needs time to develop. She also knows when to exit. Ironically, most traders are most cautious when they should be most bold, and vice versa. When you catch a winner you think the sky's the limit; when the market is about to run, you are scared to death, so you let a good opportunity slip away. Or, worse, you wait for a breakout and take on substantial risk.

I was looking for a way to help me suspend my emotions, and trade based on market probabilities, not what my fears dictated. My market intuition was good, but, like many traders, I had a hard time listening to it. After years of struggling with the problem of uncertainty, I formulated the notion of what I call the "paradoxical event," which changed everything. Now, I could accept—and really expect—the very opposite of the conventional wisdom to come true. At the bottom of what I was striving to understand was that there was some pattern as to why the market behaved at it did. That led to the notion of market symmetry that W. D. Gann had pioneered so many years ago. There was a pattern in the market, and it was right there in front of me.

TIME AND PRICE

This is the way to measure market symmetry. So many minutes, days, weeks up or down and so many points up or down. Rallies are followed by profit-taking market breaks just as declines are followed by bargain-hunting rallies. Once the news is out, the information needs to be processed by the market, resulting in choppy price action. Finally, there is a consolidation or equilibrium in the market. And the rally or break is resumed, often in an identical pattern.

This is the application of math to market patterns. I have such confidence in the notion of time and price that I say you should never take a trade unless you know where it should go—to the tick—and the very minute it should get there! Persistent time and price patterns manifest themselves in the market every day.

The market has its own wisdom. You don't tell it how to behave; it tells you. Fortunately, it announces its intentions for everyone willing to observe and listen, but it takes skill to learn to read the patterns and make intelligent assumptions about market direction. Because of the symmetrical nature of markets, a market that cannot rise will fall—usually in keeping with the symmetry already evident in the price pattern. That's why you often experience a V-pattern, down and up, or the inverted V-pattern, up and down. It is not an accident that the pattern often exhausts itself right where it started.

I was excited by the prospect of having a numerical answer to the age-old question: Where will the market go? What's more, by factoring in the notion of time as well, you can answer the timing question also: When will it get there? To this I added an approximation of risk: Where can the market trade and still be viable? Or, put another way, where do you have to bail out? In short, I'm telling myself all the key answers I need to know: Where is it going? When is it going to get there? And where am I in trouble? To this I would add the following valuable piece of advice. If the symmetry fails, it signals a market reversal. Learning to calculate these figures gave me a whole new way of evaluating the market.

Never again would I have to guess about market direction. Sure, there are always going to be misleading breakouts and false moves. Witness the notorious false breakouts, or the classic stop-running patterns. Now I could say that based on the evidence before me the market should, with a high degree of probability, trade at level A or level B within X minutes.

When I started using time and price, I was impressed with the accuracy of a trading strategy that could pinpoint a top or bottom within a tick or two, and often to the exact minute. But I soon found out that time and price trading is most effective when you've found the genuine trends of the day, usually one in the morning and one in the afternoon, not one of the many gyrating crosscurrents that make up the bulk of the price action. You have to be selective and patient if you are truly going to capitalize on this method of trading. Moreover, I soon learned that the winning strategist must monitor the market closely. By doing so, you can monitor any price failures and be ready to reverse your position. It is important to know what *should* happen in the market. When a price pattern doesn't materialize as expected, you can often profit by fading trading against the move. This is only possible, of course, if you know what to expect and can spot a failure. Typically, a good trend is easy to see. The sheer magnitude of the move speaks volumes about the seriousness of the market's willingness to rise or decline. When I spot such a move, I know from experience that I'm looking at an 80-percent or better chance of winning. There is no more reliable trade.

As I came to understand the nuances of time and price trading, I felt as if I were in possession of a great secret. Understandably, most traders are skeptical of trading "systems," especially totally mechanical ones that don't allow for flexibility. But here was something that, given a modicum of common sense, provided a virtual roadmap to profits. I realized that this type of trading was not for everyone, so I expected some resistance to my ideas. I was shocked to learn that so many would dismiss the ideas simply because there was some substantial work involved. "How do you know they are running the stops?" a questioner challenged me at a seminar in Las Vegas. "Why do you have to spend so much time watching the market?" another asked. "I don't have a computer," said yet another. All were excuses for my failure to provide easy answers. Meanwhile, I was able to parlay my ideas into significant winning streaks with very low risk.

Using time and price, I knew I could make a lot of money if I could find the two major daily trends. Having identified a single leg—there are two legs in each trend—I knew, with a few simple calculations, I could identify the target exit price, the pullback stop-loss price, and the probable time the trend would take to develop. In short, everything I needed to know to capture that leg. But there was still another piece of the trading puzzle I wanted to solve. We'll turn to that next.

DAILY PATTERNS

Some of my most successful trades have come from anticipating the day's trend. For years, I've loved trading on Thursdays. There was something about Thursdays that seemed to yield significant profits for me. I knew this on a deep, intuitive level. But only in recent years have I gained the insight into the reason why my trading did so well on this day of the week as opposed to others. The simple reason is that I like to sell. And Thursdays, put simply, are the best day of the week to sell. I say this unequivocally because we have done the research to demonstrate the validity of this assertion. If you have just one day of the week to sell, sell on Thursday—*if* the market has been rising. In a bear market, Thursday will be the countertrend day, or rising day.

From a bullish perspective, you have to give the nod to Monday. Here, again, the statistics, based on more than 13 years of research, prove that Monday is the day to buy the stock market or S&P 500 stock index futures. Of course, it is not quite as easy as saying that you always buy on Monday or sell on Thursday. That would be too simplistic. But you want to learn to explore the different days of the week in terms of market trends. This is especially true when viewed through a filter of other vital indicators such as the previous day's range, the recent 5-day strength, and the previous day's strength. These can generate some pretty sophisticated analyses. But it is precisely this type of examination that can give you a valuable edge in the market.

In *Profitable Day-Trading with Precision* I mention the LSS 3-day Cycle Method, which is based on a cycle that repeats in the market. But I didn't look at the cycle in terms of any daily pattern. In my new "Trade for a Living" seminar and video course, I cover not just a daily trend, but actual patterns—up in the morning, say, and down in the afternoon—which are characteristic of certain days. Again, you need to observe a given day through the prism of accompaying indicators to gain a valuable handle on how that day's trend is likely to be played out. Students who devote themselves to this task are likely to be repaid handsomely in the market for their diligence.

To research markets that are far apart in time, you need to translate price patterns into percentages, so as to make them equivalent. This was just one challenge we had to overcome. When you compare low- and high-volatility markets, you cannot readily relate the absolute price numbers with one another and come up with anything valuable. During the summer of 1987, I remember being able to buy a steady-to-lower open, day after day, and reap profits. If adversity set in, one simply had to buy more. The market went up almost every day that summer. Today, 13 years later, while the theory may still hold, the volatility makes this tactic extremely dangerous. How do you know the market won't swing 1,000 points prior to staging a rally? Nevertheless, the so-called composite price charts we have created provide an invaluable insight into how the market *should* trade on any given day—provided, of course, one is matching up other vital indicators.

What are these indicators? Well, there are a bunch of them. I use a pivot breakout buy and sell number that tells me whether the market is at a key support or resistance point. These buy and sell numbers generally have a wide following in the trading community. As a result, they signal key breakout points in the market.

I use a 5-day average-range number to tell me whether the current range—and my expectations—are on target. Sure, you will occasionally have a blowout day that will put percentage players to shame. But I am looking to play the percentages here. I use a 5-day oscillator to measure the degree to which the market may be overbought or oversold. You don't want to buy a market that has already been bid up to an unrealistic level, nor do you want to sell a market that has already experienced substantial selling pressure. The oscillator tells you where you are in the bullish or bearish cycle. And, of course, I relate the specific indicator reading to a specific day of the week since history provides such a rich store of knowledge concerning how the market trades on specific days of the week. The real art comes, however, with how you put all these indicators together.

FORMULAS

There used to be a guy down on the floor who had a little cottage industry going selling support and resistance numbers. He'd stand near the entrance to the trading floor each morning and hand out his confidential information to his clients. Understandably, he considered his numbers proprietary, and insisted that they not be disseminated in any manner. One day he caught a friend of mine comparing notes with me (I had my own set of buy and sell numbers that I'd typed out on a three-by-five card) and he gave my friend hell. Don't ever expect me to sell you my numbers again, he told my friend. It was about this time that I found a simple formula in a trading book and incorporated it into an early version of my LSS system. A couple of years later, a floor trader took the formula and named it after himself. That's when people started saying to me, you took so-and-so's formula. No, I explained, I took the formula from another guy and this latest guy got the idea from me.

I once heard a very successful trader explain that you can do the wrong thing in the market and make money. The problem is, over time, the law of averages will catch up with you and you will give back most—if not all—of the winnings. Formulas are not the answer to tap the riches of Wall Street or

LaSalle Street, but they are part of the puzzle. You cannot rely solely on a formula for success. But you cannot be successful without the use of a limited number of formulas. It is how you use them and incorporate them into your overall concept of trading that determines how much you will win.

I am reminded of a winning streak I put together in the month of March a few years ago. Virtually every trade I made returned a profit. With each win my confidence soared. Looking back, that should have been a warning signal to cut back on my contracts and exercise caution. You know what happened. I spent the month of April giving back the hard-won profits. What had happened? The market had changed, but I failed to take this into account in my trading.

There are days when you can buy every new high in the market and make money. It doesn't matter if the fills are bad or if you buy each new intermediate high. If you can hold on until the close, you can make money. On other days, of course, even in bullish markets, you have to be very, very selective about where you decide to buy the market. The same applies to selling short.

The formulas help you by pinpointing areas and conditions that are favorable to your trade. They provide you with a point of view on the market that can prove very valuable. This is not to say that fading the rules won't occasionally work. The best intuitive traders know when to throw out the rulebook. But, for the less intuitive strategist, one must embrace the percentages; that's where a handful of formulas can place you in good stead from the first to the last.

Successful traders tend to do what works. This suggests flexibility in their approach to the market. Contrast this with a rule that is inflexible. The tendency is to find one rule or formula that works on a limited basis and then extrapolate out to try to make this limited rule a law of the universe. If only things were so easy. Moreover, you won't find candlestick people looking at bar charts. You won't find a stochastics guy looking at moving averages. If a moving average proved a winner in the last trade, it suddenly becomes part of a trader's arsenal and he or she is now on a mission to convince the world that this is the correct way to trade. I'm in favor of whatever works. But it has been my experience that too rigid an acceptance of one method over another only leads to confusion and disappointment down the road.

There are conditions that can be identified as favoring a bullish or bearish scenario. Under such conditions, the perceptive trader should win again and again. Given a strong Friday close in S&P futures, you usually want to be a buyer early on Monday morning—before the market makes a huge run-up. This is particularly true if Monday's opening price is a gap above Friday's high. But if you wait until the noon hour and the market is sitting on its highs, chances are you are going to witness some profit-taking and the market will probably give up some of its gains. As I learned so dramatically in my own trading, if you are trading in mid-March, the bulls are likely to be in control. But if it is already mid-April, chances are the market has already seen its near-term high and the overall seasonal trend is probably lower. This does not mean that you wouldn't buy a strong Monday open in April, only that the seasonal bias has temporarily turned down.

You will often observe a market bias. Sometimes this bias becomes almost palpable as a bull market surges off its lows and knocks at the resistance prior to breaking out. The same is true of a market about to break. While hard to describe, this market bias becomes particularly noticeable down on the floor where the ebb and flow of buy and sell orders becomes more vocal as one side or the other is about to prevail. Some off-floor traders try to capitalize on this vocal aspect of the floor by subscribing to a service that provides the bid and asked prices and occasional commentary. I've listened to this service and I like it. But it can be misleading to the new trader who doesn't understand that the market will always get noisy when attempts are made at new highs or lows, or who mistakes the commentary for market analysis—a more dangerous assumption. Indeed, I've known of some traders who have gotten in trouble by thinking they had the insider track to the floor. You are often talking to a clerk in a booth overlooking the pit. The fact that Merrill Lynch is buying may be interesting, but someone else is selling to them.

The purpose of the formula is to quantify the market's bias. Turn it into a number that you can relate to yet another number, and so on. I find this analysis of patterns particularly helpful when it confirms my gut intuition. This doesn't mean that you won't have to be patient in order to capitalize on the best trade. But sooner or later, given the right circumstances, you will find that opportunity; that's when you need to jump on the trade.

Golden opportunities won't present themselves every day. The market may be churning around in advance of a Fed report. But when they do arise, the opportunity-minded trader must be willing to commit to the market. There will always be slow periods, such as around the Christmas holidays, but given the exciting times in which we live, expect no lack of opportunities.

The key is to know on which ones to chance risking your money, and which ones to leave alone, a daunting task.

There are two key components to being a successful trader. One, you have to have the analytical skills to read the market. This is a skill that I'm confident can be learned. Two, you have to have the confidence in your trading skills to throw your money on the table. This is often called money management but, more accurately, it should be called self-management. Put another way, it is one thing to know where the market is going and another to capitalize on the situation. Some of the best analysts have no trading skills. They can tell you where the market is going, but they cannot utilize that knowledge in the marketplace.

I knew that, given a few refinements, I had a reasonably good grasp on the analytical techniques. After years of trading, I knew enough to avoid the obvious mistakes. But I was far less sanguine about my self-management trading skills. I knew that failure to observe the rules of money management would doom even the most brilliant analyst. Moreover, not only do you need to know how to handle your money, but you also need to know how to choose your spot. Although I've been trying for years, I still need to fine-tune my trade selection. Sometimes, being just five minutes too late—or early— spelled all the difference between a fabulous trade and an ill-timed loser. Indeed, I had observed two distinct syndromes—either a trader would be too cautious and never want to get in, or exceedingly reckless with a damn-the-torpedoes approach to the market. I knew I needed to formulate a trading strategy that would successfully steer me down the middle road of these two competing philosophies.

Most new traders tend to follow a traditional approach. They want to trade one-lots, place a stop, and hopefully exit a winner at a predetermined exit point. Given some success with this strategy, the new trader then looks to increase size. Though seemingly sensible, this approach doesn't work. The reason: No matter what trading strategy one uses, the fact remains that *most of one's profits are generated by a minority of one's trades.* Those who tend to succeed at trading seem to have an uncanny ability to identify big money-makers and capitalize on this knowledge by taking larger positions. One would often witness this among winning floor traders. The most successful locals would often test the waters with small positions and load the boat if they felt they were right. That is, they would vary their commitment depending upon their confidence in the trade. Moreover, they tended to place their positions within buy or sell zones where they could add with the knowledge that the trade still looked good. But once sensing that a trade was a mistake, the same trader would exit the market by going "retail," or giving up the edge to another local, to keep the losses small.

As I mentioned, the big moneymakers tend to occur on the minority of trades. That means you are likely to either lose or just break even on most of your trades. The problem becomes one of identifying the outstanding opportunities. How do you identify the winners in advance?

PATIENCE AND TRADE SELECTION

Clearly, one answer is patience. Another is selection. Put simply, there are rarely more than two or three truly good opportunities per day. Assuming that this observation is correct for the moment, how then do you justify nine or ten trades a day?

Typically, the only person making money when you overtrade in this fashion is your broker. Indeed, without much effort, one could also make the case that, at best, there are only two or three good trading opportunities per week! If you have been a victim of the search-and-destroy trading pattern, when the market just churns up and down, you know what I am talking about. Fortunately, our research has shown when to expect this pattern—typically on a Wednesday. Just knowing this simple probability can help you mark on your calendar what days to avoid, and perhaps go golfing, leaving the frustration of the nondirectional day to someone else.

Everyone wants the high-probability winning trade, but comparatively few are willing to wait for the trade to materialize. What one needs is a Zen-like patience, secure in the knowledge that things will work out. I know it is obvious but the following bit of advice needs to be stated: A day when you don't trade and don't lose money is better than the day when you do trade and lose money. Too often the novice trader attempts to capture the proverbial running water by forcing the trade. To mix metaphors, this is similar to capturing lightning in a bottle. I know it seems that there is constant opportunity in the market. This may be true. However, this is not the same thing as saying that you can capitalize on every opportunity.

Here, again, I am speaking of a middle path. As one for whom patience has never come easily, I can tell you that the market will drive home two simple lessons. On the one hand, the search for certainty will prove disastrous (there are no sure things); on the other, for those gunslingers among you, reckless trading, like reckless driving, will have predictable results.

RESPECT THE MONEY

The best traders are smart about money. They respect money and they don't believe in squandering their hard-won capital. I've been fortunate in knowing a lot of wealthy people. Except for the ones who inherited the money, as opposed to earning it, they all shared common traits. None of them was wasteful. They all understood that in order to receive, one must have something to give. And many of them gave in abundance. They were all generous and hardworking, never considering themselves victims. In short, they were—and are—responsible people. These people all have an aura that attracts money and they are comfortable in their good fortune. It is important to be able to identify the type of person who prospers in the market, since so many are ill-suited to win. While it is true that the rich tend to get richer in the market, those not so rich can benefit from emulating the successful ones.

Whenever someone tells me they couldn't care less for money—as if its acquisition were beneath them—I'm always on guard because I suspect it is a put-down. Understandably, such individuals rarely have any. Instead, they have a sense of entitlement. This means that someone else should pay for his or her lack of success. These are the same people who have maxed-out their credit cards trying to live above their means. In the financial markets, one can readily see such individuals who are driven by their desperation. They *need* to make a lot of money quickly—perferably without putting in a lot of work. I'm often amused, not angry, at people who take the trouble to call me up to tell me how useless my books and videos are because they were not able to translate them into instant easy profits. The fact is, it takes work and patience and perseverance, and perhaps a little luck, all of which such individuals tend to have in short supply.

While I know it is difficult, one has to learn to concentrate on the market, not the money. The mark of a novice trader is that she almost always thinks of her equity position to the exclusion of everything else. So you hear that the market has gone so many points against her, or that she is underwater and can't get out now. The market, of course, is totally indifferent to any given trader's position. It is going to do what it does regardless of any one trader's position. So why dwell on a situation that can only muddle one's thinking?

We know that leverage is the proverbial double-edged sword. To trade effectively, you must take reasonable risks, putting the leverage to work for you. Over the years, I've tried without success to come up with formulas for the amount of risk to take on any given trade. My general rule for margin is to have enough that you don't have to think about the money. I also like the notion of being underleveraged, having much more money than you'll ever need should your trading plans go awry. You can think of risk in terms of dollars or points; I prefer points because it eliminates the mistakes that occur when one is thinking about the money.

Again, one's focus should always be on the market—not what you can afford to lose. High-volatility markets require more distant stops. It doesn't make any sense to place stops too close to the market in a high-volatility environment. This is self-defeating because it only ensures that the trade will be stopped out. Whether you are thinking in terms of dollars or points, the only sensible approach is to get out when your position is no longer good— that is, when the market has clearly demonstrated that you are incorrect in your analysis. A better approach is to identify those areas where the trade has definitely turned negative and try to exit the market with as little damage as possible. We've performed studies with tick data in which we move the stops in and run the numbers over and over. The results prove that the tighter the stop, the more likely it is that it will get hit. Accordingly, you need to move the stop outside the line of fire, but not so far that the losses will be overwhelming.

I'm often amused by this theory that is set forth in trading books: Risk a small portion of your capital on every trade and no more. This is fine in theory. But what if you find yourself on the wrong side of the market on the afternoon when a Fed report comes out? You could lose 25 to 30 percent of your entire trading capital in 10 minutes! So much for the theory about limiting losses. If your game plan was to risk just five percent, this is a major setback.

When it comes to money management, I'm a believer in market cycles. When things are going well, you need to be a bit more aggressive. When you are in a losing streak, it seems nothing will work; increasing your size will only serve to bury you deeper. Never try to get hot when you are cold by increasing your stake. I've tried this. It doesn't work.

One's own temperament toward risk should dictate money management.

If you cannot feel comfortable with what you stand to lose on a trade, you cannot afford to trade. So ask yourself: Can I afford to lose this money? If the answer is no, don't trade until you can answer in the affirmative and see yourself going through the process of losing and winning. So many people view the market through rose-colored glasses. Despite the high odds against them, they don't believe they will sustain trading losses. An attendee at an OmegaWorld conference several years ago asked me why I didn't trade more contracts. I knew immediately that he had no idea of the risks involved. Trading merely looks easy. Try it and you'll see the difference.

When it comes to the conventional wisdom concerning money management, something that is tailored to your own attitudes toward risk is likely to suit your personal style. I don't understand why anyone would want to hold a position in the S&P 500 futures market overnight when you risk ruin on the next day's opening. But many people are quite comfortable with this approach. There are many traders, of course, who would never trade the S&P 500 futures market. For them, the potential rewards don't warrant the risks. For others with a high tolerance for risk, no amount of market volatility is going to chase them away. You have to decide for yourself what you can stand emotionally when it comes to trading. Unless you have the stomach for the risk, don't place yourself in a position where disaster could strike. Just remember that there are people out there who will match your bet in the market dollar-for-dollar.

How often do you read about some hedge fund manager who loses millions of dollars on a miscalculation? This happens far more frequently than one would think. On an individual basis, where one's own money is at stake, the losses are undoubtedly smaller, but the outcome is often the same. Ask yourself: Are you comfortable with the risk? Always trade within your comfort level. Once you go beyond that point, you lose all ability to reason.

There are two questions to ask yourself if you are overextended in the market: Do you think about the money? Do you panic? As illogical as it sounds, this should be the litmus test that every trader must pass. I never found that my trading improved if I worried about the money day after day or if I found myself getting out on panic. The ultimate test, of course, is to ask yourself if you are enjoying your trading. If you dread to see the market open in the morning, it is probably better to find another occupation.

A trader cannot operate on what some textbook says is right or wrong. You have to trade according to your own game plan, taking intelligent risks and reaping, hopefully, your just rewards. That's when trading can be extremely satisfying—when you have and execute a plan according to wise strategies and your tolerance toward risk.

With this in mind, you want to approach the market with a specific game plan in mind. You want to be selective, yet aggressive, looking for classic opportunities and capitalizing on them to the best of your ability. Is this a realistic approach? You bet. The winning trader knows how to craft his own enthusiastic approach to the market, one grounded in sound trading techniques, but tailor-made for his own personality.

All traders face the same challenge: how to identify the optimal situation. Perhaps you have already decided to concentrate on short-term, aggressive trading in the high-flying S&P 500 futures market. Perhaps you plan to focus on time and price patterns and reliable trading formulas. A second consideration, which is equally important to your success, is money management. How will you manage your money? For most new traders, the market commitment is dictated by the size of their bankroll, making one-lots a necessity. But even the most cautious trader must occasionally take advantage of the exceptional opportunities. You don't want to be locked into a rule that says you can never go for the genuine opportunity. The downside, of course, is that you may get hammered. So you need to factor in the likelihood of some substantial losses.

FINDING THE "GO FOR BROKE" TRADES

In order to manage money intelligently, you must divide your trade selection into two categories: the run-of-the-mill trades and the go-for-broke trades. If you can find enough of the latter, your odds of coming out ahead are greatly improved. How to find them? We are going to explore some of the strategies in the pages ahead. But be assured the work is worth the payoff. One good go-for-broke winner will offset a half dozen losers. I am often asked questions about winning percentages versus losing percentages. My reply is always the same. Essentially, you can win on only ten percent of your trades and still make a lot of money—if the winners are big and the losses small. So the important question isn't one of winning versus losing percentages. How much money, on average, do you make on every trade, including winners *and* losers? Do you average three or four hundred dollars a trade? Do you lose money on average? Do you make just fifty dollars? To arrive at this number, simply divide your equity gains by the number of trades. This will give you your average gain or loss. To give you an absurd example, let's say you make $20,000 on one trade and then lose $500 on the next nine trades. You have won just ten percent of the time, but the net gain is $15,500 before commissions. This translates into $1,550 per trade—a healthy profit by any standard. Take away the one gain, though, and you have a completely different result. Trading is a process, so you have to get comfortable with the up-and-down nature of winning and losing. Being more realistic, if you insist on percentages, I'd suggest trying to win more than half the time and you'll come out way ahead—if you manage your money wisely.

Those who become extraordinarily successful as short-term traders know how to manage both themselves and their money. A conservative trader might be appalled that one would risk the kind of money required to win in the futures market, but what, you must ask yourself, is the alternative? While not suggesting recklessness, I am advocating a controlled aggressiveness that will enable you to earn the occasional score that will put you far ahead. I suppose that this willingness to risk is but one of the many paradoxes that abound in the market. And, of course, it is also biblical in nature—the notion that she who will find her life must risk losing it.

This paradoxical notion extends beyond risk to trade selection as well. How often have you taken a sure thing, only to end up a loser? As certain as night follows day, the only universal law is that the so-called easy trades always end up in the loser column, while difficult and impossible trades prove to be the outstanding winners. I've never known there to be an exception to this rule. But how many people approach the market with the idea that there is an easy answer, a formula that will make them rich?

I began my trading career the way that most people do, looking for a formula that would produce winning trade after winning trade. And I never quite relinquished the idea that I could master every facet of the trading game. Unfortunately, once one hits an inevitable winning streak, the belief that one has indeed some inside knowledge about the market tends to inflate the ego. This always occurs when one's equity is at a peak. The inevitable slide, driven by one's hubris, is not a pretty sight. What begins in denial—"How could this happen to me?"—often ends in a rout with one's broker calling for more equity. I remember a day several years ago when I made $18,000 on one good trade, only to lose the entire profit the very next day! As one who has paid for his shortcomings, I can tell you that this is no way to run a business—or indeed trade. Trading is a process. First you take one step, then another. A good quarterback knows when to run for a few yards or pass the ball for small yardage. The so-called "Hail Mary" pass is reserved solely for situations when it can prove to be a game-saving maneuver with seconds left on the clock. This is the risk-reward calculation that every quarterback—and trader—must continually make. Does the reward warrant the risk, and vice versa? The market is fluid and ever-changing. This is why flexibility is the hallmark of a good trader.

From my conversations with my mentors over the years, I learned that there is nothing shameful about earning small profits on percentage plays that favor a given outcome. It is for this reason that I decided to do research on probability studies. If I could find situations where the likelihood of higher prices into the close was, say, 70 percent versus just 30 percent to the downside, then, I reasoned, I had a winning edge. While perhaps not the complete answer, these studies enabled me to couple them with other indicators or studies that would amount to setting up my ducks in a row. Moreover, it would enable me to weed out the trades that only proved to be fifty-fifty as unworthy of my commitment.

Now you are probably wondering, "If you are looking for a go-for-broke trade to load the boat, why would you waste time looking for bread-and-butter, high-probability winners?" Good question. The answer is, they are part and parcel of the same thing. The home run hitter may be always swinging for the fences, but the utility infielders who produce bunts and singles also contribute to winning the game. The fact is, you must take an inventory of your strengths and weaknesses and cultivate the confidence to move ahead, commensurate with your abilities.

FORMULATING A STRATEGY

My money management strategy is to bet more when I am winning and to back off after losses. Not long ago, I remember a day when I tested the waters by selling a five-lot of S&P 500 futures shortly after the open. The market promptly notified me that the trade wasn't going to work. I took a quick loss, but still the dollar amount was greater than $1,600. What to do? I realized I had to quickly reverse the position, but now I was risking more money and the outcome was anything but certain. I knew a one- or two-lot wouldn't do the job. I was in no mood to risk losing on seven or eight contracts. Since a two-lot was too small and an eight-lot too scary to contemplate the losses, I decided to purchase four contracts. The market quickly broke to the upside, earning me sufficient profits to offset the initial loss. I'd dodged another bullet successfully.

Sometimes the best you can do is break even. Recently, I was visiting with a very successful stock trader friend who had just purchased almost 20,000 shares of Xerox as it was breaking to all-time new lows. He was underwater to the tune of about $20,000 and the situation wasn't looking good. Because I had to catch a plane, I left, but I called him a few days later to see how the trade eventually worked out. Xerox was still below his purchase price so I didn't expect the news to be particularly good.

"Oh, that," he explained. "When it broke to the lows at 7, I purchased another 20,000 shares and sold them all on a bounce to 9."

He had broken even—no damage. Obviously, this was past history. But being an excellent trader, he had the presence of mind—and the money—to buy more and minimize the damage.

"I can tell you one thing," he'd explained to me the first morning when I visited him. "I'm a value player and Xerox isn't going out of business. I know that this stock will continue to have value." Of course, he was right.

The principle of risk management will apply whenever you trade. Don't get in over your head, and don't risk losses on a number of contracts that you are not prepared to equal in pursuit of getting back losses. About ten years ago, I tried this crazy approach to money management in the bond market by doubling each time I lost. Well, I started off with a lowly two-lot. When I lost on that, I traded four. After that loser, I moved up to an eight-lot. And, finally, one day I found myself buying 16 Treasury bond futures contracts, with each one-tick fluctuation worth $500 a tick! Talk about getting in over one's head. The funny thing is the first time I tried this it worked. I got back all my losses—and more. It even worked the second time I tried this risky strategy. It was the third time that killed me. I lost on the 16-lot trade—at $500 a tick—and now I was faced with losing on 32 contracts in a single trade. With $1,000-per-tick risk, I simply couldn't take the trade. I had reached the point of my ultimate risk. The strategy failed.

I'm reminded of a story that my mentor told me in the coffee shop one afternoon. We were talking about his willingness to share his trading strategies with others. "Most people cannot do what I do," he explained. "So what's the damage in telling them? The average guy is going to trade one-lots. So he buys his contract and goes out to the kitchen and makes himself a sandwich and returns to his screen and watches the market. Let him take a ten-lot and he won't feel like eating anymore. If the average guy had the losing days that I have, he would jump out the window."

IF YOU ARE GOING TO THRIVE, YOU MUST SURVIVE

The first rule of trading is survival. Unless you are confident that you can weather the ups and downs of trading, you won't be able to make it as a trader. The market is just too punishing to the new trader who is not aware of the downside risks. The fact is, if you trade long enough, you will certainly have bad days. All traders experience losses. The question is, can you maintain your composure in the face of incredible adversity? My friend John had an ambition to become a floor trader in Chicago. Despite being told that this was an impossible goal, that the floor traders would eat him for lunch, he persisted; today he trades among the elite S&P 500 locals at the Chicago Mercantile Exchange. In the face of adversity and inevitable trading losses, he just kept going. Gradually, his trading improved and he was able to make the transition to professional floor trader.

As a connoisseur of the misconceptions that traders often labor under, I was amused by a call I got one day shortly after the close. It had been one of those tough days when everything went wrong, the kind that prompts traders to say, "If it weren't for bad luck, there would be no luck at all." I was bemoaning my bad luck when the caller said in surprise, "You mean you still have losing days?"

At first I thought he was kidding. But he was serious.

"Of course," I replied. "Everyone who trades futures has losing days."

He seemed genuinely surprised. Like many new traders, he probably thought trading was a piece of cake once you mastered a few simple techniques. I'm sure I deflated his optimistic balloon.

Sometimes when you are first starting out as a new trader, just learning to survive is a chore. After some of the hits I'd taken as a novice trader, I was just happy to be still standing. Frankly, I've never been able to understand why such a hard-won education should be easy for others. Even after years of trading, the losing cycles persist. Looking back, I could remember using every trick, strategy, formula, or money management technique—and still enduring the down cycles. It was like trying to ride a roller coaster. In my early days, I'd occasionally go out and purchase some expensive luxury item following a real coup in the market, only to lose the profits within several days or a week. Invariably, what worked on Monday wouldn't work on Tuesday. Today, based on the research we've done on day-of-the-week patterns, I understand why. But back then, I didn't have a clue why buying a higher open on Tuesday wasn't the same as buying a higher open on Monday.

Most of the time, the mistakes I'd made were a simple lack of self-discipline. I wanted the action. Throwing out my buy and sell numbers—which were often quite accurate—I would later find myself buying the sell numbers and selling the buy numbers, the exact opposite of my intended strategy. So it wasn't the strategy that had gone awry, but rather my implementation of that plan. I had to endure many more setbacks before I recognized the problem, but once I did, I had a valuable insight into why I lost.

For years, I'd wondered about the psychology of winning and losing and why the good and bad times seemed to occur in predictable cycles. With every losing trade, I'd begin to see the self-doubts, the depression, the feeling that I just wasn't up to the task. Then I began to analyze my mental condition and realized that my attitudes contributed to the prolonging of the slump. Like a beaten animal, you begin to anticipate the next unfortunate incident. You get mired down in a defeatist mentality that perpetuates the trading losses. I'm reminded of a trade, not long ago, when I was short and the market rose and I sold more. I was confident that I had the right side, but the market continued higher and I panicked and bought the top. It was classic stop-running. I knew what had happened but I couldn't pick up the phone and sell them again. The market plummeted lower. I'd missed the move. This wasn't a matter of not knowing better; I knew what had to be done. It was a failure of will. It is during times like this that you want to quit trading for good.

Fortunately, I persisted and the slump ended. Not long after, a similar pattern occurred. I was a bit premature in my selling, but my analysis was on the money. The same thing happened. The market rose and I sold again. I love to average in my positions at varying prices. But trouble was brewing. The market continued higher and I ran for the exit. It looked like it was ready to run. I felt like I had no alternative. Within minutes, the market retreated and I realized my mistake. This time I loaded the boat—short! I was up thousands when I covered them prior to the close.

What a difference a good attitude makes! One crucial decision to make that final trade created success out of failure. I had been hammered, but I wasn't giving up. I decided to start keeping a diary that would alert me to the persistent mistakes I was making in the market. I'd seen that predictable pattern a hundred times if I'd seen it once. It was a question of execution. Was I up to the task?

I don't think the experience of most traders is dissimilar to mine. When I first read the interviews in *Market Wizards,* I was amazed how the genuine hardships of trading were spread out, even among the superstars. Indeed, overcoming adversity was the singular experience that they all seemed to share. At least I wasn't alone. Not long ago, I received a phone call from an individual who had attended a seminar in Las Vegas several years ago where I was one of the speakers. In this particular group, which was given by a well-known market guru, I sensed a strong reluctance to hear my message— namely, that the market could be beaten, but only by those who were well informed. With genuine emotion in his voice, he began the conversation by saying, "I wasn't ready to hear what you were saying back then." He'd since learned that the easy answers don't work. Who doesn't love a sinner who learns to repent?

This caller, like many individuals who don't give up at the first try, had undergone a sort of spiritual awakening, after a soul-searching review into why and how he had floundered. This is a deeply personal journey, but one that is necessary for the serious student of the market. It was only after reviewing my personal patterns that I was able to gain insights into what was going on in my own trading. For instance, winning streaks would leave me overconfident, ready to take a reckless and unwise trade. On the other hand, the losing cycle would put me in the depths of despair and anger over what I had done. I tried to be philosophical about my losses—it is only money, and all that. But I was dying inside every time I endured one of these losing streaks.

More than once I had headed to the airport and taken the next plane south following a particularly bad day or losing cycle. After a few days in the sun I'd return in a better frame of mind. But how often had I fantasized that, following one of these journeys, I'd return, only to have the security guards grab me and throw me out into the street? Although this never happened, I couldn't stop thinking that one day it could. At the entrance to the trading floor, the exchange posts the name of members who are no longer "guaranteed" by their clearinghouses—an almost certain sign that these traders have gone broke.

I remember being up in the offices of my clearinghouse one morning, retrieving my trading jacket, when I overheard several traders discussing their previous night's activities. "I hailed a cab last night," one trader said, "and you'll never guess who was driving. Remember that guy, Bob, who used to stand behind Michelle in the soybean pit?" "Oh, hell," said another guy, "I ordered a pizza last week, and remember that guy Hayward who used to throw around twenty-lots in the bonds? He delivered the pizza." I decided to be extra-careful once I got downstairs.

In *West of Wall Street,* my coauthor shared an anecdote about losing months of profits one reckless Friday afternoon in the gold pit. He said it made him want to stand in a dark closet and repeat over and over again how he would never, ever lose that discipline that is so vital to successful trading. Down on the floor, practically everyone had, at some time, gone broke. It was part of their education. So what does one do following such a debacle? Borrow a small stake of money and go back to basics—small numbers, iron discipline, slowly finding one's way. You simply cannot tell someone who has never traded about this experience and make him understand it. Ask yourself this: If this is what happens to market professionals, who spend their days trading, why should your experience be any different?

STREAKS

You need to be able to identify the end of a streak. Winning streaks tend to come to a halt in one of two ways. Either the end is abrupt or it occurs slowly with one or two losses followed by many more. The littlest things can break a streak. The first time I left the trading floor to go have a cup of coffee, my position lost $1,200 by the time I'd returned. Another time I tried to impress a date by having her visit me on the floor. That little fiasco cost $6,800. I remember these trading losses as if they occurred yesterday, but, in fact, these two events occurred more than 14 and 12 years ago, respectively. What's important is that I remember the lessons they taught me. Trading is a very, very serious business. You cannot let your concentration be broken by anyone or anything. Sometimes a temporary distraction—a phone call, a CNBC market analyst's comments, even a missed trade—can throw you off stride.

What are the clues that a streak may be over? The subtle ones are often hard to judge. You might have two or three small losses in a row. But thinking you are due, you might get aggressive on the next trade and perhaps lose on that one. Now, you feel you must get even more aggressive on the next trade; pretty soon, reason goes out the window and your trading is spiraling out of sight. You don't want your healthy self-confidence to degenerate into cockiness, which is practically an occupational hazard among young floor traders.

Unfortunately, you never know when you will turn cold. If you have been winning, you are in denial at first and simply aren't receptive to the notion that a minor setback might be the beginning of a serious losing streak. Not long ago, I was even on my morning trade. It was one of those reversal situations where I had to act quickly to get back my initial losses. So in the afternoon trade, which I patiently waited for, I was ready to make my money on the day. I tried selling, but that didn't work. So I took the loss. The problem is, I was becoming stubborn. I was convinced the market was going lower. So I sold again and added to the position when it went higher. It started to back off and I dropped my guard. Now I've got them, I thought. But I was wrong. The market took off to the upside and I had to chase the damn thing to get out. The result: big losses.

Sometimes events conspire against you. Last year, I sold short six S&P's one afternoon and had a nice $3,000 profit in minutes. I hit my speed dialer, wanting to take profits. Ring, ring, ring—no answer. Why aren't they picking up the phone? I asked myself. I immediately knew why. The market was soaring. My profit had vanished and the losses were mounting quickly. Finally, I got through to the floor. I had to make a quick decision. Take the loss—which was probably about $5,000 now—or try to trade out of it. I chose the later strategy.

"Sell me four S&P's market!" I yelled into the phone.

They gave me the fill. I was now short ten contracts.

The market momentarily started to trade lower and I had that warm feeling that I was suddenly going to make some nice money.

But, just as suddenly, it propelled higher and I knew the party was over.

"Buy me ten S&P's market!" I could hear my heart beating this time.

The total damage was over $12,000, almost enough to buy a modest economy car. I never complain about bad fills or my desk's service. But the next day I called the desk manager and explained that their failure to pick up the phone cost me some serious money. I didn't bother telling him that I'd sabotaged myself by adding to the position.

"Look," he explained. "We've got eight clerks and 30 phone lines. We get busy."

It took me three days to get the money back, including one day when the phone rang off the hook, but this time I was long and the market was going my way. Their failure to pick up the phone this time actually worked in my favor, making me a couple of thousand dollars. After the third day, I was exhausted, but pleased to know that I was still standing despite a rare and bizarre event. There was never another incident when they didn't pick up the phone.

In looking back, I can honestly say that it was focused, disciplined trading that made me whole again. I don't think I ever panicked in the market and didn't regret my action. There are still days when I feel the panic rising in me and I try to calm myself down before grabbing the phone. The bottom line is this: When it comes to trading, I can be my best friend or worst enemy. I know that my mental discipline is what keeps me winning when I win, and the loss of that discipline is what short-circuits my profits.

PUTTING IT ALL TOGETHER

I became a winning trader when I discovered the existence of predictable patterns, a technique that embraces both time and price studies and day-of-the-week probability studies.

I was enthralled with the notion that a market would often "tip its hand," telling you exactly where it was going, often well before the scenario would be played out. I took the best intuitive trading that my mentor had used to earn himself a fortune, and translated the intuition into a set of numbers that told me not only the likelihood of a precise target goal, but also the exact minute when the target price would be hit. To this I added a longer-term, daily scenario pattern—the day-of-the-week probabilities—which indicated whether the market would likely rise or fall and, significantly, whether the move would occur early in the morning or late in the afternoon. The resultant numbers gave me a whole new way of looking at the market.

Never again would I have to guess about market direction. The answer was right there in front of me. Now I could say that the next leg should rise (or fall) so many points in so many minutes. It was simply a matter of learning to measure the market.

When I started using this approach I was amazed by the symmetry in the market. W.D. Gann, the market pioneer who had once predicted the price of Penn Central railroad shares to the exact eighth of a point, was correct when he asserted that there are predictable patterns in the market. Moreover, using this approach, which I called time and price, I realized I could identify the downside risk. If the market broke a predetermined threshold, the pattern was likely to fail, but, significantly, the symmetry of the move was still intact since the move would play out a symmetrical pattern in the other direction. If I locate a pattern that "fails" in this fashion, I know from experience that the initial move will be retraced almost 100 percent of the time. I know from experience that the move will only halt once the stops are run—a time-honored trading tactic of savvy floor operators. There is no more reliable trade.

As I learned to place trades only when I knew where the market was going (to the tick) and when it would get there (to the exact minute), I realized I was in possession of a valuable trading tool. The skeptics, of course, didn't believe that such an analysis was possible. So I'd tell them not to take my word for it, but simply to follow the patterns themselves and tell me what they found. Not a few who rose to this challenge became believers. In the meantime, I began collecting big profits on trades that the public often overlooked.

Today, I see no change in markets. Although the volatility has risen immensely in recent years, the basic market patterns have not changed—nor have the proverbial games that floor traders play. The fact is, human nature remains the same, and this is the strongest argument one could make about the future. Human fear and greed are likely to remain the same and so are the mistakes that unsuspecting traders will make. The vast majority of traders will continue to lose—and a good thing, too, since these are the people who supply the profits to the winners. With this in mind, let's turn to mechanics and see if we can fashion a sophisticated and viable approach tailored to your particular trading style.

1
Learning How to Trade

The Basics

When I was first learning to drive, some forty years ago, I remember getting in my father's Volkswagen Beetle only to let out the clutch too quickly and have the car stall. It took some time to learn how to gradually release the clutch while simultaneously applying pressure to the gas pedal. As I remember, learning to parallel-park was a bit of a challenge as well. And trying to pop the clutch on a hill remains a difficulty to this day.

Like most kids, I was a motivated learner when it came to learning how to drive. I remember getting top grades in driver's education because I wanted my driver's license. I still drive a stick shift automobile because I like sports cars, but I rarely think about the process of operating the car while I am driving. The shifting, speeding up and slowing down, is pretty much second nature.

For someone wanting to learn to trade, the process, like driving, becomes pretty much second nature once you get the mechanics down. As someone who has done this for a long time, I know that I take for granted many of the basics which, for many, still require a conscious effort. I know this because one day when I was a Chicago trader, I was at the airport talking with the airline agent about replacing one ticket with another and I said, "Oh, then it's a wash," and she looked at me like I was crazy.

"A wash?" she said. "What's a wash?"

"One cancels the other," I replied. I'd been so used to talking market nomenclature with fellow traders that this language we spoke had become a permanent part of my vocabulary. It never occurred to me that in the real world no one knew what we were talking about.

To this day, Chicago is the only city in the country where you cannot go into a restaurant without hearing people talk about getting the edge, hitting the bid, running the stops, lowballing the market, and fading the paper. I knew I'd stayed in town too long when one night, trying to relax in the Jacuzzi after a punishing day on the floor, I had to listen to a local relate his trading coup of the day.

"So I said to him," he explained to a friend. " 'I sold you a hundred, *#?!@. They're yours!' " Spare me. It wasn't long after that that I moved over to the lake to get away from the inbreeding so close to the exchange. It was bad enough to rub elbows with these guys all day, but at night one wanted to get away from the rough-and-tumble culture of the trading pits for a while.

But there was no escaping the market. Looking back, I can remember having parties where virtually all the guys in attendance were traders. After all, these were the people we knew. The women would want to come because they wanted to meet traders, and pretty soon I was getting calls from people I didn't know who wanted to attend. A highlight of these parties was to stand around with drinks and tell trading disaster stories. My favorite was about my friend, Greg, who once bought soybeans limit-up and sold them limit-down on the same day. We all had a good laugh at Greg's expense. Acting as bartender that night, Greg proved to be a good sport. Be we all knew we were vulnerable every day we walked into the exchange. I think because we all lived and died by our wits, there was a lot of gallows humor that accompanied that life.

It was about this time that I went to the Palm Restaurant with my friend, Barry, who was a leading S&P trader. As we were being led to our table, there was a chorus of "Hi Barry," "Hey Barry," "What's up Barry?" "Did you see those bonds?" It was obvious we were in a spot virtually populated by the S&P 500 pit—probably a place where the patrons had too much money to spend.

When you live and work in an environment where the market plays such a dominant factor in your life, it is difficult sometimes to gain perspective.

But when the opening bell rang on Monday morning, everyone was sober and professional. The game had begun again, and there was serious money at stake. The professional floor traders all knew the rules by which the game was played. They had to know or they couldn't survive. So the basics were really second nature to them and everyone understood them. It is only when you encounter the mistakes of the novice trader that you realize not everyone understands the basics.

WHAT THE FLOOR TRADERS KNOW

Although it is hard to overestimate the importance of managing risk, the floor traders are masters of risk aversion. You will find few traders who, when wrong, won't run as quickly as the professionals who populate the trading floors. They know that there is no future in holding on to losing positions. Contrast this with novice traders who hold on to losing positions in hopes of the market turning around. The fact is, a losing position rarely becomes profitable. While it is true that the floor traders don't pay commissions, thinking about the commission costs is rarely a good idea. Better to find yourself a bare-bones low commission and trade like a professional for whom this is not a trading factor.

While the floor professsionals are good at what they do, I doubt that their capabilities are any greater than yours. You probably underestimate your own capabilities. Successful trading is not so much the exercise of brilliant intelligence as it is one of having so-called street smarts, knowing when to run from risk and when to run toward opportunity. If educational background were a criterion for good trading, most of the floor professionals would be in a different occupation. As I said before, market success is often more a matter of managing oneself—especially one's emotions—than of outright intelligence. If anything, the overeducated are at a disadvantage on the floor, because they are busy analyzing everything, i.e., it could go up, but then again it could go down. Meanwhile the move is under way, and the overly analytical types have missed it!

The floor traders know you play your own game. I can always tell a novice trader because she is trying to play too many markets. Professionals are specialists, and you should be as well. Professionals trade in one pit. They don't run from market to market. They become experts at one method of trading within their given specialty. When you trade against them by throwing an order into the pit, you are betting that your expertise outweighs theirs. Chances are, you are going to have a difficult time beating a professional at his or her game. So how can you win? You have to out-trade them. You have to have a point of view on the market that the edge floor scalper lacks. She wants the edge, the difference between the bid and the asked price, and you want to win by predicting the direction of the move. Whereas the non-commission-paying floor trader can scalp the market, the off-floor trader cannot. She provides the liquidity that you, the off-floor trader, needs. Both parties play an important function in making the market work efficiently.

The floor trader knows you don't change the rules in the middle of the trade. Take the simple notion of a day trade. By definition, this means you enter and exit a trade during the same trading session. There must be no exceptions to this rule. Again, this is second nature to a seasonal professional. But you find novice traders who take what was supposed to be a day trade and turn it into a two-week debacle. I can remember several trading days when my losses were in excess of $10,000 each day. Each time, I took the loss because I knew the alternative, in going overnight, was to risk being out $20,000 on the next day's open. You must have that discipline.

The same applies to stop placement. If you have good reason to believe you are on the wrong side of the market, it makes no sense to move the stop from being hit. There are many ways to allow small losses to grow into large ones and this is one of them.

Listening to opinions is another mistake that the novice makes. There's a saying down on the floor about a given anatomical part, that everyone has, that is likened to opinions. And when you find someone trying to convince you of their point of view, it almost always means they are "talking their position." This is a sure sign that they are wrong or, in the parlance of the floor, a good fade—something to trade against. One reason I like trading from my office in Florida is because I no longer have to listen to all these opinions that are floating around; it is also why I push the "mute" button on CNBC. I have a friend in Oregon who won't even watch television because he is afraid it might influence his trading decisions. There is a well-known anecdote about a floor trader in the mid-eighties who was short a rising S&P 500 market. Realizing his position was deteriorating as the market shot higher, he did the only thing he could to make the market break. He spread a rumor on the floor that President Reagan had had a serious heart attack. Of course, the stock traders in New York probably didn't hear the rumor and the market failed to break. The strategy failed him.

There are other desperate measures that traders have taken, but in this case I think they are instructive of what not to do. One, in particular, remains vivid in my memory because it was emblematic of trader desperation. The fact is, desperate money never wins. Despondent over trading losses, one trader several years ago took to holding up convenience stores in the Chicago suburbs. Needless to say, he was caught. I guess the notion of getting a job never occurred to him.

The hallmark of a good professional trader, whether on or off the floor, is flexibility. She can change positions as the market swings back and forth. You see this all the time on the floor. A trader will purchase contracts in anticipation of higher prices and, sensing a change in market sentiment, suddenly sell them and go short. There was a time when a friend of mine decided to start a hotline service on the floor. The idea was that subscribers to his service would call his desk on the floor and his clerk would tell them whether he was bullish or bearish. The problem was that it took the clerk three or four minutes to pick her way through the pit where he would hand her the instructions on a trading card. More often than not, by the time she returned to the desk, he had changed his mind. He gave up the service because he couldn't turn around his clients fast enough.

A few years ago, a magazine approached me with the idea of an end-of-day hotline service that would be sold as a 900 number. The charge would be $4 for one minute of market commentary. Because I knew the average range was approximately so many points, I simply picked a direction and placed the numbers in the range of the previous day's close. The results were predictable. Occasionally I was right on the money; at other times, I wasn't even close. What amazed me was that so many people actually thought someone could accurately predict the future. My feeling was that for $4, you got a $4 opinion.

There is nothing wrong with trying to predict a given day's market scenario. The problem rests with insisting that your scenario must occur. A better approach is to have an idea of what might occur and then remain flexible to change your mind. One sees this every day down on the floor. You think you might get a higher open and the market will run up. Then you get a lower opening and the market breaks. The opening was the clue. Can you see how having opinions or trading on tips can get you in trouble here? Whenever I encounter anyone who insists the market must do this or that, I immediately know they are wrong. In fact, I usually file this information away in my brain and try to fade—or trade against—their opinion.

Not long ago, I hired a house painter to paint my house. Because he knew I worked in the markets, he would try out his stock market ideas on me. At the height of the bull market when Lucent Technologies was trading above 80 (the high in the stock was 84, I believe), he insisted that Lucent was a wonderful buy. No, no, no, I told him. The stock had just powered its way up from 60 and, while perhaps it had been a good buy at 60, you didn't want to touch it at 80. He insisted he was right.

"Why don't you buy Lucent?" he asked me.

"No way," I replied.

He knew I had a stock account. "Well, instead of paying me for this paint job, why don't you buy Lucent for me?"

"Because Lucent is trading at 80 and I don't owe you $8,000," I said. "But I could buy you the call options. You say you are certain that Lucent is going up?"

"Absolutely," he said. "Over 100."

"Then you could make a lot of money on the calls."

"Let's do it," he said.

In lieu of payment for the paint job, I purchased an equivalent amount of Lucent Technologies 80-strike calls. You know what happened? The stock tanked. The money he should have earned on the paint job was lost in the market and he learned an important lesson.

Later that year, Lucent Technologies shares traded below 20. They later fell another 10 points before bottoming at 5½. This is the kind of uninformed opinion that can be a good fading opportunity. One only has to observe the crash-and-burn nosedive of the dot-com stocks in recent memory. While I didn't get rich on the boom in Internet stocks, I also didn't lose a dime on the big break that ruined a number of portfolios. Today, every time I go to have my teeth checked or for a routine physical, I have to listen to tales of woe from physicians about the beating they are taking in the market. If only medical intelligence could be translated into market intelligence. "I don't do brain surgery on weekends," a floor trader commented to me years ago. "What makes these guys think they can play market maker during the week?" The classic story about market opinions goes back to the days of the late twenties right before the Great Crash. Joseph P. Kennedy, father of President Kennedy, was having his shoes shined and the shoeshine boy started giving him stock tips. Kennedy went out and sold short all the stocks he could. He made a fortune on the crash.

I relate these stories not merely for entertainment. They illustrate an important point. No one knows where the market is going. And those who insist that they do, usually don't know what they are talking about.

THE STOP-RUNNING GAME

Now that we've covered the fallacy of placing stock in market opinions, we need to look at specific examples of what floor traders know that can prove dangerous to your wealth. The most important bit of information that floor traders know is where the stop-loss orders are placed. Isn't this illegal to reveal where resting orders may be? It is, but you don't have to be told where the orders are to know where they exist. You have to understand that the trading pit is populated by two key groups of people. You have the locals, who trade their own money for their own account, and you have the order fillers, who execute orders for the investing public. The order fillers have what are known as "decks"—the so-called "paper" or paper orders. The locals "card" their trades on hardbound "trading cards," printed red on one side for selling and blue on the other for buying. For public orders, the trend in recent years has been toward the new wireless technology. So the trades are entered into hand-held computers and relayed back to the brokerage desk. Nevertheless, there is still plenty of "paper" floating around exchange floors.

I'll never forget the day a broker filling orders yelled out into the pit, "Whoever get the order, get the stop!" This generated a good laugh. The hapless public investor had placed the stop-loss order too close—the distance between the bid and the asked price—and the broker actually filled the stop before he filled the order. Good on his word, the broker let the same local have both sides. So the public investor was actually out before he was even in. In this instance, the public investor deserved the blame because he placed his stop too close.

The fact is, however, you don't need the public order filler to announce where the stops are placed. You have every broker in the country telling their clients to place a stop just above or below the respective highs and lows of the day. There are also plenty of intraday highs and lows that attract stops. Moreover, the floor brokers keep their decks in their pockets arranged by price; once they pull out their deck and begin shouting out orders, it turns into a feeding frenzy. When the stop orders are filled, the situation quiets down. The brokers' decks are now depleted and the locals go back to trying to nickel-and-dime one another.

If you find your stop being hit repeatedly, it means it is either too close to your original position or it is placed in an area where there are many stops. One of the favorite games of locals is to either highball or lowball the stops. This means that they will either bid the market up or offer the market down to a level where there are a lot of stop orders. Once that level is reached, their mission is accomplished, since there will be a temporary panic as the order fillers join the tumult in trying to execute the public orders. How is this accomplished? Very simply, by taking the market to a level where there are many stops. Once a stop is triggered, it becomes a market order. A market order will be filled at the best prevailing price in the market. So how is the order filled? By having both buyer and seller agree on the same price. So if the market is rising, you may not have many sellers. The sellers will sit on their hands as the buyers bid the market out of sight.

To understand how this works, you have to understand what goes on in the pit. Every trader acts as his own auctioneer. If he wants to buy, he bids; if he wants to sell, he offers. Most of the time, there is both a bid (the price at which the buyers are willing to buy) and an offer (the price at which the sellers are willing to sell). For a trade to be consummated, both sides must agree to a single price. The rule is, a bid must be at or above the last immediate bid that was yelled out in the pit. So if I'm "half bid," meaning 50, the whole pit must be half-bid or higher. If you want it more, you have to bid sixty, seventy, or higher.

Can you see how a bidding panic begins? One trader yells out "Half bid!" Another immediately screams "Sixty!" Another "Seventy!" And you are off to the races. Chances are, the sellers at this point are absolutely quiet. It is in this frenzied environment that your broker must get your order filled amid the total chaos that reigns when the market runs. Sooner or later, you will have sellers entering into the fray; then you may have a race downward as the sellers offer down the market. When selling, the rules are reversed. The sellers must offer "at" the prevailing offer or lower. So when the momentum swings the other way, you get "At twenty!" "At ten!" "At even!" and so on. The word "at" must be used when selling to differentiate the seller from the buyer. The difference between where you placed your stop loss order and where it is filled is known as slippage. This slippage can be considerable in markets that suddenly swing one way or another.

Why do the floor traders want to get the market stops? Because that's where the orders are that will propel the market higher or lower—at least temporarily. Highballing and lowballing can be risky. That's because if I bid higher, a seller may like my bid and sell to me. That may attract other sellers and the market may break. In this case, I just bought the high of the day. The same is true in reverse for sellers who try to lowball. For this reason, the knowledgeable insiders only risk doing this with one contract. So what if they lose on a one-lot? Chances are, they are much bigger players. And the small loss generated by a one-lot position is more than offset by the knowledge gained. Accordingly, you get a lot of attempted raids on the stops that aren't always successful. For example, late in the day, you may see the floor trying to sell and sell and take the market lower, but it fails to break. The sales are met with buying. Sooner or later, the sellers give up, you have a wholesale switch to the buy side, and the market soars higher.

People think you need high volume to move the market. But this is not so, especially when it comes to floor-generated forays into the stops. The rule is that one's bid must be at the prevailing bid or higher, and that one's offer must be at the prevailing offer or lower. To fully appreciate what goes on in the trading pit, you also need to know the rule on size. Small size trumps large size. No one can force you to take on more contracts than you want to buy or sell. So if I'm a local who wants to bid on two cars—lots or contracts—and you're a local who wants to sell ten, we do two. It's that simple. For this reason, the one- and two-lot locals trade with others who want to do similar size. The ten- and twenty-lot traders likewise want to deal with bigger traders. This is also why you sometimes get split fills. Let's say you wanted to buy six contracts. You might have paid "eighty on two" and the higher "even on four." This is because the person filling the order was only able to get a seller for two of the contracts at eighty, and the remaining were purchased at a higher price on the other four. You can't blame the seller at eighty for not wanting the other four. The market was going against her and she was out money by the time she carded the trade.

There is an important implication to this rule that not every trader appreciates. The one-lot trader, by bidding higher or offering lower, can effectively take the power out of the multilot trader's hands. He can manipulate prices to the extent that he can get the market to a level—with very little risk—where other forces (namely, the public stops) will play an effective role.

Can you see how a floor broker, trying to fill a large order at a limit price, might not enjoy some wise-guy local bidding over her? Because she holds a limit order, she cannot pay more, and here's some one-lot guy preventing her from doing her job by taking the market higher. You can be sure that these two probably don't like one another.

In the pandemonium that frequently prevails in the pit, you sometimes get a situation where one or more bids may be "off the market." Due to market tumult, one side of the pit may not hear what someone on the other side yells out. So one trader might start shouting, "Even bid! Even bid!"

This inadvertent mistake is quickly brought to a halt when someone yells out, "Hey, shut up! We are ten bid over here!"

This aberrant mistake is quickly erased and the market resumes its normal volatile course.

Now you take these two rules and you can see how some smart floor traders can temporarily manipulate the market to their own advantage despite the overall daily trend. First, you have the rule about the lowest bid being the prevailing last bid and the highest offer the prevailing last offer. Second, you have the rule that says no one can make you take a larger size than you want. So if the market has been declining, and is approaching an intraday low, the floor can make some nice money by running the stops.

Here's how this scenario might be played out. First, our hypothetical stop raider quietly takes his position. Since he wants the market to break, he will sell short, let's say, five contracts. Let's assume the market has been churning around the sixty-to-ninety area and he is able to sell the five at seventy. Now he is short five cars at seventy. Let's assume the intraday low is at the lower ten. Below that number there will be sell stops because that was a major intraday low and public traders like to place stops just below the low of the day. Obviously, the cash market will have to show some weakness or the futures market won't be able to decline. Again, let's assume it does. The market drifts lower—fifty, forty, thirty. Typically, you will find some bargain hunters buying in a scenario such as this. So don't be surprised if you don't get a bounce. On the second or third test of the lows, however, the stops will become approachable. At thirty, you could have a 30-bid, 40-asked market. Our market engineer, who is now short from the higher 70, will typically offer to sell one at thirty. Now you have a 20-bid, 30-asked market. As others begin to offer at thirty (they cannot offer it higher because that is the last immediate offer), the stop raider will offer one at 20. Now, all the would-be sellers in the pit have to offer at 20 or stop offering. Chances are, however, they will increase their efforts to sell. Anticipating a freefall, the sellers realize this is a now-or-never scenario. The stops, remember, are at ten, or possibly even. More sellers join in at 20. At this point, the stop raider may simply offer one at even—and all hell will break loose! With a tremendous roar, all the order fillers will now start selling their stop orders. They will start hitting the bids as fast as they can. In the absence of bids, they will simply offer the market lower.

"At ninety!"

"At eighty!"

"At seventy!"

And so on. At times, the spread between bid and asked will widen out and the difference will be "half a handle," or 50 points. So the sellers will offer "At even, at half, at even," sometimes for hundreds of points. When the market breaks like this, there are very few orders executed on the way down, although if you looked at a chart, you would think the market broke in a steady fashion. This phenomenon is known as painting the tape. The result, for the hapless public trader who had the misfortune to place her order amid a bunch of stops, is a disastrous fill. And who is the beneficiary of all this market madness? You guessed it, the stop raider.

With palms in for buying, the former seller will suddenly have an appetite to cover his position. "Buy 'em! Buy 'em! Buy 'em!"

If he covers his five-lot position at the lower seventy—100 points below where he initially sold—his profit is $1,250 on the five and, let's say, another $100 on the lowball sale at ten. That's $1,350 in a matter of minutes. This is a very conservative scenario. Big players can win small fortunes in minutes. So much for the conventional wisdom about putting your stops just under the market.

If you are wondering if this strategy is illegal, the answer is a resounding, "No, it isn't."

No one told you to place your stop under the market. The broker didn't mishandle your order. On the contrary, he probably did a pretty good job. He can only fill the order at a price where both buyer and seller agree. Buyers are not readily available when the market is freefalling.

What you find among public traders is an "I've been robbed" attitude when this happens. As you can see, though, the public trader plays a prominent role in his own demise.

I can tell you this. I've never seen a day when the stops weren't run—at least in a temporary fashion. Typically, the open itself is a massive stop-running exercise of the overnight stops. Position traders like to protect their profits by placing stops above or below the market. These stops, of course, offer little protection when the so-called opening gap swallows up the stops in a huge buying or selling frenzy. Now you must be thinking, "Isn't there a way to profit from this stop-running madness?" Of course there is.

On average, I'd say the stops are run nine or ten times a day. Some are minor exercises and others draw blood. But when the market is making a major move, the first target is always the stops. One way to capitalize on this is to exit your position when the stops are hit. Accordingly, if I'm long (having bought) and the market is approaching an intraday high, yesterday's high, this week's high, or, even better, a life-of-contract high, I'm going to sell as soon as that high is penetrated. Why? Because there will be enormous buying at that price and I will be selling into a crowd of panicked buyers. People do crazy things when they panic, among them paying too much for something. Once reason sets in—and the stops are all filled—prices tend to settle down.

Another strategy is to fade the overnight gap opening trade, although this is not always such a cut-and-dry technique as it may seem. Essentially, due to the large volume of stops that are hit on an opening gap, a temporary dislocation in prices occurs right after the open. The simplest strategy is to fade, or trade against, the initial trend. That is, you buy lower openings and sell higher openings. Paradoxically, so-called extreme gap openings call for the reverse strategy. There you have to buy strength and sell weakness, the reason being this is much more significant than stop-running. The market wants to go somewhere.

WHEN UP IS DOWN—AND VICE VERSA!

Another common market phenomenon that most novice traders don't understand is the run-the-market-one-way-to-go-the-other strategy. I call this my perversity theory of the market. If you turn everything on its head—a 180-degree turnaround—you will have a pretty good idea of how this phenomenon works. For instance, the market wants to soar to the moon. It will. But first there will be a raid on the sell stops at the day's lows. Only after every last weak-handed buyer has sold out of fear (and, conversely, every last knowledgeable buyer has purchased out of confidence), will the market go up. The reverse works at major tops, where the short sellers are virtually murdered in a bloodbath of short covering at the top. Once that is accomplished, the market is free to fall. This, by the way, is why the rich get richer. One, they understand the phenomenon, they know what's going on. Two, they have sufficient capital to hang on.

One way to easily spot this scenario being set up is to take note of the intraday high or low at mid-morning. At this stage, chances are you have a portion of the day's range, but not the entire range. Wait for one side of the range to be penetrated. Then observe if it is rejected. There could be a one- or two-tick new high or low—or perhaps more. It all depends on the market.

If the market tried to go higher (established new intraday highs) but failed, it will probably go lower later in the day. If the market penetrated the lows (established new intraday lows) but failed, it will probably go higher later in the day.

The specific day-of-the-week pattern will help you identify the precise timing. Just remember that things are not always as they seem. In a nutshell, the market is frequently engineered to go down by first going up—and vice versa!

LIMIT ORDERS

Much as I want to believe that the futures market is a 100 percent fair game, I begin to wonder when I hear stories such as the one my friend Charlie (a fictitious name) related to me not long ago. Just as some people are drawn to train wrecks, I am a connoisseur of the market disaster—even if, as in this case, the story has a silver lining. Charlie had purchased multiple S&P 500 contracts in anticipation of rising prices. His judgment was wrong. The market began to break. So he did the only intelligent thing and called his clearing firm's desk on the floor of the exchange and told the clerk to sell his position.

"Sell me five S&P's market!" Charlie shouted into the phone.

"You want to sell five," the clerk repeated.

"That's right."

Charlie held for the fill. The market was breaking like a rock. Even on the phone, the sound was deafening.

Seconds later, the clerk announced, "You bought five at forty."

"Bought five?" Charlie yelled. "What do you mean I bought five? I told you to sell! Now I'm long ten. Sell ten!"

Flustered, the clerk did as he was told. But the market was freefalling and there were thousands of dollars in losses in Charlie's account due to this clerk's error.

Normally, this is a cut-and-dry situation. The clerk or the clerk's house eats the error. The client is made whole.

Later, Charlie called me and asked me what he should do.

"They have the conversation on tape," I explained. "The house has to eat the error. You are entitled to get out where you told them to sell."

"But he bought," Charlie sighed.

"I know," I told him. "That's their problem."

Apparently, this wasn't the first error this clerk had made. Realizing that he would lose his job over this, the clerk pleaded with Charlie to give him a few days. He would make good on the mistake. Soft-hearted Charlie went along with the scheme. Knowing that clerks don't earn the big money, I was reluctant to endorse this idea. How did this guy plan to make good?

A few days later Charlie got a call from the clerk on the trading desk.

"You sold ten S&P's this morning at seventy-three half on the open," the clerk said in a conspiratorial tone. "It is time to cover them." The market was then breaking through seventy. This was a gain of over $8,700.

"What are you talking about?" Charlie said. "I'm not even in the market. I was out walking my dog."

"We're buying them back for you right here," the clerk insisted. "Done! The trades will be in your account in the morning."

"Whatever you say," Charlie said. He wasn't going to turn down $8,700—especially since this was close to the amount that he'd lost on the prior fiasco. The clerk had made good.

When Charlie later called me and told me what had happened, he couldn't stop laughing. We did some investigating. That morning, a public trader had put in a limit order to sell at seventy-three half. The market had traded to that price, but not through it, and the broker filling the order had been able to get the edge on the trade, selling all ten at the offer. The market immediately moved lower. Realizing he had a nice profit on his hands, the broker, wanting to help the hapless clerk, gave the trade to Charlie. Meanwhile, the client with the limit order was told the trade was "unable"—bad luck, he'd missed a great move by one tick!

I can hear the shouts already. "Can't happen!" It did. And I believe it happened exactly as I've related it here.

Looking back, I can remember a number of times when I had limit orders that just missed being filled. In fact, I got so bummed out by these close calls that I stopped using limit orders altogether and just threw in market orders. At least with a market order, they have to fill you. Granted, sometimes the fills are not what you would expect. But I feel that you have to out-trade the scalpers and other floor traders if you trade from off the floor. There is, of course, one situation where you always receive your limit price. That's when the market is going against you. In that instance, the trade is always consummated.

The most bizarre story that occurs to me concerning strange trades in my account took place in the late eighties. Being a day trader, I never held positions overnight. So when I reached my trading desk down on the floor, the clerk, who knew me well and my style of trading, immediately called me over.

"George," he said, "you have some bonds in your account overnight."

"No, I don't," I said. "You know I'm flat every day at the close."

"Maybe so," he replied, "but they are in your account and no one has come looking for them."

It was only minutes to the open. I hadn't bothered to ask the obvious question.

"Well, in that case, are they profitable?"

He looked up at the board. The opening call was for the market to open at 90-12. The five bond contracts in my account had been purchased at even— a potential 12-tick gain.

"Why don't we just sell them on the open?" the clerk suggested.

"Fine with me," I replied.

We got the five contracts sold at ten, better than a $1,500 profit. No one ever came looking for the trade. And, of course, such good luck never occurred again. Normally, the out-trade clerks are all over you, looking for a misplaced winner.

STOPS

I don't use resting stops—and here's why. When I was young and inexperienced, I once placed a stop under my position in the gold market and it was stopped out below the low of the day. At the time, I didn't know whether I should protest, so I simply took my lumps. Of course, the original position proved to be a big winner, but I'd already been stopped out. I haven't had any resting stop orders in the market since.

About a year ago, I got a call from a guy named Joe who managed somehow to sell near the low of the day in the E-mini S&P and buy near the high. How, I asked him, did he manage to lose so much money on one little contract? It was the largest E-mini loss in one day I ever remember hearing about.

"Well," Joe explained, "you said they run the stops and I didn't want to be an easy target."

I couldn't believe what I was hearing. "Instead," I said, "you let them clean you out of perhaps 25 percent of your account." This was one of the most reckless stop stories I've ever heard.

Just because you may not want to place a resting stop-loss order in the market doesn't mean you don't want to have a clearly defined point where you will have what is known as a mental stop. There has to be a place where you pull the plug. Managing the losses is a major component of trading success.

Stop placement, of course, whether mental or actual, can be a tricky proposition. Understandably, most new traders get the process backward. The novice trader tends to place the stop based on what he or she is willing to lose. This is the wrong approach for two reasons. First, the market cares little for your risk tolerance. Second, if placed among many other stops, the fill isn't going to have any resemblance to the price at which the stop was originally placed. Put another way, when the market breaks below a support level, the abundance of sell stops resting there will create temporary panic selling. Conversely, when the market penetrates a resistance area, the buying stops will propel the market higher. Either way, you will find yourself paying up.

Intelligent stop placement needs to be tailored to the market environment at the time you are trading. Accordingly, volatile markets require stops that are further away than quieter markets. Otherwise, mere random moves can whipsaw you out of a potentially profitable position. A stop of three or four cents (worth $75 to $100), in a quiet market like oats, might work. But a tight stop such as this in the high-flying S&P 500 would guarantee a loss perhaps 95 percent of the time. In addition to volatility, the other key component of stop placement is where you initially entered the position. If you bought near the high of the day, and now profit-taking is setting in, you may have to sustain a greater paper loss than if you fine-tuned the entry and purchased right where the pullback should have stopped. Now this requires a certain degree of sophistication, but is not outside the realm of possibility once you can get a handle on how the market behaves. The point is, the easy answers need to be thrown out. If you cannot afford to lose more than a specific amount, and the stop calls for putting more money at risk than you care to, find another market. You need to play the game without one eye on the money. The money should be secondary. To win, you need to concentrate on market action and act according to what the probabilities suggest will occur.

I know this is a tall order. But if you handicap yourself at the outset by tying two arms behind your back, you are almost certain to lose.

PLAY YOUR OWN GAME

The tendency among novice traders is to want to change the rules in the middle of the game. I've alluded to the notion that one can always tell a newcomer by both the number of markets he follows and number of strategies he trades. The professional, on the other hand, does one thing well, and does it over and over again. In all the years I've traded, I sold the high of the day only once and bought the low of the day only once. One would think that selling the high and buying the bottom would be a slam-dunk, sure-thing profit. But, in fact, I managed to actually lose money, despite my incredible good fortune, by changing the rules in the middle of the day.

Here's what happened. It was a Friday in the early eighties when Chicago still had a viable gold market. New York had always been the primary market for gold, but Chicago traders, taking New York's leadership, would look for arbitrage possibilities between the two markets. This, of course, generated plenty of volume and liquidity. On the heels of the surge in gold prices to $850 an ounce, there was money to be made; understandably enough, I was one of those seeking to capitalize on the situation. At the time, the gold market was so vibrant that you could make a thousand dollars even before you carded a trade. That is, you would yell out "sold" and begin to write down the trade on your trading card—opposing trader ID, house number, number of contracts, price, and so on. When you looked up at the board, the market might have already moved in your favor. Those were heady days.

Anyway, on that particular Friday morning, I was out of town, traveling down in Florida. I pulled into a rest area, called my brokerage desk on the floor, and placed a trade to sell so many gold contracts. Because I was out of town, I then placed a stop loss order on the position. Told the fill, I traveled on. As the day progressed, I realized I had sold the high of the day—from Florida! What good luck. As we approached the close of trading, I decided to let a good thing ride. It had been a trend day down and the market was going to close near the low of the day.

A weak closing like that means the sellers are in control, and you can usually expect more selling on the following day once the news is absorbed. Because it was a weekend, I expected more nervous sellers on Monday morning to push the market lower. That's where I planned to cover my position.

Instead, that was the weekend that the Israeli Air Force bombed Iraq's nuclear reactor. The gold market opened limit up on Monday morning. Compounding my mistakes, I panicked and bought back my contracts at a large loss. The rest of the day, the gold market sold off.

I never took a day trade overnight ever again.

Looking back, I tried to fool myself by saying, "My rule wasn't no trades overnight. My rule was no losing day trades overnight." That is, if a day trade proved to be a winner, why not take it at least to the next morning's opening to collect a higher payoff?

This was my means of rationalizing this disaster. The problem was, on the several occasions I tried this approach, I couldn't sleep at nights because I was worried about my open position. Then, about five o'clock in the morning, I'd turn on the all-news radio station to get the London fix, or the opening price in London. This was resulting in a lot of useless worry. If the London call opened my way, I'd gloat but begin to worry that they might take it back prior to the morning's U.S. opening. If it was against me in London, there wasn't much I could do but wait several hours, go downtown, and face the music. There was very little chance the market was going to reverse direction and open in my favor in New York and Chicago. So the occasional added profit, when the overnight market cooperated, didn't compensate for the time and money spent worrying about the losers.

There are many reasons why you might want to go overnight. But don't do it if you are a day trader.

We all make mistakes. Indeed, if you are going to make day trading your profession, you will continue to make mistakes. The key is knowing the difference between what I call stupid mistakes and intelligent mistakes. The former will sabotage your trading for good, whereas the latter are just a normal part of trading. The sooner you can weed out the "stupid" mistakes in your trading repertoire, the sooner you will master the learning curve and begin to profit.

UNDERSTANDING MARKET PATTERNS

The place to begin a serious study of market phenomena is understanding market patterns. Even if you can become a master of self-discipline, a knowledgeable market sleuth of insider engineering, and a virtual encyclopedia of market lore, but not understand market patterns, you are likely to fall short in winning the trading game. This is because you need to know how to read the market. You need to know, for instance, the difference between a short-cover rally and a genuine rally. You need to know what to pay attention to and what to ignore. You need to see who's in trouble and who's in control. You need to understand the market machinations that create confusion for some but certainty for others. You need to be able to decipher the hidden footprints of the market insiders.

To start, you need to be able to measure the market—place a number on strength, speed, rate of momentum, and so on. This is the part of trading that attracts so many. Having quantified the market, these traders feel justified in expecting a given outcome. This leaves out the delicate subject of interpretation, however. How do you actually apply these numbers to a given market circumstance?

I'm a firm believer in understanding everything you can about a market—strength, support, resistance, momentum, whatever. But to effectively use these measurements, you need to know what has happened under comparable conditions in the past; in short, you need research. With good research, you know the percentages. Factor in a good money management approach and you are on your way to a strong and solid trading strategy.

So much that passes for knowledge of the markets is nothing more than opinion, pure and simple. There is a saying down on the floor that even a broken clock is correct twice a day. Some pundits would have you believe that they actually did foresee some key market event, but isn't everyone with 20-20 hindsight correct? Then, too, there is the old spaghetti technique: Throw enough against the wall and something will stick. The task is to learn to ignore the unknowable and concentrate on the few pieces of evidence that are truly valuable.

If you have ever undergone a medical examination you will know that doctors don't like to guess. To make an intelligent diagnosis, a physician will run tests: blood pressure, number of heart beats per minute, cholesterol, body weight, blood analysis, vitamin and mineral deficits, and so on. Typically, these tests generate numbers which, when analyzed, can pinpoint a real or potential problem. Certain high or low readings can spell trouble ahead. Likewise, the market analyst can look at a certain series of numbers and interpret them as well.

What are these numbers, what do they measure, and how are they used? We'll get to these answers in a minute.

In order to detect patterns intelligently, every trader must begin by maintaining the proper balance between knowing which patterns are high-probability and which are simply likely. They have to avoid the likely trades in favor of those with the most probable outcome. Otherwise, they fall into a trap of wasting their resources on lesser situations and the inevitable demoralization that sets in once equity disappears in a series of ill-chosen trades.

We are going to shine a spotlight on the best opportunities in the pages to come. To find the best trades, we are going to have to throw out a lot of iffy, fifty-fifty, coin-flip situations.

To begin, you have to understand that there are relatively few genuine opportunities. To successfully capitalize on those that do exist, you have to know what to expect, and then you have to implement your strategy immediately. Occasionally, a developing market opportunity might give you as much as 20 to 30 minutes to take action. Far more often, though, the window of opportunity can be measured in minutes. Once this opportunity is gone, it's gone.

One popular misconception about trading is that a professional can step into the market and extract dollars at a moment's whim. This is not true. On the contrary, the professional knows when to stand aside, which, given the risks that exist, is most of the time. So the trading-animal psychology, which is exemplified in movies such as *Trading Places,* has no place among the trading arsenal of professional traders.

The market novice might be surprised that one would wait an hour or two, or even longer, for a good 15-minute rally, but if that's what it takes, then the wait is justified. Besides, one is not merely waiting for one or two hours. More likely, the seasoned professional is waiting for evidence that the market is ready to run.

The fact is, the market will tip its hand. It doesn't operate in a vacuum. A good analyst will rapidly review a dozen or more indicators, place them in the context of an overall market environment, and immediately seize upon a plan. She may even back away a few steps to gain longer-term prosperity. She might look at seasonal patterns, for instance. Above all, she will remain flexible and adjust her level of commitment as the fluid market situation dictates.

I understand the novice trader's tendency to want to jump whole hog on the first good trade that comes along. This is a mistake because there is always the risk, no matter how certain the outcome, that one is simply wrong. Accordingly, one must demonstrate some restraint in first starting out.

There are the go-for-broke trades that I have already alluded to and bread-and-butter trades that are much more commonplace. The professional realizes it is these latter trades that pay the rent. When starting out, try to get your feet wet first lest you end up drowning. Go slow in the beginning. There will be plenty of opportunities to make a killing later on.

I say this at the outset, because I know how dangerous a little information can be. You read about a pattern or market phenomenon, you observe that phenomenon occurring three or four times, and pretty soon you are ready to mortgage your home to get aboard the next move.

There are many ways to discern market patterns, but I will concentrate my comments on the three with which I am most familiar. They are:

1. *Support and resistance*—the measurement of levels that dictate where prices will cease rising or declining.

2. *Time and price*—how patterns will repeat in duration and magnitude.

3. *Day of the week*—why the specific daily pattern is important in deciding how the market will trade.

In a nutshell, these three approaches, when used together, should give you a pretty good idea where the market is heading. The first two are opposite sides of the same coin. Support and resistance levels measure key price levels. Time and price measures the amount of time it took the market to reach level A or level B. Factor in the specific day and now you have a market bias.

Over the years, I've used all three of these pattern-recognition techniques, and today I use a combination of these three that works for me. I've never been one to say, "Try this because it works." Rather, my attitude is that you have to make yourself a believer. Only then will you have the confidence to incorporate a given strategy into your overall trading arsenal. So today I tell people, "Don't take my word on this. Try it and see if it works for yourself." I'm always amused when I get a wide diversity of views on trading techniques. A caller will tell you your XYZ strategy is the greatest thing since sliced bread. The very next caller will tell how worthless it is. A difference of opinion is, I suppose, what makes the market, whether for soybean futures or trading strategies.

I've related this story in previous works, but for the first-time reader here it is. After making all the dumb mistakes that new traders make, I was driven by desperation to find something that worked. I discovered an unreadable, torn copy of George Douglas Taylor's "Book Method" in the library at the Chicago Mercantile Exchange. In the 1950s, Taylor used this strategy to track the grain market. He said that there was a three-day cycle, that the market was engineered from within. The market would be engineered lower, according to Taylor, offering an opportunity for the knowledgeable buyers to purchase contracts at bargain prices from sellers who were unaware of the phenomenon. Then, after two days of rising prices, the market was engineered higher, causing hapless short-sellers to panic and cover their short positions, only to collapse later in the day. This was an interesting theory. But did it work? I began to monitor the market. Sure enough, it would often open lower and gain support and surge to the highs at the end of the day. Conversely, after a couple of days of this high-flying bullishness, there would be a final surge to new highs, and—you guessed it—the market would collapse. I couldn't figure who was doing the engineering or manipulating. It just seemed the same old fear-and-greed syndrome one witnessed everyday—but who cared? I was finally able to join the winners.

I did observe one other thing. The same winning floor traders made money every day off the paper orders that seemed clustered together at key support and resistance levels.

After witnessing the floor brokers offering the market down in an effort to execute their trading decks, I began to notice that when the stops were all gone, the market would reverse and surge the other way. I didn't see this happen once or twice, but dozens of times. Once the public was out of the way, the market was ready to run—in, of course, the opposite direction. Moreover, as Taylor had so accurately pointed out, the market stopped at predictable levels at, through, or above the prior high or low. A true believer, I began to track all the Taylor numbers and keep them on a card in my shirt pocket. I finally realized I had an enormous advantage over the public traders. I knew where the stops would be run—if only the market could trade at that level. These numbers later became the genesis of my LSS 3-Day Cycle Method.

There are a million ways to screw up a good trading system and I've made my share of mistakes over the years. Using my Book Method numbers, I'd come in all ready to trade, relax my guard and take a reckless position, only to find myself buying my sell numbers, or vice versa. Or I'd get caught up in the emotionalism of some big trader pushing the pit around and join the crowd of locals, only to get killed when the market suddenly switched direction. Only then would I consult my trading numbers that I'd written down after the previous day's close and see that my system was right on the money. It was only after a "report" day fiasco that I vowed to get a grip on my trading. So I took an inventory of my strengths and weaknesses, and told myself to buckle down.

It was about this time that I began to observe that the most successful traders were always in the pit at certain times during the day and conspicuously absent at others. You would always see them in there early on—at the open and first hour—and then they would reappear late in the day, usually when the market was about to make a run. Was this my first glimpse of the time-of-day syndrome that I would later incorporate in my time and price trading? It probably was. You would see the same guys elbowing their way into the pit every afternoon and you knew something was up. Like clockwork, the market would begin to run. Looking back, I now know this wasn't happenstance.

It was about this time, when I'd become a believer in my LSS numbers, that early one morning I was standing in the bond pit when a report hit. The report must have been extremely bullish (I'm purely a technician and care little for the fundamentals) because the locals began bidding the market up in a panic. That's when I saw my opportunity. The market surged up to my sell number. I immediately began hitting the bids. "Sold! Sold! Sold!" I hit the three closest guys standing near me. The market promptly sailed higher, but then the Fed must have adjusted the number, for there was panic selling like you wouldn't believe. The market broke like a rock under the weight of a ton of sellers.

I covered my short positions on the break, but not before the floor and probably not a few public traders had gotten caught in a classic bull trap.

Once the panic was over, the trader standing next to me, one I had sold to, turned and said, "How did you know to sell 'em there?"

I smiled. "Just lucky, I guess."

I wasn't about to get in a long discussion about Taylor's numbers and how they had rescued me from ruin. The less said the better.

I had been lucky. Government reports are notorious for destabilizing the market. There is always the chance you will select the right direction prior to one of these reports. But there is also the likelihood that you will have your share of losers if you try to outguess the reports. A better approach is to let the dust settle after a report and begin your analysis from there.

Taylor's contribution to technical analysis cannot be underestimated. He believed in measuring everything—market declines and market rallies, how far one high or low exceeded another—and then averaging the results. He divided up his numbers between the buy envelope and sell envelope and then averaged those as well. The net result of all this averaging was a buy number and a sell number. I know it would be convenient if these two numbers were the final answers. But the market is far too complex to be able to predict in advance the actual high and low. We have done extensive studies over the years in trying to predict the actual high or low. The results are conclusive. No simple mathematical formula can accurately predict a day's range in advance—at least none that we tested. Nevertheless, when taken in conjunction with some common sense, the Taylor numbers can provide some valuable insights.

For instance, once the market is open and a range is established, the Taylor (or LSS) average range numbers can be superimposed on the early range. Utilized in this fashion, they can provide a pretty good assessment of where the high and low will be. This, by the way, is one of the strongest arguments for trading the same market day after day. If I'm a soybean trader and I know that the average range is approximately 15 cents, then I can make an educated guess about where the market might end today—once it has already opened and been trading for a while. If I haven't traded this market before, I haven't got a clue. I think you will agree that this is a lot different than simply picking numbers out of the air.

Let's say I'm trading the S&P 500. My calculations tell me from high to low, the range is approximately 20.00 points. If the prior day's close is 1400.00, I might say we are looking at 1420.00 on tomorrow's high or 1380.00 on tomorrow's low—if the market opens unchanged. But it is far better to be able to work with tomorrow's numbers after the market opens. This is because now you can throw out a number of opposing scenarios after the open. For example, take the following statement: There is a high degree of probability that, after one hour of trading, either the high or low of the day has already been established. How can this help me? By telling me that the probabilities favor one of two scenarios—that either the high or low of the day is already in existence or that the range is probably within 20.00 points of that number.

Now let's put numbers to this proposition. Assume the market closes at 1400.00 and the next day's open is 1404.00. After one hour, the intraday range high is 1407.00 and low is 1400.00, or 7.00 points. Well, if the market averages 20.00 points, we are probably going to see another 13.00 points. Nothing, of course, is ever certain. One sensible strategy is to add the average range of 20.00 to the low, or subtract the average range from the high— or 1420.00 on the high or 1387.00 on the low. Will you get both? This is unlikely. Will you get one? This is quite possible. Which one will it be? There are a variety of questions that need to be answered before you'll know.

What day are we in the trading cycle? What was the sequence of the highs and lows yesterday? Did the high occur first or last? What day of the week is today? What's the market's overall strength or weakness? Has the recent momentum been up or down? What conclusions can you infer from today's open? We will discuss all these questions in the pages to come. The point is, a multitude of considerations have to be given to the specifics before you trade.

You have to understand that the market action is a fluid situation that is evolving before you. Yesterday's resistance becomes today's support as the market powers higher. Moreover, there are levels upon levels of major- and minor-stopping points along the way, each of which will have its own significance—and, I might add, its own opportunities and pitfalls.

On a daily basis, a market finds its own equilibrium level. There is what the technicians call the *value area,* an area around which prices rotate. Also known as a *consolidation area,* this value area acts as a powerful magnet; one can usually fade any move away from this area. Particularly significant is the value area established on yesterday's close, or at least on the last 30 minutes of trading in the day session. This is where buyers and sellers were in agreement. It stands to reason, unless there is a compelling reason to think otherwise, that fundamentals haven't changed that much overnight. Accordingly, whenever the market is stretched out of the open, often creating a so-called *gap* on the charts—I liken this to extending a huge spring—the probable outcome is that the spring will resume its normal shape. We've already discussed the notion of running lots of overnight stops on the open, creating a sort of mini-panic that feeds on itself. All this drama is frequently just a prelude to the real price action of the day. These fireworks on the open are generally used to separate the unfocused players from their money. But the serious action is still to come. For this reason, I may play the open to improve my concentration (nothing causes one to pay attention as much as the prospect of winning or losing money), but I'll save the real commitment for later in the morning, or even afternoon, when the legitimate trend begins.

Armed with a slew of numbers, the professional can be overwhelmed if he or she is not careful. This is because so much happens so fast that there isn't time to process all the information. Sometimes you just have to go for it. Let me give you an example. You get an immediate upside gap on the opening bell. You know from experience that there is a 75 percent chance that a normal opening gap like this will be filled. So the probabilities are 75 percent that you will win if you sell immediately—or are they? I said the probabilities are that the gap will be filled. I didn't say the market couldn't carry another two, three, or four hundred points against you first. There is always the one-in-four chance that the gap won't be filled at all, in which case a sale on the open might indeed be at the low of the day! The fact is, you never know for certain.

There is a high likelihood that the market isn't going to open up higher and die, not when you are looking at a range of a couple of thousand points. (Note: In markets that are known to lock limit, this comment doesn't apply. So be careful.) At any rate, you need to make a decision regarding this trade quickly. Here's why: The market *should* fill the gap rather rapidly. If more than 20 or 30 minutes goes by and the gap isn't filled, something is probably wrong. One strategy is to sell some right at or just after the open. Given some adversity, sell more, averaging up your sell price. If you are very aggressive, you might take a third stab at the sell side. But you need confirmation almost immediately that you are correct on this trade. That is, the trade should begin to work. If it doesn't, run like crazy.

I say this as someone who has had the market die shortly after selling a gap opening. This is not a good sign. Without a preponderance of sellers, the market cannot break; new buying is probably holding it there. And why is there new buying if this was a simple stop-running exercise? After the buy stops are executed, the market should break. If it doesn't, something is wrong.

Another alternative is to do nothing. In this instance, accept the fact that you have probably missed the trade. If it starts to move your way, you'll probably want to jump aboard. But resist this temptation. By the time you decide to sell, a lot of other would-be sellers will also be jumping in—and what's that going to do to your fill? If you want to sell, do so on the initial upward surge, or when the market is rising. You'll know soon enough if you are correct. The safest place to sell is always when the uncertainty is greatest.

Why risk money on the open amid all this uncertainty? Because it is also an opportunity to get the day off on a good foot. Moreover, by sending out a few soldiers in this fashion, you can often get a genuine feel for what is to come. I cannot explain the difference between looking and doing, but I can tell you that it makes a fundamental difference in how you'll trade the rest of the day. On a day when I get killed for selling early, I'm going to be a much more reluctant seller later in the day. The same applies, of course, to the buy side. You could make the case that this creates a bias in your trading opinions. But I believe that it provides the kind of information that enables you to go for the big win later in the day.

With the prior day's close representing the value area, there is a high probability that the market will trade at that price at some time during the day. Using simple support and resistance patterns, one can create buying and selling *zones,* areas where they are comfortable doing one or the other. Contrast this with the novice trader's approach of taking a position and placing a stop. If the initial order and the stop are within the same zone, you unnecessarily lose money because the position was still good when you folded your cards.

To prevent this from happening, you need to know what constitutes a legitimate buying or selling zone. Taylor's Book Method provides a pretty good handle on where the support and resistance zones exist. The point is, you have to understand the paradoxical nature of using this zone-type strategy. Specifically, the market is a better buy higher up than lower down; the market is a better sell lower down than higher up. You mean it is okay to sell it higher up, but it is a buy even higher? That's exactly what I'm saying. Strength begets strength and weakness begets weakness. Look at what happened in October 1987. First, the weak hands with close stops sold; then, as the market went lower still, more selling developed; by the end, the whole world wanted to sell—big funds and all—and that, of course, was the bottom. In a lesser fashion, one sees this same phenomenon practically every day. Take the difference between what I call a *normal* gap and an *extreme* gap. You can fade the normal gap, but you better jump aboard the extreme gap. It isn't coming back.

How do you tell one gap from the other? You are not going to like this answer. I know one when I see one. Yesterday's extreme gap is today's normal gap. So much depends on current volatility that it doesn't make sense to quantify the number of points at one moment in time.

The concept of zone trading is nothing more than support and resistance. There isn't a trader who doesn't swear by his or her own numbers or indicators—whether they be trend lines, Bollinger Bands, moving averages, stochastics, or old-fashioned support and resistance. They can all help you get a better handle on the market.

Another way to look at market patterns is to measure symmetry. So much of market action seems random and haphazard. But to one familiar with market patterns, there are distinct, telltale signs that the market wants to trend higher or lower. I call this type of market analysis *time and price;* I've even created a workbook and video called "Sniper Trading" that describes this trading strategy. The other side of the support and resistance coin, time and price, looks at market trends and tries to predict the next trend, based on current market action.

How would you like to predict a high or low of the next move within a few ticks? How would you like to know the exact minute when a high or low will occur? With time and price trading this is often possible. Market symmetry provides a virtual roadmap to profits when correctly applied. Moreover, because it tells both the magnitude and the duration of a move, it alerts you when something is wrong, when a pattern fails. Even then, not all is lost. A failure pattern suggests the reverse will occur; now you'll have symmetry in the opposite direction. I know that these are startling claims. But if you remain open to the notion that there is a rhyme and reason to the markets, you'll see that these patterns are indeed knowable—and that anyone able to read these patterns will no longer have to guess about market direction.

While support and resistance trading and time and price trading are totally different, they are not mutually exclusive. You can use both in your trading and one can enhance the other.

I know that hindsight is always 20-20. The amazing thing is that foresight can also be 20-20 when you understand time and price. Once again, don't take my word on this. In the pages ahead, we will explore this simple concept in-depth and you'll be able to apply the principles yourself.

This notion of market symmetry is nothing new. It goes back to the early work of the market guru, W.D. Gann, whose pioneering work into market cycles remains unchallenged to this day. The problem with Gann, of course, is that he was a bit of a mystic and no one, to this day, can readily translate what he wrote into anything that anyone can understand. At bottom, however, was the idea that everything in the universe was governed by a cycle—tides, the phases of the moon, whatever—and that the market had its own cyclical nature as well. A deeply mystical man, Gann was an unsung prophet in his time and a controversial one as well.

I won't attempt to do justice to Gann's work in a few sentences. But in a nutshell, he said this: Markets, like many forces in the universe, move according to predictable patterns. These patterns are symmetrical in nature both in terms of price and time. Put another way, a market will trend X points in Y time, the two being directly related to one another.

Although I had followed Gann's work for years—and even written about it in some of my previous books—I was unprepared for a call I got from my trading friend, Bill, who lives out on the West Coast, in the early nineties.

"When are you coming out here?" Bill asked. "I've got some very interesting trading concepts to show you."

I get calls like this all the time. Usually the caller thinks he has discovered the proverbial holy grail when in fact he just has a new wrinkle on interpreting stochastics or some other indicator. I told Bill that I'd planned a West Coast trip for October and that I'd be able to spend a couple of days with him. I ended up staying an entire week.

"See this trend here?" Bill said the first morning, pointing to his computer screen. "The market has traded three hundred points in exactly eight minutes. The next trend should be identical."

"When will that be?" I asked, puzzled.

"We don't know yet," he explained. "It's still consolidating."

We watched the screen silently. Profit-taking was pushing the market lower, but there was a clear-cut consolidation being formed. The market was choppy. To my mind, it was anyone's call as to which direction it would go.

Bill saw what he was looking for. "It's setting up to run," he said. "See these two prices. They are identical. Prices are in equilibrium. The train is about to leave the station." He pointed to the screen. Then he tapped out some numbers on his calculator and showed me the result. "That's the top," he said. "It should be there at 10:44 A.M. Chicago time."

At precisely 10:44 A.M. Chicago time, the December S&P 500 futures traded at exactly the price he indicated. It was a new high on the day. The trend was exactly eight minutes long. I know because I counted the one-minute bars on the screen.

"It's over," Bill announced. "It's almost lunchtime in New York. Time to take a break." After the top had been quickly reached, the market drifted lower.

I was amazed. "How in the world," I later asked him, "did you know that?"

"I didn't," he said. "The market told me."

"Told you what?"

"Where it would go," he explained, "and when it would get there."

Bill related to me how the symmetry worked. He explained how a mirror-like effect would occur whenever a trend occurred. It was like when you threw a rock into a pond. There would be ripples. These were universal laws. The symmetry in the market was there for everyone to see.

The first thing I told him was that I enjoyed teaching people. Because I was a writer as well as a trader, I couldn't agree to keep such information secret.

Bill laughed. "George, you are my friend," he said. "If I help you or some-one else become a better trader, so much the better. What goes around, comes around." Like most generous people, Bill was a spiritual person as well who felt that bread cast upon the waters came back to him in dividends.

This generosity of spirit appealed to me. I'd seen it many times over in all the wealthy people I knew. What you give away comes back to you. What you try to grasp tightly, you always lose. It is a good metaphor for trading itself. One who takes intelligent risks is rewarded; one who insists on cer-tainty is punished. The paradoxes abound.

We spent the rest of the week identifying symmetrical patterns. The amaz-ing thing is how consistent—and identifiable—these patterns could be. And even when the market throws you a curve, when perhaps your initial estimate is wrong, you'll find that later the symmetry exists in the opposite direction.

The implications of what I was about to learn that week were formidable. By identifying an initial leg in a trend, one could measure for time and price and come up with a precise target number and minute. What's more, based on this analysis, one could identify the downside risk and create a buying or selling zone. The bottom line was this: You never took a trade unless you knew where it was going and when it was going to get there. And, of course, you knew what to expect in terms of downside risk. If a leg were to fail, you knew it immediately and you now had a new set of variables to tell you the significance of this failure swing. Looking back, there was rarely a day when these patterns were not evident. Looking forward, of course, the analysis was understandably more difficult. You needed to factor in a number of variables.

Flying east, I couldn't wait to get home and begin using my new time and price studies in the market. If what I'd witnessed in Bill's office was true, I was about to embark on a whole new path in my trading career. For years, I'd been what I call a *long-term* trader—in on the open, out on the close. While often profitable, this could be a frustrating endeavor. You would frequently find yourself taking one step forward and two steps back. Why give back what had already been so hard-won? With Bill's approach, you never took a trade unless you knew where it was going and when it was going to get there—often to the exact minute and tick! It was a one-way street to profits. Moreover, the risk, being closely monitored, was small. You knew all the components of the trade before you entered: where it was going, when it was going to get there, and, in the event of failure, when to run for the sidelines. What more could one ask for? Understandably, my excitement caused me to think about how I was going to use this new insight into market symmetry.

Just as I never asked anyone to take me at my word about trading techniques, I wasn't going to take Bill's word. Perhaps I'd just witnessed a lucky week. No. I wanted to investigate some more and do a little research.

I almost never make a serious commitment in the market unless I'm fairly certain I'm not making a foolish mistake. If you can successfully outline a scenario for a successful trade in advance—win or lose—you, at the very least, have a handle on what's going on in the market. This puts you miles ahead of the guy who is simply guessing. In short, if you understand what should occur—and have a game plan for capitalizing on that occurrence— you will likewise know when a trade isn't shaping up and you can take defensive action. Once-impenetrable market patterns were finally coming into focus. Clearly, fully understanding market symmetry was going to prove a difficult challenge, but I felt I was up to it. Sometimes the right opportunity comes up at the right time.

I'm a firm believer in serendipity. This word derives from the Persian fairy tale "The Three Princes of Serendip." The dictionary describes the term as meaning "the faculty or phenomenon of finding valuable or agreeable things not sought for." I might add that the harder one seeks to find the answer, the more elusive the answer becomes. I think this is true in the markets as well as in life in general. How often have you tried to make something happen in your life—or in the market? It never works. There is a Zen component to this phenomenon. The harder you try, the more difficult the task becomes.

My discovery of time and price symmetry had been extremely serendipitous. If I hadn't met Bill, who'd been a student of mine, I never would have learned about market symmetry. This requires a certain amount of humility, the notion that one never has all the answers. If I hadn't been planning a West Coast trip, independent of Bill's phone call, I wouldn't have made my way to his door. If I hadn't studied Gann, I wouldn't have known about his notion of symmetry that embraces the concept of time and price. I might have dismissed the idea altogether. So much of success depends on simply being in the right place at the right time. But you must be open to the experience.

When I look back on the many frustrations of becoming a trader, they pale in comparison to the many wonderful things that have happened. I think back on the conversation in the greasy coffee shop with my first trading mentor. What were these conversations worth in terms of keeping me alive when I was at the brink of disaster? The luck that caused me to discover Taylor and the notion of the market engineering. Some twenty years later, I can still remember reading that the market is taken lower to go up—and vice versa.

I can remember paying my first programmer to test some tentative theories and how disappointed I was when he informed me that the testing proved that, over time, my strategies didn't work. Presenting me with the computer print-out of the results, he said: "Sorry they don't work, but thanks for the $1,500." I immediately realized that I'd have to find another programmer. And, because of serendipity, I did. Over the years, there have been many, many more such instances where the answer was waiting just over the horizon.

If you have ever traveled, you know what I mean. If you are open to experience, you will find what you are looking for. I was coming out of a Left Bank cafe with a friend in Paris not long ago when I suggested we visit a church across the street. I don't know why I suddenly had the urge to visit this church, but I did. Dating back to the 14th century, St. Germain des Pres, the most important church in Paris before Notre Dame, is a magnificent example of Gothic architecture, both dignified and magical. On the wall was a sign announcing a concert of Mozart's "Requiem" scheduled for that evening. We immediately decided to attend. Later that evening, walking back to the hotel in a gentle rain, the Chorus of Versailles still resounding in my ears, I realized how valuable a serendipitous event can be. It proved to be the highlight of the trip.

I could provide you with many more instances of chance happenings resulting in profitable experiences. Let me relate a more mundane example. Several years ago, we were putting together a promotional brochure for a two-day seminar. We had done our homework and had an excellent product, but it was proving difficult to advertise without sounding too self-serving. We could list the statistics that demonstrated the profitability of the software, but our prospective clients had seen the same thing a hundred times from less reputable sources. Exactly why should we appear any different in the eyes of a prospective customer? Then my partner came up with a novel idea.

"Why not give it away?" he suggested.

"Give it away?" I asked. "We've done months of research here. How could we possibly get back our investment if we give it away?"

"Not the entire system," he explained, "but enough to demonstrate that we have something good."

The strategy worked. The people who attended the subsequent seminars were delighted with the nonpromotional information we had provided to them. Some had even paid for the seminar with the money they had made using the formulas. Those who learned to embrace the uncertainty, as I'd suggested at the seminars, made even more money. Months later, I was still receiving phone calls from people who had found the brochure buried under a pile of papers. Some explained that this free information was worth more than expensive software programs they had purchased. Once again, a serendipitous event had led a number of people to discover a valuable trading tool.

The final component of understanding market patterns is to take the macro view of the market, day-of-the-week trading. If you had asked me several years ago if I thought there was any difference between the days of the week, I would have dismissed the idea immediately. But research has made me a believer. We now have incontrovertible evidence that each day of the week has its own unique pattern. There is, for instance, a high probability of the market rising on Monday and declining on Thursday. This is not the same, however, as saying that the market must rise on Monday and fall on Thursday. The probabilities only favor these typical patterns when the circumstances on the prior days fall within a given set of parameters. So don't be tempted to take the easy approach. On average, Monday will be strong if Friday closes strong. But a weak Friday with a close at the lows will probably suggest a weak Monday. Moreover, while Thursday is typically the weakest day of the week—in a bull market, at least—it will be the strongest in a bear market when the prior three days have been weak.

I say this based on looking at almost 600 day-of-the-week samples. Using our research, I can tell you exactly what a typical day should look like. Granted, there will always be exceptions, but even the exceptions can be anticipated if you know what to look for. I don't want you to think that day-of-the-week trading is a simple task. Over the years, I've lost my share of supporters who refused to believe that trading wasn't easy. The fact is, there isn't one formula or one pattern that can identify a winner in advance. Rather, ferreting out a winner requires an understanding of the nuances of the market. Market analysis is like putting together a complicated puzzle. There are a variety of competing trends that must be blended together.

The nice thing about day-of-the-week trading is that it gives you the big picture, a blueprint of what to expect on a given day. Moreover, while it zooms out and provides you with an overall daily pattern, it dovetails with both the time and price and the support and resistance approach to market analysis. With day-of-the-week trading, you still have the two clear-cut trends, morning and afternoon, separated by the noon hour sideways action. Zooming in, time and price enables you to fine-tune the trade, further separating the trends into two legs of equal magnitude and duration. The most amazing thing about these different approaches is that, while they are arrived at by totally different means, they complement one another.

For most traders, making the calculations necessary to find a winning trade is a laborious, often tedious task. For me it is an art that represents creating order out of chaos. There is no more satisfying endeavor than to successfully map out a winning strategy and then implement that strategy. The amount of money that is at stake is secondary. Indeed, looking back, I can remember losing trades that I felt better about than winning ones. Why? Because the winners were simply the result of a lucky guess, whereas the losers were monitored correctly and losses kept to a minimum. Trading is a process. If you do the correct thing on a consistent basis, you will win. The occasional big score, on the other hand, is often the result of recklessness. Do it long enough and you will end up losing.

I've encountered this phenomenon many times among new traders. They get a lucky break or, operating out of ignorance, they throw caution to the winds only to win big. One mistake leads to another. They now think they have the inside track to profits, but the inevitable losses end up ruining them. Far better to concentrate on what works and take a disciplined approach. In the years I've spent observing every type of trader, I've never known the reckless types to last for long.

The first thing novice traders always ask is, "How much money can I make?" This is almost always a signal that they will soon be separated from their money. It's better to immerse yourself in the challenging task of understanding market patterns and mastering the discipline to utilize this hard-won knowledge. Breaking even is not such a bad situation when you are first starting and beginning to compete with professionals.

When I first started out in the futures markets, I too was bewildered by the confusing mass of data confronting me. Nevertheless, like most novice traders, I plunged ahead, often to my severe regret. After numerous inevitable setbacks, I began to recognize patterns emerging from the market haze. Most of the time, one could recognize these patterns on an intuitive basis. It wasn't until I was able to quantify these events that I truly began to understand what was going on; I could evaluate momentum and strength and sum up the market's condition with a series of numbers. The figures gave me an overall understanding of the market, and they eventually became the source of my success. It is to the construction and understanding of these numbers that we will now turn.

2

Time and Price

Sniper Trading

Sniper trading is a hit-and-run approach to the market, in which time and price play the key roles. It is based on the notion that a specific pattern or symmetry can be identified and quantified. Learning how to measure market trends in terms of time and price is the basis of successful trading using this approach.

The *ideal* pattern, when time and price are identical, consists of two legs in perfect symmetry completing one trend. The idea is to use the appearance of the first leg to forecast the magnitude and duration of the second leg. Ideally, there are two trends a day, one in the morning and one in the afternoon.

While this ideal pattern is simplicity itself, you have to understand that there are a number of variations on this theme. Significantly, these variations can cause stumbling blocks for the trader who is not prepared for their appearance. Nevertheless, even though a portion of time and price patterns fail, their failure does not always constitute a violation of the market's overall symmetry. For example, let's say the market rallies 4.50 points in 13 minutes. With market symmetry you might see an identical decline—4.50 points in 13 minutes. In this instance, the failure was not a failure at all, although the second leg failed to materialize as anticipated.

In learning to identify market symmetry, one must be willing to settle for *partial* symmetry. The market might fail in time but not in price, and vice versa. To further complicate matters, you need to understand that the symmetry extends outward from two legs comprising one trend, to two trends comprising one day, to two weeks comprising one-half of one month's trend, and so on. The symmetry is there if only you take the time to correctly identify it. Using this concept of market symmetry, you can identify long-term market objectives as well as where you may wish to exit the market on a minute-to-minute, tick-by-tick basis.

When it comes to extracting dollars from the market, sniper trading is the closest thing to a legal printing press that I can think of. This is because it is extremely short-term in its outlook. You aren't thinking about a week or a month from now—not even today's close. Rather, based on a five- to fifteen-minute rally or decline, you are betting on a similar pattern occurring sometime in the next 30 to 60 minutes. The trip is short, sweet, consistent, and extremely profitable. What's more, the risk is manageable. It is not what you stand to make but what you have to risk that determines a good trade. This style of trading keeps the risk both manageable and small—the two vital ingredients of a good risk-reward equation.

There are many ways to complicate your trading. One of them is to ask too much of the market. The more you want, the more risk you must be willing to undertake. As I get older (and, hopefully, wiser), I'm considerably less enchanted with the high-wire art of making market killings than when I was younger. My goal is consistent, low-risk profits. Like many experienced traders who have had their fill of extreme equity swings, I just don't have the stomach for the high-risk trade anymore. I realize that this is a matter of risk temperament. The youthful trader with little to lose may feel justified in taking on a lot of risk. The older trader, who has spent years building up his net worth, may not embrace that idea. Sniper trading actually applies to both temperaments. To keep the risk small, though, you have to focus on small moves.

What do I mean by a small move? This is relative since the market has changed so dramatically in recent years. When the S&P 500 futures contract first started trading back in April 1982, 3.00 points was considered a good day. Today, the average range is approximately ten times that amount. Accordingly, today's small move was yesterday's big move. At $250 per hundred points (what's known in floor parlance as a *handle*), a 4.00 move generates $1,000. On three or four contracts, that's $3,000 or $4,000, all quite possible in today's five- or ten-minute rally or break. If you want to go the other way, you can always trade the E-mini S&P, which is one-fifth the size. The same four-point move in this contract would generate a $200 profit or loss.

The principles of time and price trading apply to all markets under all circumstances since the laws of market symmetry appear to be universal in nature. This doesn't mean that you want to trade most futures—only that the symmetry persists in all types of market trends, long and short.

CAPTURING THE "PURE" TREND

From the sniper perspective, the shorter the trend the better. The reason for this is simple. In the shorter term, you have the so-called *pure* trends in which the market does indeed move in one direction. This means you endure little or no adversity while you hold the trade. The longer you hold a trade, the greater the likelihood that you will encounter crosscurrents—consolidation phases, profit-taking, and the like. This means the more likely you are to get out in error on a temporary pullback.

Sniper looks for two trends a day, one in the morning and one in the afternoon. You could make the case that there are more trends, but I'm talking about two major trends a day. Because these trends are comprised of two legs apiece, you are trying to capture 50 percent of each trend. The first leg provides you with the information you will need to find the second leg: duration (length of leg), price objective (magnitude of move), and maximum adversity (stop placement).

Because these short-term, intraday moves tend to form quickly, the subsequent moves tend to mirror them. This means that your profits should be quick and certain, if you entered the trade correctly. When the market runs, it tends to do so in one direction. This is the pure move you are looking for.

Although the market allows you a little leeway in entering a successful Sniper trade, it can be unforgiving if you make any serious mistakes. Let's say you are anticipating a breakout to the upside. Rather than entering the trade when prices are still consolidating, you wait until the breakout occurs and you buy on the penetration of the resistance. Now you are bidding against a crowd of buyers and your fill will be understandably awful. In fact, under this scenario, you are probably buying when most of the smart money is getting ready to sell.

Or let's say you have correctly identified the point of maximum adversity. Rather than trying to determine whether the market is simply running the stops or getting ready for a major move against you, you place a stop and are picked off. Now you are out of the market and prices are ready to run your way. You'll have a loss and you probably won't have the confidence to get back in on the right side. No one holds a gun to your head and makes you trade. Rather, your own fear of loss is likely to accomplish the same thing. This is what the other side is counting on. After all, your mistakes are their profits.

How do you guard against making mistakes? Simply by understanding how the market works. It seems that the market is designed to fool as many people as possible, hence these forays into the stops just prior to a huge move in the other direction. Who hasn't witnessed the situation where you get out just before you would have been proven right—if only you'd hung on!

To illustrate this point, take a price chart of one-minute bars and draw a horizontal line across from early-morning, intraday highs and lows. Then look to see what subsequent price action violated those highs and lows, then retreated. These are all stop-running exercises. Sooner or later, of course, you will get a legitimate trend in one direction or another. But in the meantime the market is going to churn up and down.

The key to winning is avoiding the crosscurrents and properly identifying trends. This is what time and price trading is designed to do. Once you learn to do the simple calculations, you'll see that the real trends are easy to find. If you are having trouble finding the best trades, take a printout of a completed day and work backward. You'll want to use one- and five-minute bar or candlestick charts. Once you've mastered the technique going backward, try to find the trends going forward. You'll find that this is somewhat more difficult, but still a relatively easy process.

Most new traders fail at time and price analysis because they lack the patience to find the best trades. In a trading day of approximately six hours, you may find only 15 or 20 minutes of truly good trending activity. If you are patient, you can capitalize on these trends. However, if your impatience drives you to take reckless trades, you can pretty well count on being demoralized when the genuine opportunities occur. Not wanting to be on the sidelines when the market is about to move is understandable, but you shouldn't have to guess when the trends will occur. With time and price trading you won't have to.

There are confirming indicators that make the selection of a trade easier to make. You can use divergence techniques coupled with the time of day (the market trends best early in the morning or late in the afternoon) to capitalize on the very best trades. Just remember that discipline—waiting for the opportunities and withstanding the lure of easy profits—is the key to winning with time and price trading.

USING WHAT WE KNOW

The place to begin any intelligent discussion of time and price trading is with an inventory of what we know about a market prior to a given day's open. Statistical studies tell us that one end of the day's range will typically occur in the early going of a trading session. They also tell us that the percentages favor the other end of the range being registered in the final hour of a trading session. They don't tell us, however, whether the probabilities favor the high or low being made first or last. Taylor's 3-day cycle, however, covered in Chapter 3, can provide you with a clue on this score. Depending where you find yourself in the 3-day cycle, the probabilities favor one side or the other. Moreover, our probability studies, using a total of six different parameters, can also demonstrate a market's propensity for rising or falling prices.

We know that most markets will move somewhere during a given day, even if it is not a *trending* day. Indeed, some of the best Sniper trading profits occur on small moves on nontrending days. This is because certain market patterns become very predictable once a range is established. A case in point is the well-known search-and-destroy pattern when the highs and lows are repeatedly penetrated.

There are many more things we know. On any given day, we know the previous day's close. Should an opening gap occur, this prior close works like a magnet, drawing the market back to where it found equilibrium on the day before. In the Standard & Poor's 500 futures market, for instance, the probabilities favor better than a 75-percent chance that the gap will be closed, assuming that the original opening price didn't exceed the prior day's high or low. This is valuable information.

We know that a trend of some magnitude should occur during the first two hours of trading, and, in the unlikely event that it does not, that this trend will be pushed into the noon hour. Likewise, an afternoon trend, occurring at two o'clock or later East Coast time, is a strong probability as well. We know that today's open is often a continuation from the prior trading day—and almost certainly from the overnight Globex trading session. The rule is, weakness begets weakness and strength begets strength. But you must not take this statement to suggest you simply sell following a weak close or buy following a strong one. You can usually fade—or trade against—these openings since the trend is frequently nearing its completion. Indeed, by using time and price calculations, you can often pinpoint exactly where the move will end.

USING WHAT WE DON'T KNOW

While it is hard to get a handle on the unknown, the uncertainty is what makes the market so profitable. It is precisely because the market is uncertain that so much opportunity exists. For this reason, we might want to explore our attitude toward risk. That's why we listen to the pundits, subscribe to newsletters, and take our broker's advice—all in the vain hope that someone out there *knows* what he or she is talking about. But trying to eliminate risk is like trying to capture running water in a sieve. Once the certainty exists, the opportunities evaporate.

I recently had a person approach me with an opportunity to make 100 percent on my money in a week, with no risk! It would have required, unfortunately, a $100,000 payment up front. I had to stop myself from laughing. No such animal exists.

Learning to embrace uncertainty in a world that is filled with experts is a necessary, but difficult, task for the new trader. We have experts testifying—often at cross-purposes—in court trials. We have pundits of every stripe appearing on television. We have specialty upon specialty in every field from cooking to real estate. Why can't we find someone who can tell us where the market is going? Expert advice is often not quite as valuable as some of the pundits would suggest. Remember the story about the monkey throwing darts at the newspaper stock tables? The dart thrower's stock selection methods showed better results than the picks of seasoned Wall Street analysts.

The fact is—apart from the age-old question "Is it hot enough for you?"—no single question in history has rivaled "Where do you think the market is going?" No one knows the answer to this question. Yet the airwaves are filled with an earnest army of pundits eager to provide the answer.

The first rule for a would-be trader, therefore, is to assume a mantle of humility. Accept the notion that you don't know. Failure to acknowledge that we are often clueless in the market is usually a major mistake. I treat this with the seriousness of an alcoholic in a twelve-step program saying that he is powerless over his addiction. This, to my mind, is the only way that you can open yourself to the notion that a greater power is calling the shots. Contrast this approach to that of the market braggart who is screaming to the world how wonderful he is. The mystery of the market needs to be approached in a spirit of humility.

While the great unspoken market secret is that no one knows what the market will do on any given day, the good news is that you don't have to know the future in order to trade intelligently. But you do have to have sound practices. In short, you have to know how to trade.

By learning to read the hidden clues of the market, you can learn to capitalize on what it is telling you. This is the secret of becoming a good trader. How it opens, how it trends, the overall tone of the market—these can all provide valuable clues to what may or may not occur in ensuing moments. By emphasizing a short-term approach, you can see how some valid inferences might be drawn from certain market behavior. You might say, for instance, I don't know about this afternoon, but given the last ten minutes of price action, I suspect the market is headed higher—or lower. Next week, a month from now, even this afternoon might require a different—and less probable—analysis. But given A, B, C, and D, I can make a strong case for one scenario or another occurring in the not-too-distant future.

Take the simple notion of a ten-day average range. This number is calculated by taking the range of the last ten days and dividing by ten. It tells you the average number of points in a daily range. I'm sure the statisticians could tell you the probabilities of the market having a range greater or less than this average range, the standard deviation. But used in an elemental fashion, you can take this average and add it to an early low or subtract it from an early high and have a ballpark idea of where today's high or low might be. There are more sophisticated methods of generating range numbers, such as the LSS system's notion of the anticipated range, which involves more calculations, but in the end an average is an average. In short, this means the probabilities favor one event over another.

How do we deal with the unknowable? Embrace the probabilities. If nine times out of ten the odds favor one scenario over another, which one are you going to choose? Exactly. All good trading involves doing on a routine basis that which favors a positive outcome.

The problem rests not with embracing uncertainty, but rather insisting on certainty, the sure-thing. If you wait until the market rallies to buy, you will probably be providing profits to the earlier, less risk-averse buyers, who are now selling. In short, you will buy the top because that's where the crowd is most bullish. All the true market success stories are about individuals who took risks when no one else wanted to.

FLEXIBILITY

No two days are ever alike in the market; if they are similar, they may be weeks, even months, apart. It is for this reason that rigid, inflexible approaches to the market never work. To win, you have to be like a reed in the wind, blowing from side to side. So one minute you might be an aggressive buyer, averaging down, and the next you might want to sell short.

You need an approach, a point of view, a plan, something to work with that will give you the confidence to pick up the phone (the hardest thing in trading) and place a trade. The Sniper approach is designed to help you accomplish that goal. In the following rules, you will find specific guidelines for identifying a profitable trade. You must accept the fact that only a portion of your trades will be profitable; this is acceptable if you maximize the profits on the winning trades. After all, the first rule of sound trading is survival.

The goal of time and price trading is to correctly identify winning trades. More specifically, you want to take a trade only when you know exactly where the market is going (to the tick) and when it will get there (to the minute). This is a tall order.

To begin, you want to forget about making money and concentrate on finding the patterns. Down the road, the money will take care of itself if you do the necessary homework. There are two important components to successful trading: One is knowing how to spot the best opportunities (the theoretical side of the equation); the other is knowing how to capitalize on them (the practical side of the equation). You cannot succeed as a trader if you have one and not the other. You need both.

As you will find, both take work. But the place to begin is with the theoretical. You'll want to immerse yourself in the market, study the patterns, and convince yourself that market symmetry exists. You'll want to obtain a charting program that gives you one- and five-minute charts. There is nothing wrong with looking at two-, three-, or four-minute charts. For that matter, since the symmetry appears to be universal, you can look at longer-term charts if you prefer. The point is, you'll want to study a variety of markets in detail before even thinking of taking your first time and price trade.

SYMMETRY OUT OF CHAOS

If chart patterns appear as meaningless chaos to you, welcome to the crowd. One is not born with a trained eye for technical charting analysis. You may be familiar with the basics of technical analysis—trend lines, support and resistance, head-and-shoulders patterns, and so on. A good book on elementary technical analysis can bring you up to speed on how to identify these market patterns. The problem with most technical analysis, however, is that so much of it is subjective in nature. Many such patterns are difficult to spot in their formation stages. Even once identified, many technicians would argue over their meaning. I think you can see some of the shortcomings of traditional technical analysis. The patterns are often only identified late in their formation, and by then it is often too late to do anything about it.

With time and price, you are looking at specific patterns that are easily quantifiable. There are some subjective interpretations of time and price chart patterns, but they are relatively few. There will always be an element of uncertainty no matter how rigorous your analysis. In general, though, we are looking at cut-and-dry calculations that eliminate the guesswork.

You'll want to start by finding the two major daily trends. Depending on whether you want to look at one-minute bars or, say, twenty-minute bars, you need to get an idea of what a day looks like. Whenever I feel that I cannot find the forest for the trees when looking at a chart, I always switch to a longer-term configuration. If the one-minute bars are confusing me, I'll switch to five-minute bars. If I still cannot find the trends, I'll look at ten-minute bars, and so on. Sooner or later, I'll find what I'm looking for. By the way, at this stage of your analysis, forget about finding the trends going forward; we just want to look backward in time and see if you can identify the major trends. Looking at an entire trading day, therefore, what can you see? Do you see a morning trend? An afternoon trend? Are there more than two? If so, how many are there? Three? Four?

The importance of identifying these trends is to demonstrate the money-making potential of the market you are trading. Even if you typically hold a trade an entire day, you must realize that most of the profits are gained during a relatively short period of time—namely, when the market trends. The rest of the time, you are gaining a little or losing a little. This, by the way, applies whether you are concentrating on a ten-minute trade in the futures market or holding a long-term stock position for six months. The money is made when the market trends.

You need to go through at least ten trading days and identify the daily trends. If you can identify only one trend per day, you are probably looking at a chart where the bars are too long in duration; if you can identify more than two or three, you are probably looking at a chart that is too short in duration. In general, I use a one-minute chart when I trade, but a five-minute chart to identify the pattern. I find charts with bars that are greater than ten or twenty minutes useless because I am solely a day trader. I'm really not that concerned about where the market will be a week from now. If you intend to use time and price to identify long-term trends, however, you would be perfectly justified in using longer-term charts.

Assume we are in agreement about the two daily trends. What kind of observations can you make about these two trends? When do they occur? Morning? Afternoon? Both? What is the magnitude of each? Are they similar? Dissimilar? Use your charting program to zoom in on the trends. If you identified them on a five-minute chart, look at the same price action on a one- or two-minute chart. Blow up the chart. What do you see?

It is important at this stage to view as many trends as possible. You'll find that the magnitude of the moves will vary widely, as will the duration. Can you see how looking for the same move every day will lead you to trouble? Can you see how most of the time the market is only getting ready to move—and not really moving? Can you see how Monday's huge bull rally was followed by Tuesday's more modest gains? Every day is different for a variety of reasons. You may have a Fed report drive the market one day, but on another the lack of news causes the market to consolidate. The trader who settles for modest profits on a barn-burning day is cutting his or her own throat. The same profit objectives on a less volatile day may be right on the money. Can you see why a flexible approach makes more sense than a rigid one?

Let's look at time elapsed. If you are looking at one-minute bars, you will be able to measure the length of time it took for a market trend to occur. If you are looking at five-minute bars, you will be able to measure the length of the trend within five minutes. Now look at the length of time that it took for these two trends to occur and compare this amount of time with the total time in the trading day.

For example, if the S&P 500 futures market trades from 9:30 A.M. East Coast time until 4:15 P.M., it is open for six hours and 45 minutes—or a total of 405 minutes. If the day you are looking at had two 30-minute trends, for a total of 60 minutes, or one hour, then the market trended for just 14.8 percent of the trading day, or approximately 15 percent of the day. To derive this number, simply divide 60 by 405.

Would it be fair to say that most of the time the market wasn't trending? I think so. I know what you are thinking: If I'm not in the market the entire day, then I am likely to miss the trend when—and if—it occurs. Perhaps. But this assumes several things. One, that you are on the right side of the market when the trend occurs. How do you know that the trend will be up and not down? Two, that the adversity you will sustain on countertrends (even assuming you have the right side) will not cause your stop to be hit or otherwise shake you out of the market. There are always risks when one holds a position. Given the perversity of price moves, chances are a longer-term perspective will undermine the most well-thought-out position.

Now let's turn to time of day. When do these trends occur? At ten o'clock in the morning and three o'clock in the afternoon? You'll find that the precise time of day will vary. Nevertheless, assuming we are getting the two daily trends, you will, in general, find a morning and an afternoon trend. While there are always exceptions, I think you will find that the market will adhere to a given pattern for a period of time and then change. This is why general rules can be misleading. For example, there will be periods when the morning trends are clear-cut and easy to identify and when the afternoon trends are difficult to identify. Then the patterns will shift and you will have excellent afternoon trends and choppy morning trends. There will be times when the morning trend doesn't occur on schedule and is typically pushed into the noon hour. But this is rare.

The point is, with study you will begin to see a pattern to the market. You will begin to anticipate trends; this will be the very first glimmer of seeing the symmetry in what was previously market chaos. Remember what I said about the very best traders showing up in the pit just before a big move began? I don't think their sudden appearance was accidental.

Once you have identified the two major daily trends, you'll want to scrutinize them further. Zoom in on the trends and count the number of one-minute bars. Count from the lowest low to the highest high. Each trend is comprised of two legs, a leg being defined as a series of price moves when there is no countermove. Now count the number of bars. Let's say you count eight one-minute bars when the market does nothing but rally. Following this rally, you will get the inevitable profit-taking phase when prices are pushed lower. This is called the consolidation phase. Within this phase, you will typically get a two-minute period of time when an equilibrium is formed, characterized by two consecutive bars with identical closes. With one leg intact followed by a subsequent consolidation with an equilibrium, you now have everything you need to calculate the entry point, profit-taking point, and point of maximum adversity.

We have been talking about time—when the trends occur, their typical duration, and the notion of two legs comprising a trend. As you can see, there is no generalized rule. The trends can occur at different times, they will most certainly have different durations, and you don't always have two symmetrical legs. For this reason you cannot accurately determine in advance when and how the market will advance or decline. The best you can do is anticipate some type of move. For the precise time and price information, you have to rely on the market to provide the information.

You'll want to monitor price to determine the duration of the move. Because of the symmetry in the market, you will find two legs of, let's say, approximately 4.00 points apiece, comprising a single trend. Whatever the magnitude of the first leg, expect a similar second leg of approximately the same magnitude. For this reason, you won't have a 7.00-point leg followed by a leg of 9.00 points. They tend to be comparable in size. When they are not, the second leg is typically smaller. This is a significant development because it suggests the second leg has failed. This failure swing often signals a trend reversal.

The symmetry in the market extends to both time and price. This is not to say that you won't have occasions to observe the market when it fails in time but not in price, or vice versa, but that the patterns repeat. It is important to stress that any given day is time- and price-specific. This means that yesterday's time and price patterns have no bearing on today's time and price patterns. Accordingly, on Monday, you may have the market rallying 5.00 points in eight minutes several times. But on Tuesday, the legs of the trends may take six minutes to form and only carry 3.50 points. The exception to this day-specific rule is when you have a continuation pattern on the morning's open. In this case, you may have symmetry with the prior day. Let's say you have a market rally in the final moments of a trading day. The next day, the market opens lower and churns sideways for five or ten minutes (the consolidation phase). The next move is higher. When you compare yesterday's late-day rally to today's early-morning rally, you see the symmetry between time and price because they are identical in magnitude and duration.

TIME AND PRICE RULES

This theoretical discussion of time and price strategy is simplicity itself. In a nutshell, there are two trends a day. Each trend is comprised of two legs that are equal in duration and magnitude. Following the formation of the initial leg, one need only do several calculations to establish critical criteria for the second leg—namely, where the market will go, when it will get there, and the downside maximum adversity one should sustain. Here are the rules:

1. *Identify the first leg.* This is the place to start. Did the market rally or decline? How far did it rally or decline? How long did it take for this rally or decline to occur? You want to measure from low to high. You want a specific number of points. It is important that you measure only significant, pure, one-way moves. If the market has been jumping all over the place, it is not a trend. Try not to identify minor moves as significant trends. This can cause you to overtrade because there may be many minor moves on a given day but only one or two significant moves. In general, you will find one trend in the morning and another in the afternoon.

Trends are characterized by two distinct and comparable legs. The two components of each leg are time and price; put another way, how long did it take to move so many points? You also need to observe the direction of the move. Because of market symmetry, you need to use this information to create a market scenario for the second leg.

Here are the steps in measuring the first leg:

a. Measure low to high, or vice versa.

b. Measure elapsed time of move in minutes.

For example: The market moved 8.00 points higher in 14 minutes.

The implication is that the market will mirror this pattern on a second leg. In Figure 2.1, the first leg of a trend is clearly marked.

2. *Establish the equilibrium point.* The equilibrium point is defined as two consecutive closes at the same price following the first leg of a trend. It is the point where supply and demand come into balance following a rally or decline. Identified by two consecutive identical closes, the equilibrium level is used in calculating the parameters of the second leg. While you may occasionally observe more than one equilibrium point following a trend, you

05/02/2001 9:30pm   (ES1M)   05/03/2001 10:20am

ES1M-10 min 05/08/2001 C=1270.25 +6.75 O=1266.25 H=1277.00 L=1259.50 V=0

First Leg

Second Leg

5/08 9:10am Printed using TradeStation © Omega Research, Inc. 1997

Figure 2.1   The first downward leg is followed by
a consolidation in prices. The second leg is of
comparable value.

want to take the first equilibrium in calculating price objectives since there
may not be another.

The equilibrium point occurs within the consolidation following a trend.
Because a trend is created when buyers or sellers predominate and drive
prices higher or lower, respectively, the inevitable profit-taking will create a
halt in the market's rise or decline. It is at this point that prices will retreat,
providing an opportunity for the knowledgeable time and price trader to
enter his position.

As we've pointed out in Rule #1, the first thing you want to do when the market trends is observe the direction and measure for price and time. Once you know these parameters, you need to establish the equilibrium point, since this is the price level that will determine the profit objective.

Whereas the profit objective is measured from the first equilibrium level, you can have secondary profit objectives if you see additional equilibrium levels. If you wait for a second or third equilibrium level, however, to predict the profit objective, you may miss the move since many trends do not have second or third equilibrium levels.

You must wait until an equilibrium level is established before you take a trade or establish a profit objective. Equilibrium levels are easier to identify when you are looking at one-minute bars rather than bars of a longer duration.

There will occasionally be a pattern where no precise equilibrium level exists. When this occurs, draw a horizontal line midpoint across an area within the consolidation where a great deal of trading is taking place (see Figure 2.2); use this price as your equilibrium point. If you are observing one-minute bars, however, and no equilibrium price is readily visible, it is often because you have not waited long enough. The complete consolidation may take as long as 15 or 20 minutes to form even if the leg was only 6 to 12 minutes in duration. At the other extreme, you often get only one or two minutes following the creation of equilibrium to enter a trade.

One of the unknowns in time and price trading is the length of the consolidation phase. Prices may consolidate in as little as 5 or 6 minutes, or the consolidation may take as long as an hour, or even longer, to form prior to the breakout of the second leg.

3. *Add the first leg to the equilibrium point if the market is rallying, or subtract the first leg from the equilibrium point if the market is declining, to establish the profit objective of the second leg.* The second leg of the trend should be identical in length to the first leg. By adding the first leg to the equilibrium level in a rallying market, one establishes a profit objective. For example, if the first leg is 7.00 points and the subsequent equilibrium point is 1309.00, you simply add 7.00 to 1309.00 and get 1316.00 as your profit objective. In a declining market, the reverse is true. If the first leg of 7.00 points is down, the market will consolidate upward as buyers bid up the market, covering their initial short positions. With a similar equilibrium level of 1309.00, the new profit objective on the second leg would be 1302.00—or 7.00 points below the equilibrium price. (See the example in Figure 2.3.)

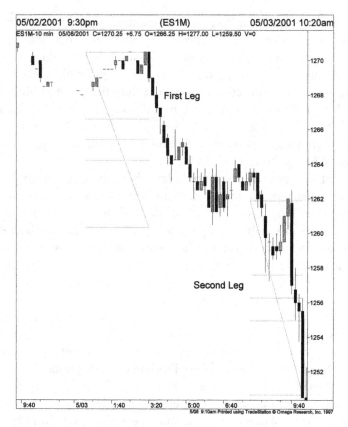

Figure 2.2   A horizontal line drawn across the mid-point of the consolidation shows the equilibrium level.

4. *Calculate the .618 retracement level, or point of maximum adversity.* The .618 retracement is the maximum amount of adversity one wants to sustain on a trade prior to exiting at a loss. If a market retraces more than this amount, chances are it is reversing direction. The exception to this statement occurs when the stops are run at the .618 retracement level. When this happens, the retracement level may be penetrated two or three times prior to the market reversing in the opposite direction. Stop-running is characterized by swift countertrend moves in the opposite direction. Therefore, if the first leg is up and the trader buys in the consolidation on a pullback down, the .618 will always be below the level of entry. When selling, of course, the reverse

Figure 2.3   Following an 8-point break on leg one, the market consolidates and forms an equilibrium at 1263. By subtracting 8 points, you get a target of 1255.

is true. If the first leg is down, and the trader sells in the consolidation of the pullback up, the .618 is always above the entry point. How the market trades once the .618 is violated is important. If the market is breaking below the .618 retracement level and stays below that level, chances are prices will break lower. However, if the market is breaking momentarily below the .618 and is immediately rejected, it is most likely stop-running and the market will subsequently trade higher. In this latter case, you do not want to exit the market. The same is true in reverse for sellers.

Here's how you calculate the .618 retracement. You take the first leg and multiply it by .618. You then take the product of this multiplication and subtract it from the high of the first leg in a rallying market. In a declining market, you will take the product of this multiplication and add it to the low of the first leg. For example:

First leg = 6.00 points

.618 of first leg = (.618 × 6.00) = 3.70

First leg high = 1303.70

Therefore, assuming rising first leg, the .618 retracement = 1300.00

The .618 retracement level price helps set up a safety zone within which prices should consolidate prior to breaking out. Within this zone, it is safe to add to a position. This is known as *averaging.* When you average on a buying position, you buy more as prices trade lower; when you average on a selling position, you sell more as prices trade higher. Averaging lowers your overall buying or raises your overall selling price. It also has the benefit of allowing you to take additional positions with relatively low risk as you approach the .618 retracement level. This assumes, of course, that you are quick to exit the trade should prices violate the .618 level. Under no circumstances should you count on the .618 retracement level being approached on all trades. This is simply the maximum adversity that you want to sustain on a trade. The best buy positions attract aggressive buying well before the .618 retracement level is reached; conversely, the best sell positions attract selling well before the .618 retracement level is reached. The .618 rule, therefore, has two important advantages for the time and price trader. It creates a buy or sell zone and it provides a point for stop placement.

5. *Buy or sell at or near the equilibrium price.* I used to insist that you buy below or sell above the equilibrium price, but experience has shown that by insisting on this rule, you miss a lot of good trades that go your way immediately following the creation of the equilibrium. Ideally, you enter at or near the equilibrium and than add to the position if prices approach the .618 retracement price (see Figure 2.4). When buying, the buying zone extends from the equilibrium price down to the .618 retracement price. When selling, the selling zone extends from the equilibrium price up to the .618 retracement. As a practical matter, you'll find that there are opportunities to fine-tune the entry once the equilibrium level is created. However, I find that by

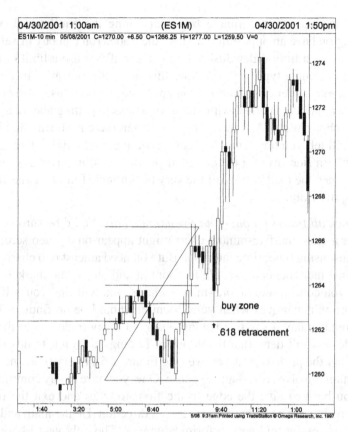

Figure 2.4 The buy zone exists from the equilibrium point down to the .618 retracement level. It is safe to buy at any point within this area.

waiting you often miss the best price, and, of course, by not waiting you are often premature, meaning you could have gotten a better price by waiting longer. So, over time, I suspect one cancels the other. The one thing you must do, however, is take the trade within the buying or selling zone. Waiting for the market to break out is a highly risky strategy and one I don't recommend. At that point, the market is poised to run and you probably haven't sufficient time to jump aboard without sustaining substantial risk. If you don't believe me, try it and see for yourself. Chances are, the fill will be truly bad and, before you even receive the fill, the profit point will be reached.

Once the second one-minute bar establishing the equilibrium price is reached, you have an opportunity to take the trade. You can buy or sell at the market or use a limit order. Just remember that if you use a limit order, the market price must typically penetrate this price for the order to be filled. With a market order, you'll know you are filled. I tend to use market orders because I am not concerned with one or two ticks in getting aboard a market which is about to run. As I mentioned, however, there is no way that I know of that will tell you how long the consolidation period will be. I've seen the market churn sideways for over an hour prior to fulfilling market symmetry. I've also seen the market take off the very next minute following the creation of the equilibrium.

6. *Track all trades on one- and five-minute bars.* You'd be surprised how different a one- and five-minute chart might appear on a video screen. I'm not against using other time intervals. But you need at least two charts of different time increments to be able to zoom in and out on the market. Otherwise, if you concentrate on one-minute charts, you will find yourself trying to capture minor moves when your attention should be on finding the two major trends a day. I say this having observed many traders over the years overtrade. I won't deny that the allure of finding the minor trends is compelling, but the profits are deceptive (see Figure 2.5). Every trade, no matter how certain, involves risk—and expense. One, you have to pay commissions. Two, you have to give the edge to the floor to enter and exit the market. Three, you have to be right on the market's direction. Do the math and you'll see that successful trading is a formidable task. The only way I know of to come out ahead is to concentrate on those trades with the highest possible risk-reward ratio and aggressively trade the market.

7. *Calculate when the second leg should end—to the minute!* This is a tricky rule to follow for several reasons. Once the equilibrium level is formed, you immediately have a target profit objective. To successfully complete the time and price analysis, however, you also need time. But you don't know this because you don't yet know when—and if—the market will break in your direction. It is important to stress that while the symmetry often persists in both time and price, you do get situations where the market may be symmetrical in price but not in time, and vice versa. For this reason, you need to know both time and price. In Figure 2.6, looking at the completion of the first leg, you do know both time and price. But, significantly, you don't know where to start counting the time until the breakout occurs and the

Figure 2.5 You want to sell at or above the
equilibrium.

trade is starting to work. For this reason, I suggest that you count forward
from every intraday high or low depending on whether you want the market
to rally or break lower.

For example, let's say you are anticipating a rally on the second leg comparable to the one that occurred on the first leg. You already know the price
and time, let's say 4.50 points in seven minutes. With the creation of the
equilibrium you now know the top should occur at exactly 4.50 points added
to the equilibrium price. But when should it occur? Well, you might answer,
after seven minutes. Fine. But the market won't accommodate you by reaching the high seven minutes after you bought. The seven minutes refers to a

05/03/2001 10:50am   (ES1M)   05/03/2001 2:30pm

ES1M-5 min   05/08/2001 C=1269.25 +5.75 O=1266.25 H=1277.00 L=1259.50 V=0

5 minute chart

Leg 1

.618 retracement

Leg 2

10:50   11:15   11:40   12:05   12:30   12:55   1:20   1:45   2:10

5/08 9:37am Printed using TradeStation © Omega Research, Inc. 1997

Figure 2.6 On a five-minute chart, the significant trends can readily be seen.

significant breakout rally that equals the first leg in time. Where do you measure from?

The answer is: You have to take every significant intraday low inside the consolidation and measure from that moment forward. So a low is formed and you begin counting. After two minutes, let's say, the would-be rally fails inside the consolidation and retreats under the prior low. Now you have to start counting again. You keep counting forward from lows until the legitimate rally begins. Sooner or later, you should get your breakout; now you have a viable tool to work with, telling you precisely where the trend should end.

Let's say after several minutes inside the consolidation (and after the equilibrium has been formed and you hold a long position), the serious rally begins and the market shoots into new high ground. The time on the last low is, say, 2:07 P.M. East Coast time. The seven-minute rally should end at precisely 2:14 P.M.—seven minutes after it began. This may have been the third or fourth attempt of the market to rally in the past 30 minutes. But this one's the real thing. By knowing the time when the rally should end, you can prepare to get out. I know from experience that you cannot wait until that very minute to pick up the phone. The market moves so quickly that a 2:14 P.M. top must be anticipated by at least a minute and perhaps more, depending upon the speed of your brokerage firm. I also know from experience that not trying to anticipate the top is a big mistake. Once the tide turns, the exuberant buying will turn to panicked selling if you aren't careful. Far better to sell into a jubilant crowd of buyers just before someone turns out the lights and tells them the party is over. That's how you get a good fill.

Why not hold on in anticipation of still better profits? A big mistake. What will happen is this: You'll get the move you anticipated using time and price just as you expected. You won't get out because your enthusiasm for winning on this trade has grown because you were so good in picking the entry point. Profit-taking will push the market lower—and perhaps lower still. After having failed to sell at the top, you will soon grow demoralized and sell your position at the bottom. Your profits will be a fraction of what they would have been had you handled the trade properly. Don't take my word on this. Try it and see what happens. For your sake, I hope you try it on a trade when I'm wrong.

Not to muddy the waters, but there is another consideration here. What do you do if you take such a trade and it works in time (time to get out?) but not in price (we need another hundred points!)? Now you are in a quandary because you don't know whether you should get out on time or price. I wish I had a straightforward, easy answer for you. But I don't. Except to say that sometimes the patterns work in time (but not price) and sometimes they work in price (but not time). In this instance, I realize I have to make one of those difficult judgment calls, but I try to do so using some common sense. The one thing I don't do is think about the money. How much money I've won does not come into play. My thinking is, rather, something along this line: "I've taken this trade and everything is working according to plan except that I'm about to run out of time. The symmetry suggests the market has so many points to run (see Figure 2.7). But I only have two minutes to reach that level

Figure 2.7   In the second leg, the trend took two
additional minutes to complete.

and it's probably not going to happen. I think I'll monitor the cash prices (for
the S&P 500) for a moment and see if they are firming up or softening." I
then let the near-term direction of the cash price dictate my action. If cash
prices continue strong, I might stay with the trade; if they start to weaken, I'll
take my profit and run. I want to stress that the dollars at stake in the trade
play no role. The only thing that counts is the direction of the market.

   8. *Act quickly if the pattern fails.* Since you have a projected target price
and target time, you will quickly know if a pattern fails (see Figure 2.8). The
surest sign of a failure is when, following a breakout, the market trades back
into the consolidation zone. When this occurs, you must exit the market as

Figure 2.8 Once the .618 retracement level is violated, the second leg has failed. You must exit immediately.

soon as possible—and perhaps even think about reversing. By knowing what should occur, you can easily spot a failure pattern when the market fails to reach its target in either time or price. The best way to deal with a failure pattern is to exit the market as soon as possible.

9. *Pay attention to the Rule of 3.* The Rule of 3 states that a significant penetration of a support or resistance will often occur on the third attempt. Why this works as well as it does, I do not know. I do know, however, that there are many examples of the market running on the third attempt. (See Figure 2.9.) By knowing when the market should run, you allow yourself to

Figure 2.9 Notice how the market broke down on the third test of the support.

get positioned for the subsequent move. Used in this fashion, the Rule of 3 becomes a timing technique. Should the pattern fail to penetrate on the third attempt, you can often anticipate a market reversal.

10. *Always buy or sell inside the consolidation.* There is no excuse for breaking the rule. If the market starts to run before you have an opportunity to take your position, let it go. There will always be another opportunity in the next trading session. By the way, I break the day into two parts—the morning and afternoon trading session. If the morning is missed, I simply wait for the afternoon trade. The normal tendency is to want to chase the

market once a breakout occurs. This is almost always a mistake. The first leg is always a precursor to the second leg (see Figure 2.10). Whenever the market runs—up or down—there is always profit-taking. The first leg tells you everything you need to know: market direction, time, price, and possible adversity. You need to take your position before the second leg becomes manifest.

11. *Use confirming indicators.* The purpose of using confirming indicators is to line up all your ducks in a row. Time and price trading works just fine by just concentrating on price bars, but the confirming indicators are the

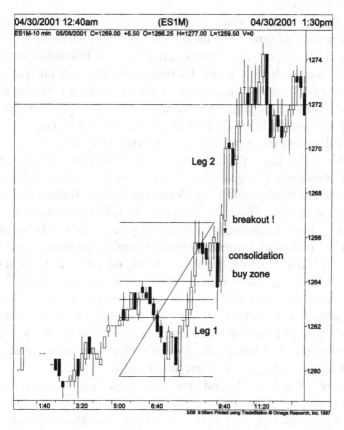

Figure 2.10   You always want to enter the position within the consolidation zone—*before* the breakout occurs.

icing on the cake—added confirmation that you are on the right side. The ones that work best for me are those that give a market divergence. By this, I mean you have a leading indicator that often turns prior to the actual move in price. This can be very valuable because it gives you evidence that the market has reversed direction before it is widely known.

One popular indicator that I use is slow stochastics. I run the slow stochastics at the bottom of my price screen. At the top of the screen I will have my one- or five-minute bar charts running. I've grown partial to candlestick charts in recent years, but it really doesn't matter whether you prefer bar charts or candles.

Slow stochastics are oscillators that measure relative market strength for different periods of time. I use the default setting on whatever program I'm running. But I suspect the settings can always be fine-tuned to whatever number of bars work best for you. There are many different interpretations of stochastics, but I'm only interested in the *divergence* between what the prices are doing and what the *stochastics* are measuring. For instance, let's say the prices are declining. What will the stochastics do? They will fall and the two will point to the same thing, lower prices. The same is true in reverse when prices rally, but at the key turns, when the market is about to reverse, you will often get a divergence between the two. Prices may still be declining, but the stochastics will fail to decline in parallel fashion; indeed, they may even start to rise. This is a divergence that tells me the market has probably seen its lows. Likewise, at market tops, prices may still be soaring. But the slow stochastics may rally only to fail to make new highs along with the prices. This is a divergence, one that is telling me prices are heading lower. One of the most significant patterns is when you are approaching a market top. Your time and price analysis tells you to sell your position in so many minutes at such-and-such a price. You then consult the slow stochastics at the bottom of the chart and see that a divergence is forming. While prices are going higher, the stochastics indicator is struggling and failing to take out the previous high reading. This is a sure sign that the top is near.

In Figure 2.11, I've indicated how a divergence can help you pinpoint a top or bottom.

In using an indicator, such as slow stochastics, the absolute reading of the indicator is unimportant. Rather, you are looking for a pattern, or relationship, between prices and the indicator that suggests a reversal is near.

Another place to look for a divergence to occur is between indicators. In

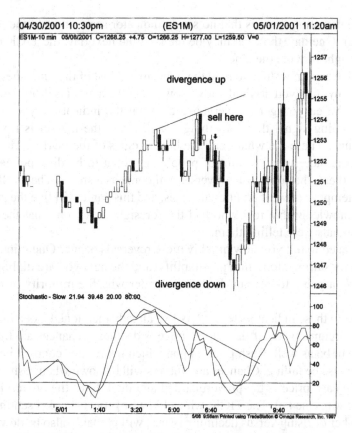

Figure 2.11 Notice the divergence between the slow stochastics and the prices. This is often a certain sign that the market is about to reverse in the direction of the slow stochastics.

trading the Standard & Poor's 500 futures contract, I track four indicators—the S&P cash price, the Dow Jones Industrials, the TICK (which is the number of rising issues minus the number of declining issues on the NYSE), and, most importantly, the premium. I keep them on the same page in order to more easily spot a divergence. Moreover, I track them on one-minute line charts as opposed to bar charts. Their absolute values are not as important to me as their relative direction.

The interesting thing is that no single indicator serves best as the leading indicator. One day, the cash may be the key; the next day, the TICK or premium might provide the clue.

You have to know how to read the indicators. Most of the time, they won't tell you anything you don't already know—that the market is dropping or rising. But when you get a divergence between the indicators, you have an early-warning signal that something is amiss and the market is ripe for a turnaround. These are what I call the hidden clues of the market. Their sudden appearance suggests a lot of people are about to be disappointed. For most of them, the soon-to-be-reversal will come as a shock. They will panic in an attempt to prevent additional losses, and this panic will line the pockets of the knowledgeable few who had the foresight to act on what the divergence signals were telling them.

Do I need to tell you how quickly these reversals occur? One minute you are calmly sailing along into profitability, and the next you are dialing your broker in a panic to get out. Is it any wonder why the minority of traders win?

What do these indicators tell us? As I've already mentioned, not a lot under normal circumstances. If the futures price is declining, chances are the indicators will be as well. Cash prices, upon which the futures contract is based, will likewise be falling. Chances are, futures will be down when cash is down since the cash price is the proverbial dog and the futures the proverbial tail. The dog wags the tail. The TICK, which likewise reflects market sentiment in the number of rising versus declining issues, will probably also be down. The 30 Dow stocks will also be lower when the overall market declines. And the premium, which measures the difference between the nearby futures price and the cash index, will probably also be lower. So what do they tell you? What you probably already know. The market is going down.

To be helpful, the indicators have to create a divergence. That's typically when a reversal will occur. And since you want to be the first one off a sinking ship, they can tell you when the first bottom leak occurs, not just when the gunnel is awash with water. While there are a variety of ways that a divergence might occur between indicators, one prominent way is when the premium signals a reversal. For example, let's say the market is declining. If you have been fortunate enough to sell short at the top of the move, you are no doubt enjoying the market break. This is understandable, but you must be cautious; the market can spring back in a heartbeat. So let's say you are monitoring prices along with the confirming indicators. All the indicators are pointing lower. Then, suddenly, with futures prices, cash, Dow, and TICK all pointing down, the premium line starts to soar higher. What is going on? Chances are, the pit has spotted an imminent reversal in the making. The pit traders are now purchasing contracts to take profits on short sales or, perhaps, to initiate new buying positions. It doesn't matter; this buying cannot be hidden. Even as prices trade lower, the relationship of the futures to the cash price is changing, and this is causing the premium value to rise. This is the clear-cut signal that the market is about to reverse. Floor traders might have spotted a single leading stock starting to gain value. Knowing that there is a lag between the time the stock rises and when it may be reflected in the cash value of the next index calculations, they are seconds ahead of the market. This can mean big profits for them and big losses for the unsuspecting who are unaware of the importance of this divergence phenomenon. So as the premium begins to shoot higher and the cash readings remain soft, the selling begins to slow. The divergence between the now-rising premium and the still-declining indicators will be evident. If you are short contracts, you must cover (buy) immediately. If you are thinking of initiating a new long (buy position), you must do so immediately (see Figure 2.12). There is no time to spare. Following such a divergence, minutes—even seconds—can mean the difference between a profit and a loss.

There is another phenomenon that deserves comment here and that is the notion of the market getting temporarily out of line on the unbridled enthusiasm that occurs when the market turns. I must stress that this situation is temporary. When the market runs, either up or down, there are always winners and losers. Both tend to let emotionalism get the upper hand. So the winners become careless and overly confident while the losers likewise lose their heads and tend to panic. The result is a market that becomes very emotional and volatile, providing opportunities for those who remain rational amid the chaos. This emotionalism, by the way, is why throwing market orders into a market that is running—assuming you are buying when panicked traders are selling, and vice versa—can be so profitable. Your market orders will get that extra profit that comes from being on the right side in a panicked situation. Do not try to take advantage of this situation, however, by throwing your time and price numbers out the window. The tendency, for those traders who find themselves on the right side of the market in this situation, is to listen to the voice of greed: "I think I'll stick around a little longer

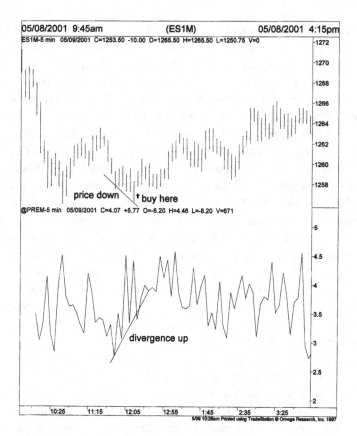

05/08/2001 9:45am   (ES1M)   05/08/2001 4:15pm

ES1M-5 min   05/09/2001 C=1253.50 -10.00 O=1265.50 H=1265.50 L=1250.75 V=0

price down   ↑ buy here

@PREM-5 min   05/09/2001 C=4.07 +5.77 O=-8.20 H=4.46 L=-8.20 V=671

divergence up

5/09 10:29am Printed using TradeStation © Omega Research, Inc. 1997

Figure 2.12   Notice the divergence between prices and the indicator. The indicator is usually right.

and increase my profit." That's always the point where the market reverses and your paper profits vanish.

12. *Trade the continuation of the overnight trend.* There are several ways to look at this trade. First, as a continuation of a leg that occurred toward the end of the prior trading day. The market might have rallied going into yesterday's close. Now, on this morning's open, the market opens down and consolidates, creating an equilibrium point shortly after the open. Here's what you have: first leg completed going into yesterday's close; profit-taking

on today's open, driving the market lower. The completion of the second leg will probably be the first trend of the day. Second, you might get a gap on the opening. Let's say the market sold off into yesterday's close. On the morning open, you now get a gap up. This is an excellent selling opportunity. Not only will the market retrace the ground that it covered on yesterday's close, but it will be drawn back to the prior day's close even if the legitimate trend is up on the day. The general rule is that the gap will be filled, especially if it doesn't take out a completion of the time and price trade. This presents an excellent fading opportunity since the pattern is now fulfilled. For example, let's assume that the market sold off near the close and then rallied slightly in the final minutes of trading. Today's open is now sharply lower. Doing some simple calculations, you realize that yesterday's final leg was exactly 5.00 points. Now the market is down another 5.00 points from the prior day's close. The pattern is complete and the market will almost certainly rally. This is also the spring effect: The market is pulled apart only to return to the middle. This is also the classic Taylor pattern. The market is taken lower to go up. Figures 2.13, 2.14, and 2.15 illustrate these three patterns.

13. *Never place the stop at the .618 retracement.* If you are confused about this rule, reread Rule #4. While the .618 retracement is the maximum adversity you stand to suffer on a winning trade, it is also a target for the stop-runners. Accordingly, you must monitor the trade once the .618 is approached. Does the market price violate the .618? If so, does the market reject this price? Price rejection, which is characterized by a rapid reversal in prices, occurs when stops are run. The market may momentarily shoot through the .618 retracement level only to be rejected. This is the surest sign of stop-running. Another way to make a reasonable judgment about this phenomenon is to use the Rule of 3. If the .618 is violated twice and rejected, the third attempt (assuming there is one) will be the deciding factor. If the third attempt is rejected, load the boat in the opposite direction. The reason? The market should run on the third attempt. If, however, the third attempt is successful, the market isn't coming back. Should that occur, you are better off selling new lows or buying new highs. Last, you want to keep an eye on the amount of time the market spends searching for the stops at the .618. The window of opportunity to buy near a low or sell near a high will exist only for a very short period of time. So if the market is poised to run higher, it will drift down toward the lows for only five to ten minutes prior to strong buying

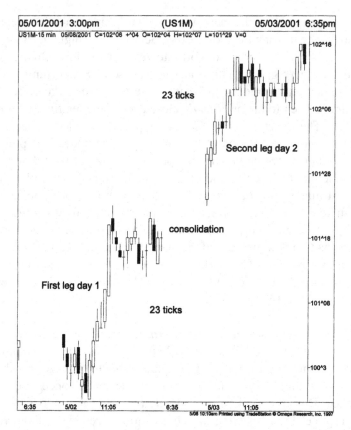

Figure 2.13 Notice the slight move down following the open. This is the early countertrend off the open. The real trend was up. On the second day, the symmetrical pattern for the two-day period was completed.

entering the market. The reverse, of course, is true when selling. Once the .618 is approached, I always start my stopwatch. Since this is a clear touch-and-go situation, I'm always ready to run—and perhaps reverse—at this point. Does the market spend five minutes at the .618? Six minutes? Seven minutes? Should it violate the .618 and stay violated, you have no choice. You must run immediately. If, on the other hand, it is stop-running, the price rejection will be evident and the market will run—in your direction!

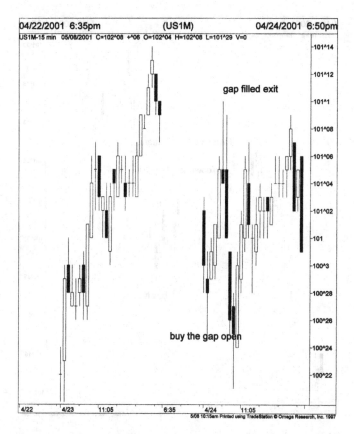

Figure 2.14 When you get gap openings, the rule is the gap will be filled. Once the gap is closed, you should exit the trade, since the market will often go the other way.

Figures 2.16 and 2.17 show the difference between price rejection at the .618 and a market that clearly wants to go the other way.

14. *Use MOC (market on close) orders.* If you are trading late in the day and your target exit price is scheduled to occur in the final ten minutes of trading, you are usually better off getting out MOC. The reason for this is that the market occasionally becomes quite irrational and panic-driven late in the day as those on the losing side of the market find themselves with nowhere to go.

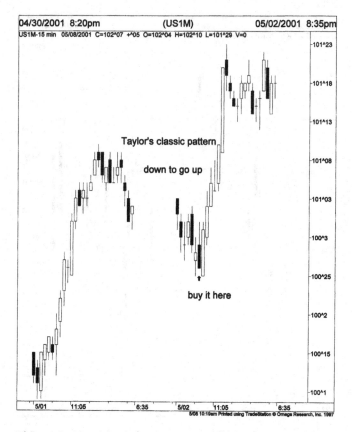

04/30/2001 8:20pm   (US1M)   05/02/2001 8:35pm

US1M-15 min 05/08/2001 C=102^07 +^05 O=102^04 H=102^10 L=101^29 V=0

Taylor's classic pattern

down to go up

buy it here

Figure 2.15   You often get a small countertrend early in the day. This is frequently the best place to fade the early trend.

Thus, in a rising market, the short-sellers will panic in the final moments and buy in a rush to exit. In a declining market, the opposite will take place. The buyers will panic and sell contracts to avoid additional losses overnight. As a result, the market will tend to get out of line at the close and be brought back only in the overnight market or the following morning.

In trying to decide where the market will go on the close, time and price are the best tools. However, if you are concentrating on one-minute bars, you

05/03/2001 7:05am   (ES1M)   05/03/2001 11:35am

ES1M-5 min 05/08/2001 C=1259.00 -4.50 O=1266.25 H=1277.00 L=1257.50 V=0

First leg

.618 violated, stops run

Second leg

7:05   7:30   7:55   8:20   8:45   9:10   9:35   10:00   10:25   10:50   11:15

5/08 10:31am Printed using TradeStation © Omega Research, Inc. 1997

Figure 2.16   The .618 retracement level is often
violated by stop-running. Be careful not to be
shaken out by this temporary market frenzy. If you
can stay with the position, you often will be vindi-
cated within five or ten minutes.

may not see the larger picture presented by the five- or ten-minute bars. Simply put, you may exit a good position prematurely.

We know that recent market history is the best indicator of whether a market will run. So always ask yourself: Where has the market come from, and
where it is headed? The exception to minute-to-minute accuracy in pinpointing the precise high or low exists in the final minutes of trading. That's when

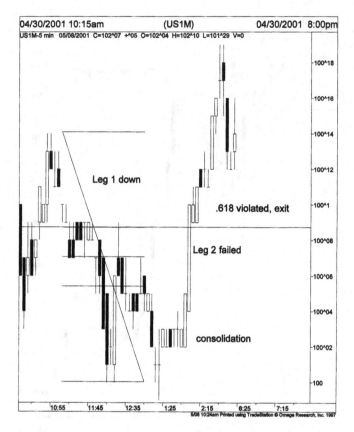

Figure 2.17 When the .618 is violated and stays violated, you must run quickly.

market panic will drive prices to extremes. The corollary should also be noted. Should you find yourself on the wrong side of the market going into the close, get out immediately! Because hope springs eternal in these matters, your like-minded buyers or sellers will wait until the final moments to panic in unison, driving prices against you and resulting in larger losses.

Having forewarned you about the downside, what are some general rules about sizing up a market going into the close? You might want to look at the big picture and consider the following three guidelines:

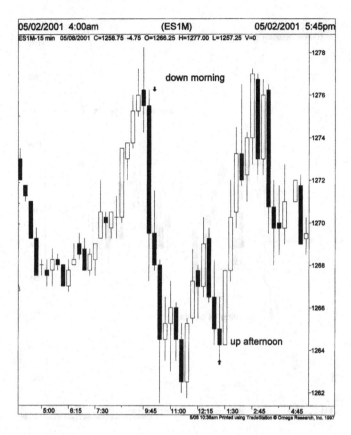

Figure 2.18   Notice how the entire break in the morning is offset by a comparable rally in the afternoon.

- When the afternoon trend is counter to the morning trend, the range often retraces the entire morning range (see Figure 2.18).

- When the afternoon trend is in the same direction as the morning trend, the respective legs of each move are often identical (see Figure 2.19).

- When you have a trendless day, the close is often in the middle of the value area (see Figure 2.20).

| 04/27/2001 6:15am | (ES1M) | 04/29/2001 5:30pm |

ES1M-15 min 05/08/2001 C=1257.00 -6.50 O=1266.25 H=1277.00 L=1256.00 V=0

afternoon 14 points

morning 14 points

5/08 10:39am Printed using TradeStation © Omega Research, Inc. 1997

Figure 2.19 The afternoon rally and the morning rally are symmetrical.

Now study Figures 2.21 and 2.22 and see if you can decide where the market will close.

15. *Look for price reversals when the TICK and TICKI get to extremes.* We've already discussed the TICK, the number of rising issues on the NYSE minus the number of declining issues. The TICKI is a similar indicator, although it only pertains to the 30 Dow Jones Industrial stocks. Because the TICKI only measures the strength of the Dow, its maximum strength reading is +30 and its minimum reading is −30.

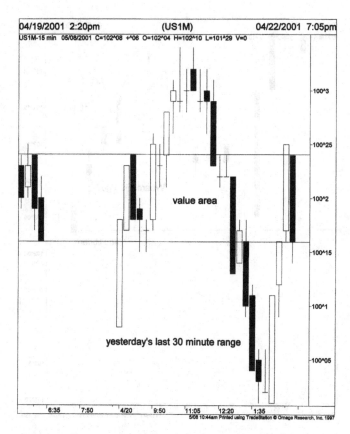

Figure 2.20 On trendless days, the market tends to close in the middle.

As I indicated in Rule #11 on confirming indicators, I chart the reading as a single line (see Figures 2.23 and 2.24). The rule for using these two indicators is as follows: When the TICKI gets above 24 or below −24, look to sell and buy, respectively. The same applies when the TICK gets above 600 or 800 or below −600 or −800. Fade high and low readings in these indicators. This is a good confirmation tool for time and price trades.

16. *Pinpoint stop-running areas.* This is a confirmation rule that will enhance your ability to exit at the correct point. If the time and price target

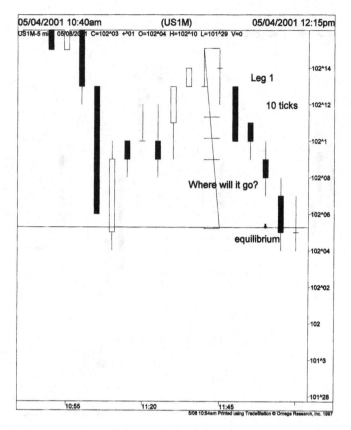

Figure 2.21 What is leg 1 telling you about the direction of the move and the potential magnitude?

is just below, at, or just above a prior intraday high or low, chances are the end of the short-term trend will be within this general area. Stops tend to be clustered above and below both intraday and interday highs and lows. As a result, when prices trade into these areas, there will be heightened volume (see Figures 2.25 and 2.26). Once the stop orders are executed, however, the market often reverses. It is important to understand that this does not mean the termination of the overall trend, only that the immediate short-term trend is likely to stop at these areas.

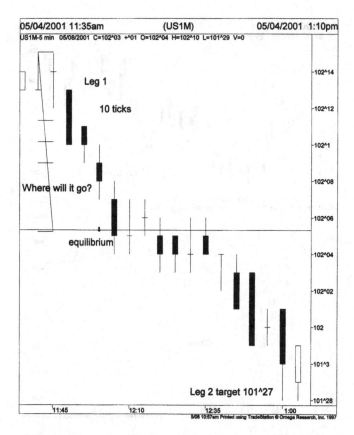

Figure 2.22 The market traded within one tick of the target.

17. *The market speeds up in the afternoon.* I am frequently asked, "When is the best time to trade—morning or afternoon?" I tend to favor the afternoon because it seems that the crosscurrents are fewer, resulting in purer moves. When, after four or five hours of churning, the market makes up its mind to run, it goes without interruption into the close. Moreover, there is another important component to this trend: It tends to go at twice the rate of the morning move. That is, the trend that takes one hour to complete in the morning is accomplished in one-half hour in the afternoon, the same move in half the time. Put another way, you make the profits in half the time. That means

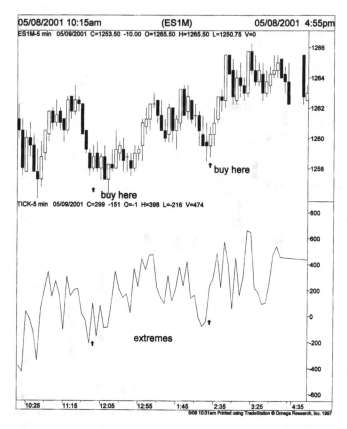

Figure 2.23 Notice how low readings in the TICK pinpoint good buying opportunities.

less time in the trade, less time for something to go wrong, and, of course, quicker adversity if you get in on the wrong side. Why does this happen? I'm not exactly certain. But I suspect that it has something to do with the herd mentality in the market. If the market starts to run after lunch in New York, the fund managers, who might fear missing the move, are apt to jump aboard lest they find themselves on the sidelines. If they miss too many moves, these same fund managers might find themselves looking for a new job if their respective funds don't keep pace with the averages. Hence, you have a rush

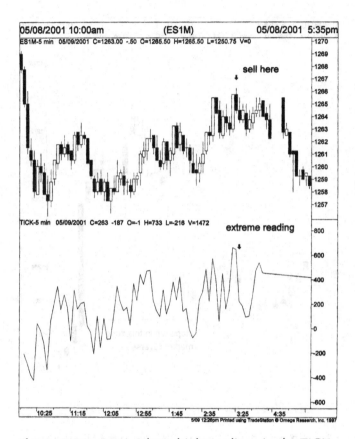

Figure 2.24 Notice how high readings in the TICK pinpoint good selling opportunities.

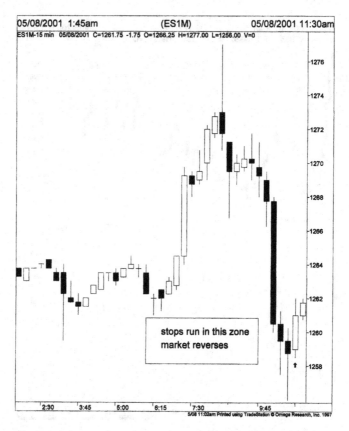

Figure 2.25 The market will often trade back to a prior support or resistance zone prior to reversing.

ES1M-15 min 05/08/2001 C=1261.50 -2.00 O=1266.25 H=1277.00 L=1256.00 V=0

stops run in this zone
market reverses

Figure 2.26 Stops are often clustered around prior highs and lows.

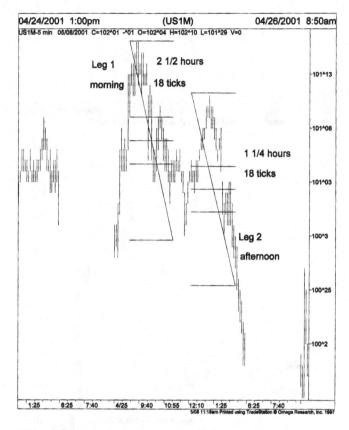

Figure 2.27 Notice how the afternoon leg 2 is purer in direction, with fewer crosscurrents than you encountered in the morning leg 1.

to join the crowd late in the day when the true trend becomes apparent. The corollary to this rule, of course, is to not fade the afternoon trend. The market may have indeed been down all morning. In a bull market, this will only provide a good buying opportunity and the afternoon trend will reflect this buying. In a bear market, a morning rally will provide the same opportunity for aggressive sellers to push down prices in the afternoon (see Figure 2.27). Lastly, the best trending cycles will vary from morning to afternoon. Look for the most recent patterns to identify whether the morning or afternoon presents the best trends.

3

Support and Resistance

How to Identify Buy and Sell Zones

No method of pattern recognition is more popular than trying to identify support and resistance zones. From the earliest days of technical analysis, traders have been trying to quantify market moves and make sense of market patterns.

Rare is the trader who doesn't have his or her own favorite indicator or market formula. A number of trading systems have been based on market formulas. Like all approaches to the market, one that embraces such formulas has both pluses and minuses. Perhaps the most frustrating aspect of relying on support and resistance formulas, however, is that market behavior cannot be reduced to a number or series of numbers. The successful analyst needs to know how to interpret these numbers, how to understand the nuances of the market, and perhaps, on some occasions, when to throw out the numbers altogether.

There was a time when I wanted to reduce all my trading decisions to the numbers on a three-by-five card that I would create following the close of trading on the prior day. I would have a buy and sell number, three or four support and resistance numbers, a buy and sell zone, and an overbought/oversold percentage number. Then, when my numbers let me down, I'd go back and try to make sense of what went wrong. The fact is, I wasn't being open to the possibility of the market changing from day to day. I sought the answers outside of myself. The numbers had become a crutch. I wasn't willing to trade without them. The fact is, despite all the help the numbers provided, they weren't sufficient to make me a consistent winner.

Today, I know why this is so. I frequently encounter new traders who only want formulas. They don't want to hear that the market is difficult to beat. The fact is, almost any reasonably good technical tool will provide you with steady profits from time to time. But the time will always come when this will not be so. This is when you need to stand back and see the formula for what it is—a trading tool. What is called for is an analysis and interpretation of a given formula within a given context. Sure, anyone can do a simple analysis and tell you the market was strong yesterday. But will it be strong today? And, in the event it is strong today, will it close strong? The market is always the most bullish at the top and more bearish at the bottom. Can you see how merely following the current trend is a prescription for disaster?

WHAT WORKS AND WHAT DOESN'T

Having expressed this caveat against relying too much on technical indicators that provide an insight into a market's behavior, I want to stress that you need a little structure in your approach to the market. The seat-of-the-pants approach almost never works. So you need the discipline that a rigorous analysis provides. But you also need the openness that comes from looking at the market in a variety of ways, the flexibility to change sides, to accept that the answer is not always as simple as you would want it to be.

The ultimate answer, no doubt, rests not with a single formula or measurement, but how you combine a variety of indicators to create an overall pattern of likely market behavior. Because most measures of market behavior, by definition, must be based on what has already occurred, it stands to reason that this occurrence is unlikely to be repeated without interpretation in the future. Nor, for that matter, is it helpful to say that the opposite must occur either. I can see you throwing up your hands in frustration, saying, "Well, in that case, what does work?"

I wish I had an easy answer, but I know from experience that those who want these easy answers are only deluding themselves. What works is a theoretical framework that allows for the subtlety of market forces to generate an overall approach that will work over time. In short, what we are talking about is flexibility.

I understand the difficulty in seeing your numbers telling you one thing and the market another. The fact is, the market is always correct no matter what your numbers say. Novice traders especially are apt to dismiss this notion. They want to believe they've found the answer, the holy grail. But this reliance on what they want to believe will only result in disappointment.

The only way to disabuse yourself of this common ailment is to accept that the fact that you just don't know every answer in advance—the old notion of embracing uncertainty.

The place to start getting a toehold on what's really going on in the market is with some simple calculations. These are the basic calculations, the ones that Taylor used some 50 years ago in the grain markets. They measure how a market tends to trade on a day-to-day basis, and they can be exceptionally valuable under certain conditions.

Taylor maintained that the market was engineered from within. He said there was a 3-day cycle that would be repeated over and over again. The three days consisted of a so-called buy day, a sell day, and a short-sell day. The sequence in which the highs and lows were recorded was critical in analyzing the respective days. On the buy day, the low was made first near the prior day's low and the market would rally. On the sell day, there would be a lot of trading activity near the prior day's (buy day) high. (Taylor was not a day trader. He used the sell day to exit the position taken on the buy day.) And on the third day up (the sell short day), the high was made first, providing the opportunity to sell before the market broke. Finally, with prices trading near the short-sell-day low, prices would be engineered lower to provide another buying opportunity for the smart money on the third day. That's the theory and you'll often be able to spot this pattern if you are careful to analyze the sequence in which the highs and lows occur in the market.

By knowing about this 3-day cycle, you can often identify the kind of day you will have in advance. This is very useful, but it is not as simple as saying you can buy every third day and make money, although I know from experience that a lot of people have tried this approach. The value in knowing about this cycle is that it tells you not to buy on the third day up—especially if you get a higher opening. And isn't this precisely what often happens? By the third day up, all the indicators are looking positive. The buyers from down below are happy because they have nice paper profits. The more cautious buyers, however, have been on the sidelines; now they want to buy as well. That's what causes all the bullish enthusiasm on the opening of the third day up. And that's precisely where the smart money, as Taylor so eloquently told us fifty years ago, is selling. Is it any wonder why the majority of traders contribute to the fortunes of the few in the market?

To know where to precisely buy or sell the market, Taylor created what he called his "book method." This was nothing more than a series of calculations based on recent market action, and the theory behind it is nothing more than common sense. How far does the market tend to rally or decline day to day? There are four key calculations:

The rally number, today's high minus yesterday's low

The decline number, yesterday's high minus today's low

The buying high number, today's high minus yesterday's high

The buying under number, yesterday's low minus today's low

When today's high is higher than yesterday's high, the buying high number will be a positive number. When today's high is lower than yesterday's high, the buying high number will be a negative number. When yesterday's high exceeds today's low (most of the time), the decline number will be a positive number. Should the market surge and today's low is *above* yesterday's high, the decline number would be negative. When today's low exceeds yesterday's low, the buying under number is positive. And when yesterday's low is above today's low, the buying under number is negative.

By averaging a series of days, you can create what I call buy envelopes and sell envelopes. [Note: I've written extensively on these calculations in five or six other books and videos and I urge interested readers to do additional research beyond the cursory examination of the calculations here. These works include, but are not limited to, *Winning in the Futures Market* (New York: McGraw-Hill, 1986), *Profitable Day-Trading with Precision* (Smithtown, N.Y.: TradeWins Publishing, 1997), *Taylor's Book Method* (Greenville, S.C.: Traders Press, 1991), *Essential Secrets of Day-Trading* (Smithtown, N.Y.: TradeWins Publishing, 1991), *How to Triple Your Money Every Year with Stock Index Futures* (Brightwaters, N.Y.: Windsor Books, 1983).] The more numbers you can generate for your respective envelopes, the more likely they represent valid support and resistance levels. The final calculation is to average the averages and come up with a single buy and sell number.

These terms can be misleading. The buy and sell numbers will have legitimacy only if the market is trendless. Indeed, when I first started working with these numbers in the early eighties, this was often the case. The market was relatively stable back then and today's rally would be offset by tomorrow's break. This meant you could buy the buy number and sell the sell number and make money. But I don't have to tell you where the market has gone since 1982, especially in the past ten years. Trying to sell yesterday's resistance in a bull market is a prescription for failure, so you need to be careful in interpreting the results.

WORKING WITH THE NUMBERS

I don't want to suggest that there is only one way to track the market in terms of putting together buy and sell numbers. Over the years, I've used three days to average results. You may want to use a different number of days to average. This is a personal preference. The principles are the same regardless of which number you decide to use. The most important point is how and why you average.

If you remember what I said about knowing your market, you'll recall that I mentioned that professionals are specialists. There is a lot of work that goes into understanding a market. Part of this work involves rallies and declines. Let's turn now to some specific measurements.

1. *The rally number.* Defined as today's high (after the close; all calculations are done following the close of trading) minus yesterday's low, this number measures how far the market tends to rally from one day to another. The only certain way to know this number is to measure it, of course, but veteran traders will have a ballpark idea of where a trend will end. A stock might rally, on average, 2.50 dollars from a previous close. A futures contract might rally 10 cents. In the example below, we are using hypothetical S&P 500 futures prices:

Day	Today's High	Yesterday's Low	Rally
1	1284.00	1260.00	24.00
2	1285.50	1266.50	19.00
3	1292.00	1271.00	21.00

In the past three days, the market has rallied between 19.00 and 24.00 off a prior day's low. By taking the average of these three prices, you will derive an average rally price of 21.30 points. This number tells us on average how much the market tends to rally over the past three days. Now, how do we use this to project a possible target price on the following day? Simply by adding the average rally to the last day's low following the close of trading.

Assume that the latest day had a high of 1292.00 (today's high), a low of 1268.00, and a close of 1272.00. You add the average range to today's low to project tomorrow's high. (21.30 average rally + 1268.00 today's low = 1289.30 anticipated high). As you can see, the answer is 1289.30. This is one number that would be a part of the sell envelope. It doesn't mean that the market must reach this number. It may fall short—or it may exceed this number. It is simply one resistance number where the market should stop advancing based on recent market action.

2. *The buying high number.* Defined as today's high minus yesterday's high, this number measures how far today's high exceeded yesterday's high. If today's high did not exceed yesterday's high, it will result in a negative number. In using this number, we will add the average buying high number to today's high to anticipate where tomorrow's high will occur. This will provide another number in the sell envelope. Assume the following:

Day	Today's High	Yesterday's High	Buying High
1	1284.00	1281.00	3.00
2	1285.50	1284.00	1.50
3	1292.00	1285.50	6.50

Over the past three days, the highs have been progressively higher. Three days ago, there was a 3.00 point gain over the prior high; yesterday there was a 1.50 point gain; and today, after the close of trading, the gain was 6.50 points. On average, the buying high number for the past three days is 3.70. This suggests that if this recent pattern is to continue, tomorrow's projected high will be 1295.70 (1292.00 today's high + 3.70 average buying high = 1295.70).

We now have two resistance numbers as a result of our calculations—the rally number and the buying high number. To finish up the sell envelope, we now need to turn to two more resistance points.

3. *Today's high.* Taylor said that resistance will always exist at the last day's high, that the market should trade slightly under, at, or above the last high. If prices stopped advancing at this number as recently as this afternoon,

chances are whatever force held it there will likewise hold it again tomorrow. You can also look at this number as a magnet. If prices open below this number, there might very well be a run to this number. Or there might be stop-running just beyond this number. Or there might be selling entering the market before this number is reached. When you create the sell envelope, the high of the day just finished (today's high) should be included as one of your resistance numbers. Using the hypothetical numbers in our example, we'll use today's high of 1292.00 as another resistance level.

4. *The LSS pivot breakout buy number (also known as the trend reaction sell number).* There is some confusion about this number because it is a resistance number when used as a component of the sell envelope, but a breakout buy number when used as a trend-following signal in my "Trade for a Living" program. This should come as no surprise because resistance means precisely that—a resistance point where prices should stop rising. Once violated, traditional technical analysis would tell you that resistance becomes support, and vice versa. It is precisely because of the dual nature of this number that it is so critical. By definition, this number is always at or above the close. In a trending market, the following formula will generate a number at which the market is considered to be breaking out to new highs. In a nontrending market, the same number will represent strong resistance which should not be violated.

This formula is as follows:

$$\frac{(\text{day's high} + \text{day's low} + \text{day's close})}{3} = X$$

$$2 \text{ times } X - \text{day's low} = \text{pivot breakout buy number}$$
$$(\text{trend reaction sell number})$$

Now let's do the math using the following numbers:

Today's high = 1292.00

Today's low = 1268.00

Today's close = 1272.00

$$\frac{(1292.00 \text{ day's high} + 1268.00 \text{ day's low} + 1272.00 \text{ day's close})}{3} = 1277.30$$

$$\text{therefore, } 2X = 2554.60$$

$$2554.60 \ (2X) - 1268.00 \ (\text{day's low}) = 1286.60$$

We now have a fourth number to add to our sell envelope. The following four numbers comprise the sell envelope:

1295.70   Buying high

1292.00   Today's high

1289.30   Rally

1286.00   LSS pivot breakout buy

The final calculation using the sell envelope is to add the four numbers and divide by four. This is the average of the four numbers, the sell number. Using the numbers above, the final sell number is 1290.70.

Before working through the calculations for the buy envelope, let's make some observations on the current market situation presented by these numbers. The market has been rallying over the three-day period shown. Each high was higher; each low was higher. Is this the 3-day cycle? Most probably. Chances are, the low was made first on Day 1. Chances also favor the high first being made on the third day up because the close (1272.00) was near the low of the day (1268.00). A steady-to-lower open on Day 4 would probably create a good buying opportunity as the market resumes its trend higher.

Now let's turn to the creation of the buy numbers in the buy envelope.

5. *The decline number.* Defined as today's low (after the close of trading) minus yesterday's high, this number measures how far the market has declined over the two-day period. Let's look at a three-day period and see what the number will tell us.

Day	Yesterday's High	Today's Low	Decline
1	1281.50	1256.70	24.80
2	1284.00	1260.00	24.00
3	1285.50	1266.50	19.00

When averaged, the 3-day decline number is 22.90. This means that on average the market has declined this amount over the past three days. Note that the most recent decline is only 19.00 points, whereas three days ago the decline was 24.80 points. This suggests that the market is finding support at higher levels. If this trend continues, the next day's decline number may be even smaller. Hence, it may not reach the support number that the average would suggest. Given the 22.90 average decline number, the support number would be 1262.20. How is this number calculated? Since today's high (the day just completed) was 1285.50, the buy support number would be 22.90 points less, or 1262.60. To generate the decline number, you take the last day's high and subtract the decline number. Hence, 1262.60 would be one of the numbers that comprise the buy envelope.

   6. *The buying under number.* Defined as yesterday's low minus today's low, this number represents how much today's market low traded under yesterday's. This will be a positive number if today's low is indeed lower than yesterday's. But, as in our example, if today's low is higher than yesterday's low, then the difference will be a negative number. As you will see, when you go to subtract a negative from a negative, you will end up adding the average number to the day's low to pinpoint the support level. Consider the following prices:

Day	Yesterday's Low	Today's Low	Buying Under
1	1260.00	1266.50	−6.50
2	1266.50	1271.00	−4.50
3	1271.00	1268.00	3.00

   Here we have two minus numbers added together and subtracted from a single positive number. The calculations are as follows:

$$\begin{array}{r} -6.50 \\ \underline{-4.50} \\ -11.00 \end{array}$$

This minus number is then added to the positive number as follows:

$$\begin{array}{r} -11.00 \\ \underline{+3.00} \\ -8.00 \end{array}$$

   This number is then divided by three (−8.00 divided by 3 = −2.70).
   This negative number is then *subtracted from* today's low (1268.00) to create the next day's buying under number of 1270.70. (NOTE: When you

subtract a negative number, you get a larger sum; when you subtract a positive number, you get a lesser sum.) This is another support level that comprises the buy envelope.

7. *Today's low.* Tomorrow's low should trade at, near, slightly above, or below yesterday's low. For this reason, today's low serves as a support level. Depending upon how bullish or bearish prices are on the following day, this price should serve some role. In a bullish environment, declining prices will halt prior to reaching this price; in a bearish environment, prices will penetrate this price. You could also make the case that stop-running will occur at this price if and when it is approached. The price at which the decline was halted yesterday (today's low) is always a key support level. That is why it is included in the buy envelope. In our example, today's low is 1268.00.

8. *The LSS pivot breakout sell number (also known as the trend reaction buy number).* Here, again, we have a single number that serves two purposes, both as the point where prices will break out to the downside and where they will find support when the market is drifting lower. Over the years, as the market has evolved from a lackadaisical affair to a runaway bull, and now, perhaps, an occasional bear, the need has existed to modify the use of this number. Even today, however, you will find that the market will often bounce off a support in the morning, but plow through the same support in the afternoon like a hot knife through butter. There is nothing inconsistent with standard technical analysis in viewing this number as the critical point it represents. The support, once violated, will indeed become the resistance. Prices will often break below a critical support only to bounce back up to the now support/resistance (the return move)—and only then break like a rock.

The formula is as follows:

$$\frac{(\text{day's high} + \text{day's low} + \text{day's close})}{3} = X$$

2 times X – day's high = pivot breakout sell number
(trend reaction buy number)

Now let's do the math using the following numbers:

Today's high = 1292.00

Today's low = 1268.00

Today's close = 1272.00

$$\frac{(1292.00 \text{ day's high} + 1268.00 \text{ day's low} + 1272.00 \text{ day's close})}{3} = 1277.50$$

$$\text{therefore, } 2X = 2554.60$$

$$2554.60 \ (2X) - 1292.00 \ (\text{day's high}) = 1262.60$$

We now have a fourth number to add to our buy envelope. The following four numbers comprise the buy envelope:

1270.70   Buying under

1268.00   Today's low

1262.60   Decline

1262.60   LSS pivot breakout sell

The final calculation using the buy envelope is to add the four numbers and divide by four. This is the average of the four numbers, the buy number. Using the numbers above, the final buy number is 1266.00.

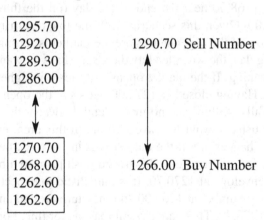

Sell Envelope

| 1295.70 |
| 1292.00 | 1290.70 Sell Number
| 1289.30 |
| 1286.00 |

| 1270.70 |
| 1268.00 | 1266.00 Buy Number
| 1262.60 |
| 1262.60 |

Buy Envelope

Note that the two bottom numbers of the buy envelope are identical: 1262.60. This suggests a true now-or-never trade should the market reach that level. This is a point in the market where prices will find support and bounce, or the reverse will occur and the market will break sharply.

By taking the difference between the buy and sell numbers, we now have an anticipated range for the next day: 24.70 points. In the studies we have performed over the years, this anticipated range has proved to be a very reliable number. We had relatively little success, on the other hand, with predicting the high and low in the absence of an opening price and early range. The exception occurred in a nontrending market where the buy and sell numbers proved very useful.

Having put together the daily buy and sell envelopes and the respective buy and sell numbers, you still have to face a dilemma. How do you use these numbers? I wish it were as simple as buying the buy number and selling the sell number, but it is not. I think you can see that if, for instance, the market is rallying and you sell the sell number, you may sell near the low of the day. Conversely, you might find yourself on the wrong side of the market if you purchase the buy number on a day when the market is breaking. There are several good approaches to using these numbers, but flexibility must always remain the key factor in deciding which approach to take.

What do you want to look for? Where the market opens, and what time of the day the market trades inside the buy or sell envelope or at the buy or sell number. In the hypothetical example above, we said that the market traded near its low of 1268.00 near the end of the day (on the third day up) and closed at 1272.00. Given this scenario, with the low occurring last and the close near the low of the day, chances are the market is setting up for a rally on the following day, the so-called buy day. But what you want is what I call a reasonable opening. If the market opens significantly higher—or lower— all bets are off. Having closed at 1272.00, let's say the open is at 1276.50. This number falls within the no-man's-land between the buy and sell envelopes. You usually want to leave it alone in this area, especially right after the open. Chances are, if the market is going to rally, perhaps the best you could hope for, in terms of a downward push prior to a big rally, is the top of the buy envelope at 1270.70. It is unrealistic to expect the market to decline to the buy number at 1266.00 and then turn around and go up to the sell number at 1290.70. There are several reasons for this. For one, on average the open tends to fall near one end of the range on a trending day. The exception would be a nontrending day when the market rotates when the open falls in the middle. For another, either the high or low tends to occur during the first hour of trading. So if you monitor the market for 30 minutes to an hour and sell an established early range, you can now do a couple of calculations and come up with a scenario. For example, with the open at

1276.50, you might find an early range of 1272.50 and 1279.50. Chances are, the 1272.50 low will hold, meaning the low has been established and now the question is one of where will it go on the upside. To generate this anticipated sell number, you add the anticipated range to the early low of 1272.50 as follows:

1272.50 early low + 24.70 anticipated range = 1297.20 anticipated high

In this case, you have shifted the envelopes higher while maintaining the range. If you don't take this approach, you will find yourself waiting in vain for the buy number or buy envelope to be reached. Where would you buy this market? Certainly not at the low. When the low is being made, you don't know whether that low will hold. So here one of the great paradoxes of the market enters the picture. This market is a better buy higher up than it is at the low. Once the low shows signs of holding, you could buy it at any price above that number, assuming, of course, that it hasn't already begun to run. So let's say you buy it at 1275.50. Having done so, you don't want to see another test of the lows. It is better to buy strength and have the market get stronger. Nor do you want to place a stop at or below the low. The stop needs to be above the low of the day because the next trip down may be the big break. You can trail the stop or place a stop in the 1273.00 or 1274.00 area. Where you place the stop should always be a question of where the market is likely or not likely to trade, not how much money you are willing to lose. Once a certain amount of times passes, the market should rally. If it doesn't, get out immediately—or get out and reverse sides. Assuming the trade does work, you next have to concern yourself with an exit strategy.

If you are willing to hold the position into the final hour, you might indeed get your anticipated high at 1297.20. This is an ideal situation. There are many factors, however, that might cause you to exit sooner. You may grow tired of holding the position. Certainly, it will probably take all day to get to the anticipated high. Once the position is profitable, you will be tempted to take profits. This is not always the wisest course, however. If your profits are only several hundred points, chances are, the next time you are wrong, the losses will be larger than this gain. So the profit might be offset. On the other hand, the anticipated high might never be reached. Unless you are going to rely on another style of trading for your exit strategy, you'll want to set up a series of target objectives. What are these objectives?

One, you want to think about holding the trade into the final hour. That's when you are most likely to get the high of the day. Two, you might want to consider holding the trade until the close. On a rising trend day, you'll get pan-icked short-sellers buying at the close. This might be the added boost you are looking for. Three, you have the new anticipated sell objective: 1297.20. Four, you have the original sell number: 1290.70. Five, you have a range of 9.70 points inside the sell envelope. Six, you have prior highs where stops exist. Yesterday's high was 1292.00. These are all legitimate profit-taking points.

On the downside, of course, you have your entry level and the day's low. You don't want to see these prices approached again once the market moves higher. You can always trail a stop, but then you have the problem of a minor reversal stopping you out just prior to another move higher.

THE NEXT DAY

Let's assume the trade works. The market rallies and closes near the high of the day. The final numbers are as follows:

Open = 1276.50

High = 1292.50

Low = 1272.50

Close = 1292.00

The range was somewhat smaller than anticipated. But the pattern was low made first, high made last—the classic buy day pattern. Let's run through the numbers for the next day.

1. *The rally number.* Taking the last three days of data, the columns would look as follows:

Day	Today's High	Yesterday's Low	Rally
1	1285.50	1266.50	19.00
2	1292.00	1271.00	21.00
3	1292.50	1272.50	21.50

The averaged rally number is 20.50. Added to yesterday's low, the rally resistance number is 1293.00.

2. *The buying high number.* The last three days of data would appear as follows:

Day	Today's High	Yesterday's High	Buying High
1	1285.50	1284.00	1.50
2	1292.00	1285.50	6.50
3	1292.50	1292.00	.50

The averaged buying high number is 2.80. Added to yesterday's high, the buying high is 1295.30.

3. *Today's high.* Today's high is 1292.50.

This is a resistance number that will be a component of the selling envelope.

4. *The LSS pivot breakout buy number.* Using the formula for the day just completed, the math would appear as follows:

$$\frac{(1292.50 \text{ day's high} + 1272.50 \text{ day's low} + 1292.00 \text{ day's close})}{3}$$

$$= 1285.70$$

therefore, $2X = 2571.40$

$$2571.40 \ (2X) - 1272.50 \text{ (day's low)} = 1298.90$$

This is the fourth number added to the sell envelope. The sell envelope for tomorrow would now look as follows:

1298.90 LSS pivot breakout buy number

1295.30 Buying high number

1293.00 Rally number

1292.50 Today's high number

The average of these four numbers is 1294.90. This is the sell number. Continuing along, let's turn to the buy numbers.

5. *The decline number.* Here are the results of the last three days:

Day	Yesterday's High	Today's Low	Decline
1	1284.00	1260.00	24.00
2	1285.50	1266.50	19.00
3	1292.00	1272.50	19.50

The average of the last three declines is 20.80. When this number is subtracted from today's high of 1292.50, the decline number for tomorrow becomes 1271.70. This number is one of the components of the buying envelope for tomorrow.

6. *The buying under number.* Here are the last three entries at the close of trading as of today:

Day	Yesterday's Low	Today's Low	Buying Under
1	1266.50	1271.00	−4.50
2	1271.00	1268.00	3.00
3	1268.00	1272.50	−4.50

When these three numbers are averaged, the result is −2.00. When this number is subtracted from 1272.50 (remember, when you subtract a negative number, you actually *add* it to the positive number), you have 1274.50 as tomorrow's buying under number. This becomes a component of tomorrow's buy envelope.

7. *Today's low.* Today's low is 1272.50. The market should find support at this level. This is the third component of the buy envelope.

8. *The LSS pivot breakout sell number.* The calculations of this number are as follows:

$$\frac{(1292.50 \text{ day's high} + 1272.50 \text{ day's low} + 1292.00 \text{ day's close})}{3}$$

$$= 1285.70$$

therefore, $2X = 2571.40$

$$2571.40 \ (2X) - 1292.50 \ (\text{day's high}) = 1278.90$$

This is the fourth number added to the buy envelope. The buy envelope for tomorrow would now look as follows:

1278.90   LSS pivot breakout sell

1274.50   Buying under

1272.50   Today's low

1271.70   Decline

The average of these four numbers is 1274.40, the buy number.
Tomorrow's numbers would now appear as follows:

Sell Envelope

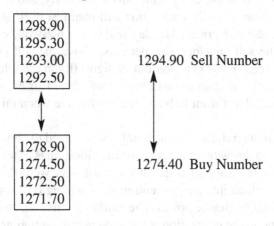

1298.90
1295.30
1293.00   1294.90 Sell Number
1292.50

1278.90
1274.50   1274.40 Buy Number
1272.50
1271.70

Buy Envelope

The calculation process is then repeated the next day, and so on. Armed with a set of reliable support and resistance numbers, the professional trader can then base his trading decisions on something more than mere guesswork. The general rule is that you want to buy within the buy envelope and sell within the sell envelope, but a breakout above the sell envelope would be a buying opportunity and a breakout below the buy envelope would be a selling opportunity. When used with the requisite amount of flexibility, the numbers provide a useful tool for judging market support and resistance.

WHAT THE NUMBERS DON'T DO

Support and resistance numbers cannot be used to predict the future. We have done studies using support and resistance to generate buy and sell points. The results don't justify taking such a simplistic approach. But this is quite different from throwing out the numbers altogether. Moreover, there are instances when the buy and sell numbers will be right on the money. You must not, however, make the mistake of thinking you can merely buy and sell these numbers willy-nilly on a daily basis and make money.

When do the numbers work, and when are they better left alone? The most obvious answer has to do with the trending or nontrending aspects of the current market you are trading. If you are experiencing a nontrending market, you'll find that the support and resistance numbers can be very helpful. Today's up day will be offset by tomorrow's down day, and the market will fluctuate. On a chart of daily prices, this will manifest itself as a consolidation period of sideways prices. The day will come, however, when the market opens in the sell envelope (or, perhaps, above the sell envelope) and you'll sell and see prices skyrocket out of sight. If you are reluctant to take losses at this point, the situation will grow more dire. This obviously will be the breakout. You don't want to be on the wrong side when this market pattern occurs.

To prevent an overreliance on the numbers, you need to know when to use them and when to throw them out. One of the oldest rules of technical analysis is that one man's support is another's resistance. Were this not so, you wouldn't find such an intense concentration of trading (buying and selling) at key support and resistance points. The market is, after all, created by a difference of opinion. The temptation is to overgeneralize a trading rule or strategy that worked yesterday or last week into a universal law. Don't do it!

THE PARADOX OF SUPPORT AND RESISTANCE

While support and resistance has traditionally been the bread and butter of professional floor traders, the off-floor trader can likewise utilize them when the market is running. And this brings us to the notion of the paradox of trending markets. After a number of years of research, we incorporated this notion into a version of the LSS system. Simply put, the market is never too high to buy and never too low to sell. What does this mean? By identifying support and resistance points away from the current market price, we were able to pinpoint areas where the market would generate enough energy to cause prices to rapidly soar or plummet. The paradox is that the market has already traveled a substantial amount in getting to these prices in the first place.

Let's take an example. If you have a Fed report scheduled to be released later in the day, what's the morning price action going to look like? That's right, it will probably open unchanged and fluctuate until the report is released. The reason for this is quite simple: No one is going to want to risk a huge loss when the news hits. So the bulk of the trading will be professional scalpers and the like trying to nickel-and-dime the market in advance of the report. But what happens once the news is released? If it is truly market-moving and unexpected, the market is going to run up or down in a big hurry. The paradox, which is defined as an apparent contradiction which is nevertheless somehow true, is that the market will prove to be a much better buy way up on the day than it was hundreds of points lower. The same, of course, is true in reverse if you are selling a plummeting market.

I know what you're thinking. Wasn't it a much better buy down below before the news was released? Not really. Down there, a negative report would have resulted in panic selling. Any would-be buyers would have been wiped out. The paradox is that the market is a better buy higher up and a better sell lower down. We have done statistical studies on this phenomenon which prove that a higher open is more bullish for a market and that a lower open is more bearish.

I used to know a trader who specialized in buying new highs and selling new lows late in the day. The late-in-the-day qualification is important since that's when the market will truly trend, as opposed to the morning when you may have a trading affair. Moreover, this successful trader used to make a big point of not abandoning his position unless the market "showed him that he was wrong." He wasn't going to let a little profit-taking shake him out of a position. Years later, when we did the computer research, we were able to prove what he'd known all along: The market was a better buy higher up. This was the paradox.

When it came to designing new software for my "Trade for a Living" seminar, we incorporated this feature into the trading system. We would add to a position at a higher price in a rising market. Indeed this presented some confusion among would-be users. "The market probably isn't going to that price," people would ask. "Why buy it there?" The point is, if it gets there it is a good buy. We are not trying to predict tomorrow's prices. This is impossible. But we are trying to capitalize on a situation if it develops in a given way. Percentagewise, there is a far greater degree of certainty that a rising market will continue to rise, than a lackadaisical market will suddenly spring to life and go soaring off into the stratosphere. For those of you who are denizens of gambling parlors, this is the same notion of the seasoned craps players seeking a so-called hot table. Take a table with a few stickmen and pit bosses standing around and no one wants to play. Crowd the table with a mob of shrieking players winning money and the entire casino rushes over. The point is, we are not trying to predict prices. We are simply suggesting that the odds favor a continuation of a given price trend. The notion of zone trading is based on this very principle.

HOW TO MEASURE MARKET STRENGTH

One simple way to determine a market's trending abilities is to measure strength. You can do this on a one-day basis or on a five-day basis depending on whether you are short- or long-term-oriented toward the market. By measuring strength, you are taking a point of view, a bias, but even here you must be careful. You must know your market. If today's strength is typically offset by tomorrow's weakness, you must interpret the strength measurement one way. But if today's strength is indicative of an overall trend, you want to use that bias to favor one side of the market or another. Let's first look at a short-term formula, the *LSS 1-day strength index*. This formula generates a percentage number based on the relationship of the close to the overall range during one day of trading. It is a simple formula that can be calculated quickly following the close of trading. The formula is as follows:

$$\frac{(\text{close} - \text{low}) \times 100}{(\text{high} - \text{low})} = \text{1-day strength index}$$

You can estimate this number simply by noting where the closing price is, relative to the range. A close at the top will be 100; a close at the bottom will be zero. A midrange close will be 50 percent, and so on.

Let's assume the March S&P 500 contract has the following range and close:

High = 1315.00

Low = 1296.50

Close = 1301.00

The calculations would be as follows:

$$\frac{(1301.00 - 1296.50) \times 100}{(1315.00 - 1296.50)} = 24\%$$

In general, a reading under 50 percent is considered bearish. So a reading of just 24 percent would suggest lower prices. I want to stress the word *general* here. This might have been the third day up in the three-day cycle. This would suggest a modest selloff. But a lower opening on the next day might be a classic case of the market being engineered lower to ultimately present a buying opportunity followed by higher prices. Moreover, this selloff might have occurred on a Thursday in a bull market. A higher opening on the following day might indeed be met with continued higher prices. We'll get to the notion of day-of-the-week trading in the next chapter.

To get a more comprehensive gauge of recent market strength, you might want to consider a five-day measurement. The following formula, which works in a similar fashion, is known as the *LSS 5-day strength index:*

$$\frac{(\text{last close} - \text{lowest price in last 5 days}) \times 100}{(\text{highest price in last 5 days} - \text{lowest price in last 5 days})}$$

$$= \text{5-day strength index}$$

Let's assume that the past five days of S&P prices occurred as follows:

5-day high = 1351.70

5-day low = 1274.50

Last close = 1294.00

The calculations would appear as follows:

$$\frac{(1294.00 - 1274.50) \times 100}{(1351.70 - 1274.50)} = 25\%$$

What is the low percentage reading telling you here? Simply that the market has been weak. Chances are, you want to capitalize on this situation by selling weakness. Prices might, for instance, open in the buy envelope and begin to slip out the bottom. This penetration of the buy envelope might be a good selling opportunity. As you can see, in an overwhelming weak market, you may not want to buy in the buy envelope. A weak to lower open in such a market could very well signal continued weak prices.

THE LSS 5-DAY OSCILLATOR

The use of this oscillator is simplicity itself. If the percentage reading is above 70 percent, the market is bullish. If the percentage reading is below 30 percent, the market is bearish. Readings between 30 and 70 percent are neutral. There are always exceptions and other factors that you might want to consider, but if you want a reliable broad indicator to measure strength, this is the best one I've seen.

All calculations in this formula and others are to be done following the close of trading. Here's the formula:

$$\text{highest price in last 5 days} - \text{open 5 days ago} = X$$

$$\text{last close} - \text{lowest price in last 5 days} = Y$$

$$\frac{(X + Y)}{(\text{highest price in last 5 days} - \text{lowest price in last 5 days}) \times 2}$$

This is a one-day calculation done following the close of trading. It is based on the previous five trading days. To keep the reading current, it must be calculated every day.

Let's plug in some numbers and do the calculations. Assume the following:

Highest price in last 5 days = 1317.50

Open 5 days ago   = 1308.20

Last close   = 1264.30

Lowest price in last 5 days = 1250.00

Given the above numbers, you can probably figure out that the market has been weak. Just how weak will be shown by the 5-day oscillator percentage. Here are the calculations:

$$1317.50 - 1308.20 = 9.30 = X$$

$$1264.30 - 1250.00 = 14.30 = Y$$

$$\frac{(9.30 + 14.30)}{(1317.50 - 1250.00) \times 2} = \frac{2360}{135} = 17$$

This is indeed a low percentage for the oscillator, one that suggests continued eroding prices.

Now, to complicate matters a little, this one-day reading needs to be smoothed by *averaging the last three one-day readings.* Assuming you had two prior one-day readings, you now add this third reading and average the three. This is the smoothed reading. Chances are, because the market's been falling, the prior two readings are also low. Let's say you had a 30-percent reading followed by a 26-percent reading. You add these two to the current 17-percent reading and then average them. The smoothed average is then 24 percent. In general, the smoothed average is more indicative of a market's bullish or bearish sentiment, since a single day could be a one-day aberration. By averaging three days, you are less likely to be thrown off by a single day's price action. When we discuss day-of-the-week trading, we place a lot of emphasis on market strength as measured by the *LSS 5-day oscillator.* We also look at the oscillator in terms of above 50 percent or below 50 percent. We also divide the oscillator percentage into thirds—the highest third, the middle third, and the lowest third. Each category has its benefits, especially when we couple the oscillator with other variables such as a specific day of the week or the prior day's close. For now, concentrate on calculating the daily LSS 5-day oscillator number and then smoothing the reading over the past three days. You'll find that this number will not only help you get a pulse on the market, but will also give you the confidence to take the best trades.

THE INTRADAY HIGH AND LOW GAME

Knowing how to identify support and resistance and how to measure market strength won't help you much unless you know how to use this information to trade successfully. One time-honored floor trader strategy is to use the early range as pivot points, buying the support and selling the resistance. This back-and-forth motion between the support and resistance may not seem like much, but when you add up the number of rallies and declines, the money becomes quite significant. I've seen the market bounce as many as a dozen times before making up its mind. The most significant number, of course, is the third attempt to penetrate the support or resistance. If the market is in a hurry, it will run on the third attempt. Once past that point, though, the market may consolidate for an hour or more. I recently saw the market make 14 attempts at both the high and the low before moving out of the consolidation area.

A truly tricky pattern to look for is when you have either a short-covering rally that fails or a simple one- or two-tick penetration of the support or resistance that fails. This is the surest sign that the market is headed in the *opposite direction*. You have to understand the psychology at work here. As long as the market rotates back and forth, the breakout players are on the sidelines. Not wanting to get caught in the whipsawing action within the consolidation, they place stops either above or below the market. These buy and sell stops are designed to get them in on a good market just as the market is beginning to run. That, at least, is the theory. These stops, however, become easy targets for the floor traders. The surest sign, therefore, that these stops are being picked off is when the market makes a new high or low and then retreats. What has happened? Well, it looked as if the market were headed higher when it penetrated the intraday high and headed into new high ground. The breakout players bought up there, as did the short-sellers from down below. But the stop-runners, typically the floor, were selling to the hapless breakout players. So now you have a new high on the day, and prices have retreated back down into the consolidation. At this stage, one of two scenarios will probably play out. There may be another run at the highs—which will fail—or the market will trend lower and break out the bottom!

The reverse, of course, occurs when a support level is penetrated. If prices trade back up into the consolidation, the market is headed higher, not lower. A temporary rally, however, to the former support (which is now a resistance) is often the last chance to sell before a big break. But a stop-running exercise is the very opposite.

How do you tell which is which? You have to observe two things: how the market trades and the time of day. When you have a short-covering rally (meaning the short-sellers are buying to get out of their positions), the market will go up, up, up—and then dead. After a moment or two at the top, there will be a race to sell—down, down, down. Those who bought at the top will feel foolish because they were just tricked into taking a loss when it was unnecessary. They didn't know this at the time, or perhaps they had a stop sitting there. In general, these forays into the stops are more likely to occur in the morning than in the late afternoon.

Now contrast this price action with the genuine rally. Once taken up, the selling that constitutes profit-taking will be met with renewed strong buying.

The market may hesitate for a moment, but the next high will be above the prior high. The market will soon find new buyers coming in and the upward trend will be under way.

Whereas a *short-cover rally* will always occur to the upside, the notion of *price rejection* can apply to rallies or declines. If you are familiar with the *Market Profile* studies, where prices are correlated with the amount of time that the market spends at certain levels, you'll know that a normal day looks like a parabolic curve. There is a lot of time spent trading in the middle with the highs and lows registered within a single, 15-minute time bracket. Indeed, were you to look at "time and sales," you'd find that typically the market trades at the high or the low for only a minute or two! The significance of this observation is that everyone loves a bargain. If the market trades lower, bargain-minded buyers will jump at the opportunity. If the market trades higher, bargain-minded sellers will jump in and push prices lower. Thus, on a so-called normal day, the big trend is back to the middle where supply and demand are in equilibrium.

As I mentioned earlier, astute floor traders can make a lot of money simply buying breaks and selling rallies, pushing prices back to equilibrium levels. The disequilibrium that occurs when the market runs is a result of one side gaining the upper hand. The key in knowing when that disequilibrium might occur is observing how prices behave at new lows and new highs. Price rejection, therefore, is the surest sign that the market is heading in the opposite direction.

There is another way to look at this market phenomenon and that is in terms of Taylor's market *engineering*. The market is taken up to go down; the market is taken down to go up. It is one thing to casually make this observation; it is another to observe it happening first-hand in a trading situation. I only wish I had back the many thousands of dollars I lost by not knowing about this phenomenon. The bottom-line is this: If you buy or sell a breakout and it doesn't work, you must reverse sides immediately! Don't think about the lost money. You don't have time. Just do it!

STOPS

The most reliable method of using support and resistance numbers is to target the areas where stops will accumulate. The first to consider is the prior day's *value area*. This is the high and low of the last 30 minutes of trading; the same could be said of the prior day's close. If the market opens above or below this area, chances are it will revisit these prices *before* moving to a new value area perhaps later in the day. It is for this reason that floor traders see little to be gained in taking positions overnight. Why take on the overnight risk if prices are going to trade back to the prior close anyway?

I liken the open to a giant spring. If it is pulled apart on the open (remember, they will be running all those overnight stops), the market will probably go back to the middle. The sole exception to this rule is the overnight news event which might cause an *extreme* gap. And here you have the paradox of the market: The higher the gap opening, the greater the likelihood that the market will continue higher. The same, in reverse, applies to sharply breaking markets.

These minority situations aside, where will the market go on any given open? Back to the prior day's close or, at the very least, to the value area. Can you see how knowing this can help you take profits at the appropriate place?

At any time, when you are holding a profitable trade, you want to set up a series of targets where you might wish to take profits. As I've mentioned, there are a variety of ways to determine where the market will trade. But the first stop is almost always just above a prior or intraday high or just below a prior or intraday low. This makes sense only because, as night follows day, there will always be stops at these levels. With half the brokers in the country telling their clients to place stops just above or below prior highs and lows, this is a virtual sure-thing. I'm not saying that there isn't more in the trade, just that stop-running occurs so frequently that there is rarely a day when you cannot count on the stops being run.

Intraday highs and lows, prior day's highs and lows, and life-of-contract highs and lows all provide easily measurable price levels where stops will accumulate. The floor traders know all the numbers. Make sure you do, as well.

Whenever I am puzzled at why the market stopped at a given level, I scroll back on my charts to look for a prior high or low. Rare is the time when I cannot find the relevant support or resistance level. It may have occurred two weeks ago, but it will be there.

You need to understand that the market moves in spurts. Seventy percent of the time the market will consolidate, the other thirty percent it will trend. This is the reason most profits are made on a relatively small number of trades. The big moneymaking moves simply don't occur every day.

FIBONACCI NUMBERS

Fibonacci numbers work extremely well with support and resistance. To use them, you simply take an intraday high and low and multiply by the key Fibonacci numbers. You then add and subtract these numbers from the intraday high and low. The selection of the intraday high and low is somewhat arbitrary. You can wait an hour after the open to measure the range—or even take a longer or shorter duration. Almost always, there is an early range that is expanded as the day continues. The key Fibonacci numbers are: 1.382, 1.618, and 2.236.

I've seen days when the market subsequently traded at the three Fibonacci targets to the top, and then reversed and traded at the three on the bottom, but this is the exception. Typically, the market will break higher or lower and trade at one or two of the numbers. The best way to explain the use of these numbers is with an example. Let's assume an early range is as follows:

High = 1292.70

Low = 1283.00

Range = 9.70

9.70 (early range) × 1.382 = 13.40

9.70 (early range) × 1.618 = 15.70

9.70 (early range) × 2.236 = 21.70

1292.70 (early high) + 13.70 = 1306.40

1292.70 (early high) + 15.70 = 1308.40

1292.70 (early high) + 21.70 = 1314.40

1283.00 (early low) − 13.70 = 1269.30

1283.00 (early low) − 15.70 = 1267.30

1283.00 (early low) − 21.70 = 1261.30

As you can see, these calculations pinpoint support and resistance levels, based on Fibonacci numbers, that are below and above the early range. With the calculations taken once a day, the numbers give you three additional support and resistance prices.

THE EVOLUTION OF LSS

LSS—the letters stand for *long, sell,* and *sell short*—is the trading program that I created based on Taylor's "Book Method." Over the years, the program, which began as the simple measuring of support and resistance, became quite sophisticated. As the market changed in recent years, we needed to go back and test some of the previous concepts. What worked so well in 1982 didn't work so well 15 years later. As a result, we had to change some of the original concepts. LSS became a breakout system as opposed to a system that faded rallies and declines. Moreover, as markets changed, it became necessary to drop certain markets which tested well in earlier years.

This doesn't surprise me. In the late 1970s inflation was raging and just about all commodities rose in value. With the taming of inflation, which hasn't been a problem now for twenty years, commodity prices in general have declined. Yet, at the same time, as the volatility of most commodities has declined, new financial instruments, such as the volatile S&P 500 stock index contract, have achieved enormous popularity.

As a short-term trader, you need two things—liquidity (many buyers and sellers) and volatility. You can make money in tamer markets, but you cannot trade them, not when you are paying commissions and are giving up the edge getting in and out. Over the years, I've seen a lot of markets become popular and then fade from popularity. I suspect the same will be true in the future.

Several years ago, I decided I'd gone about as far as I could with support and resistance and I began to explore other approaches to the market. I became very excited about time and price trading since I'd long been a believer in W.D. Gann's work. What was so exciting about the time and price approach was that it dovetailed so nicely with support and resistance; indeed, it was the very opposite side of the coin. The market did move from support level to resistance level to support, and it did so with precision. Moreover, the time and price approach enabled me to indulge the kind of flexibility I'd endorsed all along. I always knew you had to be able to switch sides during the day, but I never had a blueprint to tell me when.

The interesting thing about LSS is that, after additional testing, we turned some of its principles on their head. With fewer choppy markets to fade, we now made the trend our friend. The most notable example of this is the use of the LSS *pivotal buy and sell numbers.* We now buy strength and sell weakness. In the early 1980s we were fading the moves on the notion that the market wasn't going anywhere.

In more recent years, I've turned my attention to yet a third approach to the market—day-of-the-week trading. Armed with more than 18 years of tick data, we can now clearly demonstrate with computer proof what was only a hunch 10 years ago: The day of the week does make a difference in whether the market will rise or decline. Moreover, a strong relationship exists between what happened yesterday and what is likely to occur today.

I wish I could say that the concepts are simple. They are not. In a nutshell, they complement both support and resistance and time and price trading. Like a fine painting, they are a geometrically perfect composition, a counterbalanced completion of a finely honed puzzle. If you put in the effort to understand these concepts you'll be able to say, "Of course I see why that happened. All the answers were right in front of me all along." I know I've struggled with some of these questions for years. Now I think I can point you to some of the answers to "Why does the market behave as it does?" This is the subject of the next chapter.

4

Day-of-the-Week Trading

Why the Market Trades as It Does

The real significance of day-of-the-week trading is that it will transform your fundamental assumptions, preconceptions, and beliefs. The standard argument against short-term trading is that it is nothing more than a random gamble since the market exhibits no discernible patterns on a daily basis. For years, I agreed with this argument and indeed cautioned against favoring one side over the other lest one might become biased in one's beliefs. At the same time I had a disquieting feeling, though. Why were Thursdays so profitable and Wednesdays so difficult to trade? Why were Mondays typically rising trend days? What was the relationship between yesterday's close and today's open?

If you have ever put your faith in a single strategy or technique, you'll know what I mean. You'll use one technique on Monday or Tuesday and it will provide you with nothing but profits. The same strategy used on Wednesday and Thursday takes back all of the week's profits, and then some. Sound familiar? Welcome to the been-there-done-that club. This is a common experience for most traders.

For years, I knew I loved trading on Thursdays. But I couldn't explain why. I just knew that I tended to make a lot of money on Thursdays, often the entire month's profit. It was only later that I realized why. As a floor trader, I loved betting against the public. The public usually wanted to be long the market, meaning I was selling to them. If the market started to break, the public buyers would become panicked sellers; this generated big profits for the short-sellers. My selling wasn't limited to Thursdays, of course, but that's when the big profits tended to accumulate. I didn't think much about it at the time, but on some deep intuitive level I knew I did much better trading on Thursday than any other day of the week.

Was there a reason for this? I didn't think so at the time. I just figured that Thursdays were lucky for me.

Years later, I finally learned the secret about Thursdays. After analyzing the tick data (that's every tick of every day) of some 577 Thursdays, I was able to create a composite pattern of what a typical Thursday looked like. The evidence was overwhelming. The Thursday pattern was down. I'd been capitalizing on this tendency for years, but more importantly, I'd been fighting the odds unnecessarily on other days of the week, not realizing that the composite patterns favored other, equally compelling market trajectories.

As the spotlight moved day by day from Monday through Friday, the overall market pattern became evident. There was Taylor's 3-day cycle, the buy day pattern characterized by the down-opening followed by the up-close. The second day often featured continued strength. Then, by the third day choppiness would set in as buyers and sellers tried to make up their minds, and the cycle would begin all over again.

Have you ever been deceived by your own opinions? As a nonbeliever in day-of-the-week trading, I was highly skeptical of even examining this line of thinking, but the patterns were clear and unequivocal. Monday was the strongest day of the week, Thursday the weakest. Wednesday was by far the choppiest. If you knew when to buy, Fridays could provide you with some good opportunities. These are the generalities. In a down market, you'll find that Thursday will give you the best bounce to the upside. So before you jump, learn the exceptions. But I'm getting ahead of myself here. We must first look at how a composite daily pattern is created.

THE MARKET "SNAPSHOT"

The *snapshot* concept of creating a market composite chart is to take an average of a daily trend. If you take enough samples and average them, you will soon have a chart that illustrates how a market trades on any given day of the week. For example, let's say we want to know what a typical Friday looks like on a composite basis. We capture the price every 30 minutes and then create an average. You could, for instance, look at the price of the S&P 500 futures contract at 10 o'clock in the morning East Coast time. If you had 50 samples, you would use 50. In our study, we looked at 577 Fridays. By averaging the price over that period of time, we came up with one number, the average price of the S&P 500 on a Friday morning at ten o'clock. Thirty minutes later, we did another calculation, and so on. By connecting the lines between the 30-minute intervals, we created a composite chart.

Using this same concept, we can then create charts that illustrate specific parameters. For instance, let's say we want to look for Mondays that have a higher open than the previous day's trading. By just selecting Mondays with higher openings, we can create a composite chart and analyze its price trajectory. Do prices rise or fall on Mondays when you have a higher open? The composite chart, created from the snapshot approach, can tell you. When you are analyzing a chart based on hundreds of data points, you don't have to be reminded that this is an average chart. Any given day could be dramatically different. Nevertheless, the percentages suggest that any given day will look like the composite.

Based on composite charts, we can then begin to suggest simple rules. What if you simply bought at the open every Monday and held the position until the close? What if you bought at the LSS pivot breakout buy number every Monday and sold at the close? What if you sold at the LSS pivot breakout sell number every Monday? And so on. These are just simple rules. You'll find in analyzing a market such as the S&P 500, which has been in a virtual bull market since its inception in 1982, the buy rules make a lot of money whereas the sell rules struggle. This is understandable given the nature of the market.

What we found in doing the testing on day-of-the-week trading is that one or two rules might give you a high overall profit over time. But when you factor in commissions and slippage, you really aren't looking at a profitable strategy. By filtering out the less desirable trades, however, you can pinpoint the very best trades, trades that over time return more than $700 per contract per roundturn. The downside to this, of course, is that these moneymaking, high-probability trades are considerably harder to find. You have to spend a great deal of time on the sidelines, waiting for one with all the right criteria to present itself. This requires the kind of discipline that many new traders don't possess. Nevertheless, these trades are well worth the effort.

CHARTING THE EQUITY

Just as we can create composite charts that outline specific, day-of-the-week price moves, we can also create charts that track equity over time. The testing works like this. You outline your criteria for taking a trade and run the numbers—one for buying and one for selling. You then analyze the results. Did the equity tend to grow on a steady basis, or was the growth line choppy, up one day and down the next? How much money did the rule generate per year? Per month? Per trade? You want to know these things before risking real dollars in the market. A system that doesn't test well will probably never return good results in the market. Moreover, we still have the question about a changing market. If the results are good in a bull market, will they remain good in a bear market? My suspicion is that the results will hold up if the market continues to trend and if you are bracketing the market with both buy and sell orders.

CRITERIA SELECTION

When you are engaged in computer testing, you need to select criteria that the computer can understand. For this reason, the entry and exit rules are cut-and-dry. Buy at the open, buy at the pivotal buy number, buy on a higher open, and so on. Exit strategies are likewise easy to understand: Sell on a trailing stop, sell on the close, or sell at a specific profit objective. As you can probably deduce from previous chapters, there are a variety of ways to fine-tune your trading. I'm all in favor of anything that works for you, but once an element of judgment comes into play, you have to throw the computer testing out of the window. A computer simply cannot decide which criterion to use when presented with a variety of intangibles. Sometimes, as you probably well know, you just have a hunch that something isn't right. It is for this reason that I want to paint this picture with a broad brush.

There are positives and negatives to this approach. If you are taking a position to the close, you may gain an enormous profit on the day—if you have a genuine trend day. On the other hand, this approach may indeed give back a substantial portion of your paper profits if the market is choppy. If you use judgment in the first case, you may lock out a substantial portion of your profits, leaving them on the table. If you use judgment in the second case, your fine-tuning may maximize your profit. I point this out because there are always questions about why I selected to go to the close, or why I decided to get in on the XYZ rule or whatever.

Remember the important point that I mentioned earlier. It is not what you make, but what you have to go through to make it. There are winning systems that no sensible person could trade. The reason: You couldn't live through the drawdowns. One advantage of short-term trading is that the risk is limited. The most important statistic, therefore, is not total profits, but average profit per trade. How much do you make on average on every single trade (including, of course, losing trades)?

We have already covered some of the formulas we'll be working with. I'm happy to repeat these formulas so you won't have to page back looking for them. Others will be new. Since I already know where we are going, I will provide you with the answer first, although I suspect you may not be ready to hear it. No single formula is the answer to successful trading. Rather, a combination of formulas that are used together in a coherent package will give you the best possible opportunity for consistent profits. Having said this, I must tell you that you are probably your own greatest enemy. There are a million ways to screw up a good approach to the market. If you've been trading for a while, you probably already know this.

Now, on the subject of patience, I want to be clear. Everyone says they want only the best trades and are willing to wait for them. The minute they open their trading accounts, however, they lose all reason and do the very opposite. They listen to brokers, take trading tips from television market pundits, and throw in orders without stops; in short, they become the consummate trading hounds they claimed they would never be. The reason for all this escapes me. If you are so inclined, do yourself a favor. Remove the money from your trading account and go to Las Vegas. You may return broke, but at least you will have had a good time! On this cautionary note, let's return to our discussion of day-of-the-week trading.

WHAT WORKS AND WHAT DOESN'T

Ask any honest, winning trader what she does in the market and she will have a hard time trying to tell you—unless, of course, she says something like buy low and sell high. The fact is, there are so many things that are *market-specific* that may not help you if you are not trading that particular market. On the other hand, a knowledgeable trader does so many things that are second nature that she probably won't even think of the many things that go into making a trading decision. It is sort of like riding a bike or driving a car. You really don't think about all the activities that are taking place. These days, most bike riders and drivers are busy talking on cell phones, but that is another story.

Let me illustrate this point with a true story that took place last weekend. A couple of buddies of mine invited me to go fishing. Although I grew up around boats, I never spent much time fishing. I agreed to go, but told them I was nothing more than a rank novice. They, of course, have been fishing all their lives. They have the proven skills. I'm the new guy, the wanna-be fisherman.

On Saturday morning we all meet bright and early down at the dock. They have assembled all the necessary gear, the fishing poles, hooks, bait, various knives, tackle boxes, and beer. I don't even have a hat or sunscreen although we are destined to spend at least five hours in the sun. We speed out to the fishing grounds, kill the engines, and anchor out beyond the reef. After about two hours, no one has caught anything—not a single fish. So I'm thinking, "It couldn't be just me. These guys are experts and they haven't caught anything either."

There is a little grumbling about the fish not biting (apparently fishermen don't talk that much). Suddenly we pull up the anchor and charge over to a new fishing area. We are all using the same poles, same bait, same style of fishing. But soon my fishing buddies are hauling in one fish after another, including a whitefish that must have weighed at least 25 pounds.

Just like those unscripted fishing shows on television, there were a lot of comments, such as: "Hey, that's a fish!" "He's a monster!" "That's some fish!" "What a fish!" One even charged under the boat and refused to be taken without the gaff before being brought aboard.

By the end of the day, the boat was full of fish. But my contribution was just one little guy who got thrown overboard because he was underweight.

What had happened? My suspicion is that fishing, like trading futures or stocks, is a skill. It may look easy to the uninitiated. But there are certain intangibles that the knowledgeable practitioners know—just as my fishing companions knew how to catch fish.

What is this certain intangible quality? And how can it be cultivated? The answer is the same as for the inquiry, "How do you get to Carnegie Hall?" "Practice! Practice! Practice!"

In all fields, whether it be sports, politics, or business, the professionals always make complex subjects appear easy. Yet the novice usually approaches a subject from the wrong perspective. By focusing on results rather than procedure, the novice is trying to short-circuit the difficult process of trial and error.

When discussing a trading methodology, for instance, one frequently hears the question, "How much money does it make?" This is the wrong question. Going back to my fishing expedition, this is similar to asking, "How many fish did you catch?"

But getting to that point required a comprehensive knowledge of the strategies involved. For instance, you need to bait the hook in the proper manner. If you don't do this correctly, the fish can steal the bait without getting hooked! Assuming you have successfully hooked the fish, you then must know how to reel him in. You need to let the hook set and then raise the rod while you reel him in. You need to be both patient and aggressive; the fish won't land himself in the boat. This is an art form, no doubt about it.

Trading is no different. When discussing a trading methodology, you want to know the downside risk, the maximum drawdown. What do you stand to risk to reach your goal? It is not what you make, but what you must go through to make it.

Another misplaced question is, "What's the winning percentage of trades?" You can win on five percent of your trades and make a lot of money—*if* the winners are large enough. Conversely, you can win on 80 or 90 percent of your trades and lose money—*if* the minority of losers are too large. So this is the wrong question to ask.

The most important question is, "What is the net profit per trade?" How much do I stand to gain on every single trade I make? Once you can succeed in getting your net profit to a viable level, it means you can make a consistent, long-term profit. This net profit, however, must be sufficient to offset all losing trades and pay commissions. This is the ultimate bottom line. This is the single number that every trader must be concerned about. How do I increase my net profit per trade?

A starting point is to focus on what works and eliminate marginal strategies. I know this goes against the conventional wisdom that is constantly whispering in your ear, "Trade, trade, trade." But overtrading is perhaps the worst culprit when it comes to capturing a net profit. A losing trade not taken enhances your bottom line. Moreover, the profits must be sizable to offset the ones that barely pay commissions. So where do you start finding the best opportunities?

I think you need a way to identify the best moves. And I'm speaking here not of the day-to-day random chop that is so characteristic of many markets, but the genuine trends. How do you find these moves? One, you need to do some research into when these opportunities arise. Two, you need a formula and a point of view concerning these opportunities. We'll get to the day-of-the-week studies in a moment. For now, let's concentrate on how to identify a market that is about to move.

I've already told you about my friend who grew rich trading the S&P 500 futures contract by selling new lows and buying new highs. Very often when these critical levels were reached, the scalpers in the pit would aggressively try to push the market back. After all, they had been selling highs and buying lows all afternoon and making good money using this strategy. But my friend knew the difference between a trading-range rally and decline and the real thing. When he sensed the market was ready to run, he would buy every offer at the highs or sell every bid at the lows. The look of surprise on the scalpers' faces was a sight to see. By that point, the market was already running. His profit was assured.

He understood the paradox of the market—it is never too high to buy and never too low to sell! Just because the crowd bet against him didn't make them right. He used to explain to me that, by definition, the price had to trade through the high to go higher. Think about that for a second. It is the most obvious statement one could make; in its simplicity it revealed a profound truth.

Taking this simplicity into account, we need to *quantify* this price level. The computer demands numbers, not intuition. How do you quantify these critical levels? Again, using a broad brush, we found the answer right in front of us. It was in the traditional formula for the LSS pivotal buy and sell numbers. Here again, a paradox existed. For years, we used the low number as the buy number and the high number as the sell number. By *reversing* these two numbers—a 180-degree change—we incorporated the notion of the paradox and identified the breakout points. Why was this so important? Because it enabled us to take trades only when the market was poised to run.

Now, I won't say that we don't occasionally take a trade only to have the market reverse on us. This happens. Losses are the cost of doing business for the professional trader. What business doesn't have overhead? I've already covered these formulas, but here they are again:

The LSS Pivot Breakout Buy Number

$$\frac{(\text{day's high} + \text{day's low} + \text{day's close})}{3} = X$$

$$2 \text{ times } X - \text{day's low} = \text{buy number}$$

The LSS Pivot Breakout Sell Number

$$\frac{(\text{day's high} + \text{day's low} + \text{day's close})}{3} = X$$

$$2 \text{ times } X - \text{day's high} = \text{sell number}$$

When you bracket the market in this fashion, you have the potential to capture the breakout whether it is out the top or out the bottom. Chances are, the market won't hit one number and trade back the other way and hit the other. But if it does, there is a rule to take just one entry per day. Were this scenario indeed to be played out, the market would surely be exhausted by the time it hit the second number. The rules also call for exiting on the close; it is important that you understand why we have this rule. On a trend day, there is a high degree of probability that one end of the range will be registered early in the day (the first hour) and that the other end of the range will be registered late in the day (the final hour). By using the close as the exit point, you assure yourself of getting the lion's share of the move. Will you get the last tick? Probably not. But there are those days when the highest high or lowest low are registered in the final seconds of trading.

STOP PLACEMENT

Whether you are actually trading a system or merely testing one, you must have a stop. There are two types of stops that we use. One is the initial stop that is placed at the time the trade is taken. The other is a trailing stop that follows the market higher, if you are buying; when selling, of course, the stop will be trailed lower to protect profits.

The initial stop that we use is 50 percent of the 5-day average range. This s a simple calculation. You add the last five ranges and divide by five. Once the position shows some positive movement, you trail the stop by taking 65 percent of the average 5-day range. I know what you are thinking: Why not move the stops in to risk less? We have tested that. We have also tried making the stops larger. In the former case, you get prematurely stopped out on positions that otherwise would have been proved to be very profitable. In the latter case, you lose too much when you are wrong. There are always individual exceptions, of course.

Stop placement must be a function of market behavior, not of your personal bankroll. The tendency among new traders is to place the stop relative to what you are willing to risk. This is a mistake. Given the volatility of certain markets, close stops are almost certain to be hit on random moves. Our computer studies can demonstrate why the close placement of stops can be a mistake.

The general rule for stop placement is that the larger the potential gain, the further away the stop must be placed. You can tighten up the stops if you are using a close-to-the-vest trading style, such as time and price strategies. But when you are taking the position to the close, which may be five or six hours later in the trading session, you have to give the market room to swing.

THE BEST DAYS TO BUY AND SELL

If the market you've been trading has been rising in recent months, the best day to buy is clearly Monday, with Tuesday a distant second. You can also get some good buying opportunities on Friday late in the morning or early afternoon. In general, you don't want to buy or sell on Wednesday, the choppiest day of the week. Nor do you want to think about buying on Thursday, the weakest day of the week.

In a bear market, Monday, Tuesday, and Wednesday may all be weak. This creates a buying opportunity on Thursday, which is traditionally the countertrend day. This is the reverse of the bull market scenario.

There are exceptions to these general rules. A weak close on Friday will generally be followed by continued weakness on Monday. Strength, of course, on Friday's close will suggest continued strength the following Monday.

In a bear market, there will still be buying opportunities on Mondays, Tuesdays, and Fridays, but the follow-through will be weak compared to price action during a bull market.

These are just general rules. You still need specific formulas to measure the precise strength or weakness of a particular market.

What we have found is that no single indicator can point to a higher or lower market today. However, when you begin to examine two or three indicators, you will begin to see a pattern that correlates highly with the direction of prices on the following day.

Monday, Bloody Monday

The place to begin an examination of day-of-the-week trading is with the day that sets the tone for the week, Monday. What happens on Monday typically is a harbinger of things to come, but it is not a day you want to miss in hopes of hopping on board the trend later in the week. In a bull market, it is the best trending day, the day you want to be in on the open and out on the close. A typical Monday will see prices rise prominently early in the day, followed by some profit-taking during the noon hour, and the final rally to the highs late in the afternoon. If you think that this sounds like the two legs comprising the daylong trend that we discussed in the chapter on time and price, you would be correct. Not surprisingly, the composite charts demonstrate a market symmetry.

Because of this typical Monday pattern, we began to perform some very elementary tests. What if we purchased every Monday on the open and sold every Monday on the close? Would this be a profitable strategy? The results showed that it would be profitable, but only marginally so. Indeed, once you factored in commissions, you probably wouldn't have any profits at all. But we did learn of a market bias. You must understand that we were studying just the S&P 500 futures contract. And we were working with approximately 12 years of data (3,012 trading days), a period when the market was clearly in an uptrend.

Accordingly, should it come as any surprise that the market rose during this period? We then compared Mondays with all trading days. Mondays clearly had a more pronounced bullish bias than the typical trading day.

Buying the opening and selling the close on just any Monday, however, regardless of other factors, was just too simplistic an approach. We needed parameters to filter out the less-promising trades. So we began to think of criteria that might qualify the best Monday trades. One was: "What if Monday's open is above Friday's close?"

This improved the results. We were on our way. There seemed to be a

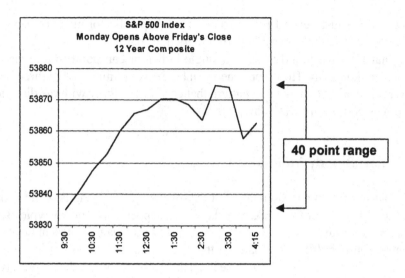

Figure 4.1   S&P 500 Index, Monday opens above Friday's close, 12-year composite.

legitimate Monday upward bias in the stock market. I need to stress here that we are talking about stock prices over a 12-year bullish period. If you did the same studies with corn or wheat, for example, you probably wouldn't find a similar bias. Figure 4.1 illustrates the composite pattern over a 12-year period for Mondays that opened above Friday's close.

The inference to be drawn from this chart pattern is that a higher opening on Monday suggests a bullish bias for the day, at least during the first three or four hours. Indeed, when you compare higher open Mondays with lower open Mondays, you'll see a clear-cut distinction. The higher open Mondays are far more bullish than the lower open Mondays. Bullish still were Mondays that opened above Friday's high. When you got a dramatically higher open on Monday, the market was clearly headed higher. Could the paradox be true—a higher open is the best harbinger of higher prices?

MEASURING THE PRIOR DAY'S STRENGTH

We mentioned the one-day strength indicator formula in the previous chap-ter. But it deserves repeating here. This is a one-day measurement of strength based on where the market closed in terms of its overall range. A close at the very top would generate a 100 percent number, a close at the very bottom would generate a 0 percent number. Below is the formula:

$$\frac{(\text{close} - \text{low}) \times 100}{(\text{high} - \text{low})} = 1\text{-day strength index}$$

We then categorize the percentages according to three general areas: in the upper third of the range (above 66 percent), in the middle third of the range (33 percent to 66 percent), and in the lower third of the range (below 33 percent).

During the 12-year testing period—from January 1, 1987, to December 31, 1998—there were 576 Mondays. Placing the previous Friday one-day strength numbers into one of three categories gave us the following results:

Friday closes in the lower ⅓ of the range = 154, or 27%

Friday closes in the middle ⅓ of the range = 166, or 29%

Friday closes in the upper ⅓ of the range = 256, or 44%

When you run the composite charts for Monday, you see that Mondays tended to be bullish when the prior Friday closed in the middle third of the range and the upper third of the range. When the prior Friday's close was in the lower third, however, the composite chart for Monday was lower. This suggests that weak Fridays lead to weak Mondays.

The 12-year composite chart for Monday appears in Figure 4.2.

The chart is characterized by two distinct legs, one in the morning and one in the afternoon. We know that Mondays tend to be bullish for the stock market and S&P 500. This bullishness is especially notable when the prior Friday closes in the middle or upper third of the range. Moreover, a higher Monday opening—especially one that opens above Friday's high—makes for an even more bullish scenario during Monday's trading.

Tuesday, the Late Rally Day

If Mondays are characterized by strength from the opening, Tuesdays need time to digest Monday's strength before resuming the climb to higher prices. In the 12-year composite chart shown in Figure 4.3, you will notice that Tuesday mornings tend to be choppy. Later in the afternoon, however, prices

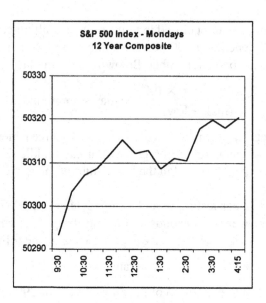

Figure 4.2 S&P 500 Index, Mondays,
12-year composite.

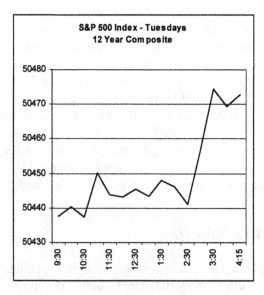

Figure 4.3 S&P 500 Index, Tuesdays,
12-year composite.

often rally, resulting in a nice upward trend. Looking at Taylor's 3-day cycle, you could make the case that Tuesday is the second day up in the cycle.

Unless Monday has been flat, and the cycle has been pushed ahead a day, Tuesday offers less promise as a buying opportunity—at least early in the day. It is understandable that some profit-taking will enter the market on Tuesday's open. This, after all, is precisely what Taylor said would happen: that prices would trade at, slightly above or below, or through the prior day's high. It takes time for this buying and selling to work itself out. The pure trend then occurs in the afternoon. This is especially helpful if you are a time and price trader because you need this good trend to make money. The composite chart also helps you identify the best time to trade. Do not take this composite chart to suggest that this pattern must occur. This simply illustrates an average of all Tuesdays over a 12-year period.

Wednesday, the Most Choppy Day

Wednesdays are, by far, the least desirable day to trade during the week. They are characterized by choppy price action. Understandably, over the 12-year testing period, when stock prices rose substantially, Wednesdays had a bullish bias, opening nearer the lows and closing nearer the highs. The characteristic, up-and-down movement of the Wednesday composite chart is shown in Figure 4.4.

Thursday, the Weakest Day

If there is one good day to sell in a bull market, it is Thursday. This is clearly the short-sell day in Taylor's view of market behavior, with the high made first earlier in the day and the subsequent sell-off occurring late in the afternoon. You will see this pronounced pattern in the Thursday composite chart shown in Figure 4.5.

Note that Thursdays are the countertrend day. In a bull market, with a higher Monday, Tuesday, and Wednesday, you will almost always see some profit-taking by Thursday, the weakest day of the week. But if you are witnessing steadily lower prices, with weakness on Monday, Tuesday, and Wednesday, Thursday will be the countertrend day and rally higher. This is an important distinction to make when you are trying to decide how to trade on a Thursday.

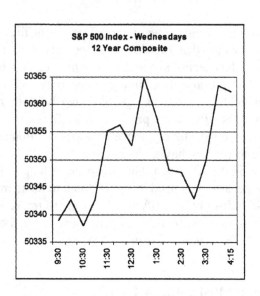

Figure 4.4 S&P 500 Index, Wednesdays, 12-year composite.

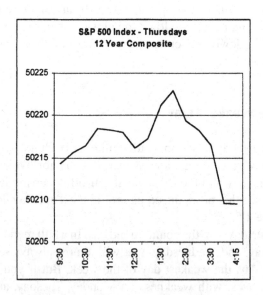

Figure 4.5 S&P 500 Index, Thursdays, 12-year composite.

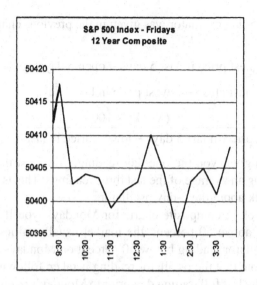

Figure 4.6   S&P 500 Index, Fridays,
12-year composite.

Friday, the Reposition Day

Friday mornings can be a continuation of Thursday's weakness, especially if Thursday closes near its lows. Yet once a final low is made on Friday afternoon, the market will often attract bargain hunters and rally into the close. This is a pattern that I've seen many, many times (see Figure 4.6). It can be enormously profitable to those who know how to capitalize on it.

HOW TO USE MARKET STRENGTH WITH
DAY-OF-THE-WEEK TRADING

There is a strong correlation between market strength and day-of-the-week trading. If you are trading on a Monday, the strongest day of the week, and you have a strong market, there is a high likelihood the market will rally.

We measure overall market strength with the LSS 5-day oscillator. When the oscillator reading is above 50 percent, we consider the market bullish; when the reading is below 50 percent, we consider the market bearish. The formula for the 5-day oscillator was given in the previous chapter, but here it is again:

$$\text{highest price in last 5 days} - \text{open 5 days ago} = X$$

$$\text{last close} - \text{lowest price in last 5 days} = Y$$

$$\frac{(X + Y) \times 100}{(\text{highest price in last 5 days} - \text{lowest price in last 5 days}) \times 2}$$

This formula gives you the one-day reading. You must then smooth this number by taking an average of the last three readings. This is the number we use when we talk about the 5-day oscillator.

When you look at composite charts for Mondays, you'll find that when the oscillator is above 50 percent, the market usually rallies. On the other hand, a low oscillator reading below 50 percent on Mondays suggests lower prices. Please note that the oscillator reading is taken following the close on Friday. This is the last full trading day prior to Monday's open. Again, we are talking about the smoothed number—the average of the last three readings.

There are two ways to use market strength with day-of-the-week trading: by looking at where the market closes on the previous day (as measured by the 1-day strength index) and by looking at overall recent market sentiment (as measured by the 5-day oscillator). When both are in agreement on Mondays, you get the strongest moves. One-day strength and five-day strength together comprise a strong endorsement for higher prices, especially on Monday. Not surprisingly, when you have both one- and five-day weakness, as measured by these indicators, you tend to have declining prices—again, especially on a leading day such as Monday.

While this tends to make common sense, it seems that Monday, above all other days of the week, serves as a market barometer. If the recent trend has been down, chances are Monday will be lower as well. In periods of rising prices, expect Monday to be strong. Clearly, how the market closes on Friday is a vital indicator of Monday's trend. Even more important to Monday's trend, though, is the overall market sentiment. If the 5-day oscillator is strong, it really doesn't matter where Friday's close occurred. The market will rally on Monday morning!

We have already discussed the typical market pattern on Tuesday, sideways in the morning followed by a late afternoon rally. Ironically, the Tuesday market will probably remain stronger *if* the recent market sentiment has been weak. This is a difficult concept to understand, but an important one

What happens is this: Following a very strong Monday, prices will be initially pushed lower on profit-taking; yet, if Monday's rally was not strong, chances are Monday's failure to rally will result in the serious buying occurring on Tuesday. Hence, you will have strong prices on Tuesday. (See Figure 4.7a and Figure 4.7b.)

Note the pullback on the composite chart, showing Tuesday prices, when the oscillator is above 50 percent. Nearly all the Tuesday morning profits are given back prior to the late-afternoon rally. When the oscillator is below 50 percent, suggesting a weaker market, Tuesday holds its gains better and makes a better run to the top at the end, probably because Monday's rally wasn't as strong as it was in the other example. This is a subtle, yet interesting, distinction. A market that cannot run on Monday may indeed find the cycle day pushed ahead one day and run the following day, Tuesday.

By Wednesday, the market is pretty much in need of a rest. But even here the market bias will follow the strength sentiment. If the overall sentiment is below 50 percent, the market will tend to decline into the close on Wednesday. A stronger market sentiment suggests higher prices into the close.

The strongest correlation between market sentiment and the day of the week occurs on Thursday; here the price action is *reversed*. A strong market, as measured by a high 5-day oscillator reading, will see prices decline on

Figure 4.7a   S&P 500 Index, Tuesdays, LSS oscillator is above 50 percent.

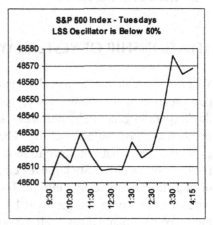

Figure 4.7b   S&P 500 Index, Tuesdays, LSS oscillator is below 50 percent.

Thursday. A weak market, as measured by the same indicator, will see prices rally on Thursday. This is the countertrend day, the day that bucks the trend.

What happens on Thursdays? In a rising market, buyers take profits. In a declining market, short-sellers take profits. The former push the market lower and the latter push the market higher. In either case, the trends are very clear.

There's another way to analyze the situation, as well. By Thursday, the uninformed Johnny-come-lately traders, who have been following the market all week, are finally ready to make the plunge. They want to get in on a sure-thing, but were cautious (when they should have been bold earlier in the week). They take the plunge by buying the top! You could make the same argument that stock investors are finally willing to sell their shares at the bottom after being hammered for the prior three days. That's the day, of course, when the market will rally—right after the uninformed abandon their positions. When you think about this, it is only human psychology. Most people are wrong at the significant market turns.

This brings us to Friday when the weekly cycle is setting up again. If the market has been weak (as measured by a 5-day oscillator lower than 50 percent), traders will use this excuse to drive the market lower in the morning. But by afternoon, once the bargain hunters begin buying, look out! This is the classic Friday afternoon pattern that I wrote about in the Introduction, "The Trade That Got Away."

RELATIONSHIP OF YESTERDAY'S CLOSE TO TODAY'S OPEN

When you decide to take a trade, regardless of the day of the week, you must pay attention to how far the market moves from the previous close to the next day's open. In general, higher opens are more favorable to buying, and lower opens more favorable to selling. There are, of course, exceptions to these general rules. What you have to look out for are extreme moves away from the prior day's close. Such moves create gaps on the charts, but not the kind of gaps that can be easily closed. The general rule for gap trades is that 75 percent of the time the gap will be filled. This means if the market gaps higher on the open, you can sell it, knowing that you have the edge. The same holds true in reverse for lower opening gaps when you can fade the move by buying. The rule is that the previous day's close will be revisited three out of four times regardless of the subsequent movement of the market.

The problem occurs when you have what I call an extreme gap. In this instance, the market has opened much higher or lower. Chances are, it won't be trading back at the previous day's close.

When you bracket the previous day's range with buy and sell orders, as you do when you use the LSS pivot buy and sell breakout numbers, you have another problem when you get an extreme move on the opening. If the market gaps down—but, significantly, not far enough to trigger a sell order—the buy order, by definition, will be a great distance from the market price. In fact, if you are aware of the five-day average range, the buy order might be an equal distance away. Can you see the dilemma if the market recovers and trades up to the buy number? At that point, the market has traveled the full range that was anticipated. Any buying at that stage will probably be done right near the top. Of course, there is always the possibility that the average range will be extended on that particular day, but this is asking a lot.

It is for this reason that you must not buy a market that has opened too low, or sell a market that has opened too high; what looks like a great opportunity very often isn't. This is the market paradox.

You always want significant potential movement left when you buy or sell a market. The same rule applies to the amount of time left when you take a trade. If you are a short-term trader, you must give the market sufficient time to generate profits. If you are rapidly approaching the end of the day and you know you want to be flat at the close, you must not take the trade. The rule of thumb that I use for this type of trade is 45 minutes. If there isn't 45 minutes left in the trading day, you want to stay out. Please note that this applies only to breakout strategies. If you find a time and price trade, where the entire move might take place in eight or nine minutes, by all means take the trade. But this is an entirely different situation.

When people tell me my breakout numbers don't work, they are usually talking about a market that topped or bottomed out near the pivot buy or sell price. I understand the frustration, but you must look at the trade in the proper context. Did it spend the day trying to reach that particular price? If so, the lion's share of the day's range was already spent. Did the trade take place on a Wednesday? Being the choppiest day of the week, Wednesdays behave like that. What about market sentiment? Was it barely bullish or bearly bearish? Perhaps the market isn't ready to run.

In addition, if you study these entries, you'll find that even those trades taken at extremes, and that prove to be winners, are only marginal winners. The risk of a substantial retracement move simply does not warrant the potential reward in this type of scenario. To avoid getting caught in this situation, always be aware of the average 5-day range, and always be aware of how much of that range has already occurred during a given day.

For example, let's say the average range is 20.00 points. If an entry point is reached when the range on the day is just 4.50 points, then you could make the argument that 15.50 points remain. There might be more. The day's range might exceed the average range. The opposite is true as well: It might be less. In any case, there is room for the market to run.

If you are looking at a 20.00 point range, however, and the market has already moved, say, 18.00 points, what's left? Those 2.00 points in potential profit aren't worth the downside risk. The market might retrace 50 percent or more. Now you are risking a lot to gain a little. It doesn't make sense.

Here's how we were able to use this information to improve our results over an eight-year period. First, we isolated this single component, measuring the percentage move from previous day's close to today's open. Second, we analyzed the equity curve for these percentage moves. What were the percentages that did and did not contribute to a positive move in the equity curve? Third, we threw out those trades that didn't contribute to the bottom line. Our studies revealed that buy trades that opened more than 7½ percent below the prior day's close did not contribute to profits, nor did sell trades that opened more than 18 percent above the prior close. Fourth, we ran the numbers without those trades. Over the eight-year period, there were 14 percent fewer trades, meaning 14 percent fewer commissions, and a 19 percent increase in profits! This is the kind of information that is very valuable.

COMPARING APPLES AND ORANGES—PERCENT VERSUS PRICE CHARTS

You'll notice that I talk about so many percentage points above or below the previous day's close. The reason for this is the enormous jump in volatility in the market in recent years. When the S&P 500 market started trading back in the Spring of 1982, a 200- to 300-point range was a typical day. Today, the number of points in the daily range is approximately ten times as large. This is why speaking in terms of points makes no sense. We routinely convert price charts to percentage charts to compare patterns over a number of years. This is achieved by making the highest price obtained on a price chart have a value of 100 and the lowest price obtained have a value of zero. Because the volatility is so much higher today, any price chart will give greater emphasis to the recent market than to the market ten or more years ago. What is interesting is how often both the price and percentage charts mirror one another. When they do, we know our analysis is often correct since it has withstood the test of time. Not to do this would give the most volatile period an undue emphasis, one that might skew the results if you are looking for long-range patterns.

BUY TRADES RANKED BY THE PREVIOUS DAY'S CLOSE

I have stressed the importance of the prior day's close in deciding whether to buy or sell. To test this assertion, we analyzed precisely what impact the prior day's close had on the growth of equity. Not surprisingly, the results revealed that it varied from day to day. When the market is at the bottom of a cycle, a lower close the prior day often resulted in profits. At other times, a strong prior close suggested the market had peaked. This, no doubt, suggested we were at the end of the cycle—Taylor's classical third day up.

For yesterday's close to have a legitimate meaning, you must understand the role that each specific day of the week has in the ebb and flow of the market cycle. If Friday closes strong, I'm ready to load the boat on Monday morning. But heaven help you if you try the same strategy on Tuesday morning following a barn-burning uptrend on Monday. By the time the Monday buying is done, the market is exhausted and ready for a pause.

Let's examine what happens on a typical Monday and see what Friday's close would suggest for Monday's price action. The rule is this: If Friday's close is weak, Monday's price action will probably be lower. Our statistics suggest you need a close on Friday that is above 35 percent on the one-day strength index in order for Monday's market to move higher.

Fridays, which are characterized by late-day rallies in a bull market, tend to offer buying opportunities for traders who anticipate strength on Monday. This buying tends to cause the market to rise on Friday afternoon.

Once you get to Tuesday morning, however, the situation changes dramatically. In a bull market, Monday is traditionally the strongest day. Hence, a strong close on Monday, coming on the heels of late-day strength on Friday, makes Tuesday the third day up. In this scenario, you have reached the top of the three-day cycle. You never want to buy on the third day up, especially if you experienced a huge rally on the second day! This is the traditional short-sale day. You can, however, buy on Tuesday if Monday's strength was only moderate. In this instance, the cycle may need to be pushed ahead a day. Our studies show that when Monday closed above 75 percent on the one-day strength index, Tuesday buy trades lost money. In short, don't buy on Tuesday if Monday was exceptionally strong. Another way to look at this phenomenon is in terms of missed opportunities. Do not try to recreate an opportunity that has been missed. If you wanted to buy on Monday and did not, do not assume you can hop aboard the bandwagon on Tuesday morning. That opportunity is gone. Do not add to one mistake (missing the move) by making another (trying to force the market higher when it is already exhausted).

On Wednesday, the relationship shifts once again. The serious money is made on Wednesday when Tuesday's close is exceptionally strong—above 75 percent on the one-day strength index. I have several theories about this phenomenon. One is that there are a number of holidays that fall on Monday. When these occur, in the absence of trading, Tuesday serves as the surrogate Monday, or even Friday since three-day weekends tend to depopulate trading floors. This places Wednesday in the popular second-day post where most of the real strength occurs. Another idea is that a lot of market-moving reports are issued on Tuesday afternoon. Wednesday would stand to benefit from a strong report issued the previous day since the news would be front-page material in the morning newspaper. A third theory is the paradox factor: A day that exhibits the most lackluster performance suddenly surprises everyone. It wouldn't be the first time that just about everyone was fooled by the market. Last, it suggests that the market is truly running when Tuesday closes strong. Nothing is going to hold this market back. Wednesday buyers benefit from this strong trend.

Figure 4.8 shows the surge in equity that occurred on Wednesday when Tuesday closed in the higher quarter percentile on the one-day strength index.

Thursday buy trades, as qualified by Wednesday's close, do best when Wednesday's strength is above 50 percent. Wednesdays tend to rise in bull markets and decline in bear markets. So this one-day reading is a relatively simple indicator of the next day's trading.

Friday's buy trades offer a truly fascinating glimpse into the relationship between the prior day's close and the following day's price action. For Friday's buy trade to work, Thursday must not close too weak or too strong. The best Friday buys occur following a bounce off Thursday's lows or a break off Thursday's high. Let's look at this event for a moment. Traditionally, we know that Thursday is the weakest day of the week, the general rule in a bull

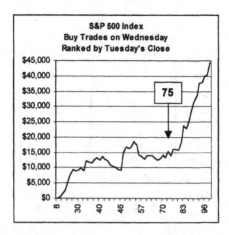

Figure 4.8 S&P 500 Index, buy trades on Wednesday ranked by Tuesday's close.

market. It is also the countertrend day, the day when prices will rise in a bear market. So let's analyze this situation.

If the market has been in an uptrend and you get the predictable break on Thursday afternoon, what should happen? That's right. Bargain hunters should step in on Thursday afternoon and bid up the market, taking it at least to midpoint by the close. If this doesn't happen, something is wrong. Let's assume that Monday, Tuesday, and Wednesday are strong, then the market tanks on Thursday and closes on the lows. This close at the bottom suggests lower prices on Friday morning—not a rally. Even if the market does regain its strength and rallies, there may be too much ground needed to get the market back to a point (near Thursday's highs) to signal a buy trade and break out to the upside.

Now let's consider the reverse scenario. The market has been weak. Monday, Tuesday, Wednesday are all down. Along comes Thursday and you get the predictable countertrend higher. What should happen on Friday? Yes, the market should resume its former pattern and sell off. How can you make money buying on a day like that?

Our studies show that you want a one-day strength reading between 33 and 65 percent on Thursday in order to have a profitable buying opportunity on Friday. Figure 4.9 illustrates the profitability of Friday trades based on Thursday closes.

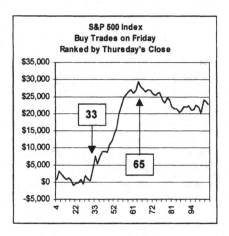

Figure 4.9   S&P 500 Index, buy
trades on Friday ranked by
Thursday's close.

SELL TRADES RANKED BY THE PREVIOUS CLOSE

We treat buy and sell trades differently. But they are similar in that they both
are sensitive to how a market closes on the previous day. You need to be
mindful that we are talking about a breakout system here that requires the
market to trade down to a sell target before a trade is initiated. It follows that
in a strong bull market, the buy signals will be more readily accessible.
With the market rising day after day, the buy signals, by definition, will be
repeatedly hit. For a sell signal to be hit, the market has to move lower at
least temporarily. For the same signal to be profitable, of course, it must
continue lower. Otherwise, the hapless seller finds himself short a market
that is rising.

Mondays present a special dilemma to would-be short-sellers. The
strongest day of the week, Monday tends to rally—especially, it seems, if
the opening is weak and the market slides on continuation of Friday selling.
The Friday one-day strength statistics suggest that a weak closing means
trouble for Monday sellers. Why is this so? Probably because Friday's weakness drives the market low enough on Monday morning to set off the sell signals. But traders, sensing an opportunity, then tend to buy the market
sending it higher. The result? Short-sellers tend to generate losses.

It is far better to have a strong close on Friday and a genuine break on Monday. This scenario presents a better opportunity for follow-through to the downside. Our statistics suggest that a bullish Friday close—above 50 percent—presents the sellers with a better opportunity for profits. Below 50 percent, the sell signals tend to generate losses on a bounce up off the lows. The chart illustrating this phenomenon is shown in Figure 4.10.

On Tuesdays, sell trades do much better if Monday's close was in the higher 70 percentile. This stands to reason because a weak day and close on Monday usually comes on the heels of a Friday selloff. By Tuesday, you are into the third day of the break with the predictable rally.

Wednesday's sell trades also favored a strong Tuesday closing above 67 percent on the one-day strength indicator, but over the eight-and-a-half-year testing period, there were relatively few sell trades. So the sample may have been too small to justify one rule or another. Wednesdays, as we well know, tend to be choppy in nature without much of an overall trend.

Thursday has an entirely predictable pattern. Any sell trade that is triggered on this day should work regardless of the previous day's close. The same could be said for Fridays. Selling later in the week seems to work better than early in the week. You should remember, of course, that we only had past history to work with. For most of that history, the market was in an uptrend.

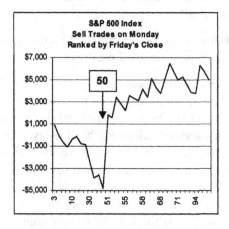

Figure 4.10 S&P 500 Index, buy trades on Monday ranked by Friday's close.

MEASURING MOMENTUM, THE RATE AT WHICH THE MARKET RISES AND DECLINES

We've discussed the calculations for both the LSS one-day strength index and the LSS five-day oscillator reading. These two respective indicators measure short-term and recent market strength. Now we will turn to an important, yet very subtle, wrinkle on market strength, the rate at which the market rises and falls.

Why is momentum important? Because it suggests when a trend is speeding up, slowing down, or about to switch direction. It is not enough to know whether a market is rising or falling; we must know where the turns are and adjust our trading accordingly. You can turn on your television to a news station and readily learn whether the Dow Jones Industrials Average was up or down today, but this just tells us what has already happened. To make money, we need to be able to make intelligent judgments about tomorrow's price action. Hopefully, market momentum can help us on this score.

We know from a previous discussion that the construction of the 5-day oscillator is a daily calculation consisting of two parts. One, we generate the day's 5-day oscillator number, which will fall between zero and 100 percent. Two, we need to take the last three readings and average them to generate the smoothed oscillator reading.

It is this smoothed number that we use when we measure momentum. The formula is simplicity itself:

$$\text{current value of the 5-day smoothed oscillator} - \text{value of}$$
$$\text{the 5-day smoothed oscillator 3 days ago}$$

This number represents the speed and direction of the 5-day oscillator. If today's number is larger, it will result in a positive number once the number three days ago is subtracted. This means the market is moving higher (remember, the oscillator measures overall strength). If today's number is negative, it suggests the opposite—prices are moving lower (negative momentum). The turns in the market tend to occur when the numbers grow large, either positive or negative. These large numbers suggest a sudden big move. Since no trend can persist without profit-taking, a large three-day difference suggests an imminent market reversal. At the very least, you want to avoid entering the market on the side of the larger reading lest you buy a top or sell a bottom.

Momentum can also tell us when the upward or downward momentum is slowing, again suggesting a reversal. It measures buying power and selling pressure. The time to look for a reversal is when market strength, as measured by the 5-day oscillator, gets above 70 percent.

Let's assume you have a rising market with the following list of smoothed 5-day oscillator numbers:

Day	LSS 5-day Oscillator
1	72.16
2	73.17
3	73.52
4	74.60
5	75.41

The 3-day difference is calculated by taking the current oscillator reading and subtracting the reading three days ago. Assuming we are at the close of day 1, yesterday's (day 2) reading will be −2.24. Today's (day 1) reading will be −2.44. This suggests the negative momentum is increasing and that the market is beginning to show signs of slowing down, if it hasn't already. The readings, of course, can go from plus to minus or minus to plus, or plus to larger plus, or negative to larger negative, and so on. It is the trend of the 3-day difference that suggests which way the next move will occur.

To study the impact of the 3-day difference, or momentum readings, we looked at markets where the oscillator suggested bullish (above 70 percent), bearish (below 30 percent), or sideways (between 30 and 70 percent) patterns. We then charted the equity against the 3-day-difference readings. The results were interesting.

As always, we looked at buys and sells separately. Looking at three different categories for each—above 70 percent, below 30 percent, and between 30 and 70 percent—we ended up with six categories. We then charted the equity runs for each as ranked by the 3-day difference. Understandably, the most bullish scenario occurred when market strength was above 70 percent and the 3-day difference rose as high as +28. This suggested that a market could become quite bullish and still generate profits from buying. But there always comes a point when the bullishness gets ahead of itself and buying ceases to be profitable. Put another way, you are buying the top.

In the 30-to-70-percent category, buy trades can be profitable when the 3-day difference is between −28 and +17.5. Under 30 percent, suggesting the sentiment is weak, buy trades still make money when the 3-day difference is more positive than −28.

I know that these numbers deserve an explanation. Let's just look at one example and see if we can make some sense out of what is going on in the market. Let's assume you want to buy when the market sentiment is low, under 30 percent. Why would you want to do this? Because you have reason to believe that the market is poised for a move higher. The sentiment therefore is under 30 percent; let's say it is just 21 percent. To get to 21 percent, the 3-day difference might have been growing more negative (rising negative momentum) for some time. At some point, however, you are going to see a *more positive negative number* in the 3-day difference. This is the clue that buying might work, especially if the 3-day difference is more positive than −28. What has happened is that the selling has already taken place. Additional selling no longer has the impact of driving prices lower because the selling is being met by increased buying. The market is now poised to run—higher!

A word of caution, however: Should the market sentiment remain under 30 percent and the 3-day difference remain more negative than −28, chances are the selling isn't finished. You don't want to buy in such an environment. The odds don't favor your success.

When it comes to selling, we divided our sells into the same three categories: over 70 percent, under 30 percent, and between 30 and 70 percent. The most problematic, of course, were those sells in the under-30-percent category when the market is already weak. Here you are typically selling deep in the hole and you have to be careful lest the market spring up against you. Be very wary of sell trades in this category that have a 3-day-difference reading more negative than −12.

You have a better chance of making money by selling when the market sentiment has been strong, above 70 percent. In this instance, any 3-day difference which is greater than +3 generated profits in our testing period.

In each of these situations, whether buying or selling, you want to measure momentum, the rate at which the market is rising or declining. At market tops, the upward momentum will begin to slow before the actual top is reached. At market bottoms, the rate at which the market declines will also slow. This is the leading indicator that you have an opportunity to step in and fade the move, perhaps catching the top or bottom. There are always risks, but momentum is one way to quantify a judgment that would otherwise remain an intuitive affair.

SOME SIMPLE RULES

I know how my readers love hard-and-fast rules written in stone. And I know how I am loathe to indulge them, simply because there are so many exceptions to every rule. Nevertheless, I'm going to set down a few examples of rules that should work if you follow the guidelines. There are a number of filters involved in these selections. As a consequence, there are only three trades per week maximum using these guidelines. Because of the filters, on some weeks there will be none.

Here are the rules:

1. Do not trade on Tuesdays or Thursdays.

2. On Mondays, buy only at the LSS pivot breakout buy number if the following conditions prevail:
   - The 5-day LSS strength number is between 65 percent and 94.5 percent.
   - The 5-day LSS oscillator is above 50 percent.
   - The 3-day difference in the 5-day oscillator is more positive than −10.

3. On Wednesdays, sell only at the LSS pivot breakout sell number if the following conditions prevail:
   - The 5-day LSS strength number is above 53 percent.
   - The 5-day LSS oscillator is below 70 percent.
   - The 3-day difference in the 5-day oscillator is more positive than −10.

4. On Fridays, buy only at the LSS pivot breakout buy number if the following conditions prevail:
   - The 5-day LSS strength number is below 83 percent.
   - The 5-day LSS oscillator is below 50 percent.
   - The 3-day difference in the 5-day oscillator is more positive than −40.

BEWARE OF HIGH-VOLATILITY DAYS

High-volatility days are fine if you are trading them, but if you base your analysis on such days, chances are you will be buying too high and selling too low. For this reason, check your current range day (the day just finished) against the 5-day average range. When the day just finished exceeds the 5-day average range, it requires another high-range day to generate profits. While this can happen, it is unlikely it can continue for long. As a result, be careful when you make your analysis on such a high-range day. The LSS pivot breakout buy and sell numbers will tend to bracket the range of the prior day. When this prior-day range is too high, you will either not get into the position or you may indeed buy the high or sell the low.

THE PROBLEM WITH LOW-VOLATILITY DAYS

When you have a low-volatility day, you have the opposite problem of the high-volatility day: Now the breakout numbers are too close. Unless the current day you are using to perform your analysis is at least 70 percent of the 5-day average range, the buy and sell numbers tend to be too close to the market.

In a bull market, as the stock index futures have experienced in the past ten years, buying too close in isn't the problem. It just means you make more money. It is a problem, though, when you begin selling on a minor move down and the market reverses. For this reason, you want a range at least between 70 and 100 percent of the 5-day average range.

I cannot emphasize enough the importance of using breakout numbers. The market is a better buy higher up and a better sell lower down. Buying or selling before these critical breakout areas are reached only increases the probabilities of sustaining a loss. Within the consolidation (before the breakout points are reached), there is a high likelihood that prices will return to the middle. (Note: This is the exact opposite of the time and price trades which require a pullback into the consolidation.) It is a mistake to try to determine in advance when the market will move in the absence of a legitimate trend. Even the time and price strategies call for the market to demonstrate that it wants to move before signaling a trade. In the absence of evidence that the market will run, you are better off on the sidelines. If you must be in the market, however, the odds favor prices moving back to the middle from the high and low extremes.

SOME RULES FOR TREASURY BONDS

Day-of-the-week trading works as well in other markets as for stock index futures. Perhaps the second-best market is U.S. Treasury bond futures. In this market, you have the two key components needed for successful day trading—volatility and liquidity.

We performed some of the same studies in bonds as we did for index futures. You have to understand, as always, risk is commensurate with reward. You will make less in bonds because the volatility is much less, but the risk is likewise less as well.

What are some of the rules for bonds? Many are quite similar, although the parameters will be understandably different. For example, here are a few of the identical rules:

1. Buy at the LSS pivot breakout buy number.

2. Sell at the LSS pivot breakout sell number.

3. One trade a day.

When we look at generating the sell trades in terms of the 5-day average range, the bonds need the following qualification:

4. No breakout sell trades when the day's range exceeds 133 percent of the average 5-day range.

A large range such as this will generate a sell number that is too low. Now let's examine oscillator values:

5. No breakout buy trades if the oscillator is below 25 percent.

In this instance, the market isn't strong enough to lift prices sufficiently to create profits on buy orders.

6. No breakout sell trades if the oscillator is above 72.5 percent or below 22 percent.

Above 72.5 percent, the market is too bullish to sell. Below 22 percent, the market is too bearish to sell. The selling has already occurred in this instance.

When you combine oscillator readings with momentum readings, as measured by the 3-day difference, you filter out additional marginal trades. For instance:

7. No breakout buy trades if the oscillator is above 70 percent and the 3-day difference is greater than 7.5.

With these readings, the market is already too bullish. You are buying strength—probably the top. Eliminate these trades.

8. No breakout sell trades if the oscillator is below 30 percent and the 3-day difference is less than −37 or greater than +5.

You don't want to sell extreme weakness. The market has already broken sharply and has been driven lower. A bad place to sell.

Now let's look at the relationship of the previous close to the entry. What are the rules for bonds? You want strength to buy, but not too much strength. Conversely, you want weakness to sell, but not too much weakness. Here are the rules:

9. No breakout buy trades if the previous close to the entry is greater than $+1\frac{14}{32}$.

Asking the bonds to rally more than one-half point ($+\frac{16}{32}$) on any given day is asking too much. Once you get past the one-half-point mark, you are counting on significant news, such as a discount rate decrease by the Fed. This is too much to ask on any given day.

10. No breakout sell trades if the previous close to the entry is more than $-\frac{6}{32}$.

In this instance, you don't want to sell them too deep in the hole.

Now for day-specific rules. Since the bonds have unique daily patterns, you want to avoid certain trades on certain days. Here are some rules:

11. Don't buy on Tuesday if the previous close to the open is greater than 17 percent of the average 5-day range.

When a substantial portion of the range takes place on the open, there isn't sufficient room for the market to rally beyond this point.

12. Don't buy on Wednesday if the previous close to the open is less than 21 percent, or greater than 41 percent, of the 5-day average range.

You have a narrow window of opportunity for buy trades in the bonds on Wednesdays. As with the stock market, Wednesdays are difficult days for bond traders.

13. Don't buy on Thursday if the previous close to the open is greater than 30 percent of the 5-day average range.

As with the stock index futures, Thursday is a good day to sell. When you get a higher open, therefore, the market is setting up for a selling opportunity—not a buying opportunity. This excessive pulling apart on the open is the spring effect. The market should trade lower after an opening which is more than 30 percent above the prior close.

14. Don't sell on Thursday if the market opens at more than 17 percent of the 5-day average range below the previous close.

Here you have the spring effect in the opposite direction. Don't sell deep in the hole. Good selling opportunities present themselves on lower openings, but not when the downward move is already in the market on the opening.

15. Don't sell on Fridays if the open is more than 42 percent of the 5-day average below the previous close.

In general, Fridays are good days to sell bonds, but not when the opening is too far down. This rule will eliminate selling trades on a very weak opening.

Last, the bonds, like the S&P's, are more likely to be weak later in the week. For this reason, we have this final rule:

16. Don't sell bonds on Monday, Tuesday, or Wednesday.

KNOW THE SEASONAL PATTERN

The final piece of the puzzle that the day-of-the-week trader wants to incorporate into her trading strategy is the seasonal pattern. You might not think that seasonality plays an important role in stock market or bond prices, but you would be wrong. It even plays a role in how a given day develops during a specific time of the year. I'd feel much more comfortable buying the stock market on a Monday in late October, for example, than I would on a Monday in April.

There's a very real reason why seasonality has been so important in agricultural commodities. The typical crop is planted at a specific time of year, harvested during another time of year, and finally consumed. There are traditional growing seasons and traditional strategies for capitalizing on the normal ebb and flow of the growing season. One would think that there would be overwhelming evidence of seasonality in most agricultural crops.

Ironically, the most predictable seasonal patterns, however, occur among stock market prices. Over many years, the patterns have been highly consistent. As a short-term trader, I don't really focus on prices six months from now, but I certainly want to know where in the seasonal cycle we stand. Just as not all days of the week are same, neither are July Mondays the same as December Mondays, or March Thursdays the same as August Thursdays. There are times of the year when you want to be more cautious, depending upon whether you want to buy or sell.

Looking back at recent stock market history, billions of dollars might have been saved if only investors had paid attention to stock market seasonality. We have researched the market back over 50 years. Here are the most basic, consistent patterns:

1. Lows the first week in January

2. Highs in March

3. Secondary highs in August

4. Lows in October or November

5. Highs into the end of the year

Does this mean that the market must make highs in late July or early August? Of course not. But the evidence is strong that midsummer highs are traditionally followed by late October or early November lows—followed, of course, by a rally into the end of the year. We have researched these patterns back to the administration of President Truman. In good times and bad, there is a very strong tendency for the market to follow this pattern.

While seasonality is probably not the single key to earning profits, it is an important component of the overall pattern of market behavior.

We now turn away from the numbers to the far more elusive notion of market psychology. Until now, we have emphasized the outer game of trading— compiling buy and sell numbers, tracking the right day in the market cycle, comparing where the market closed to where it opened. All of this is quantifiable. Yet it is the less tangible, inner game of trading, the psychological aspects, that will surely decide whether you emerge a winner or a loser. Fortunately, even within this realm there are identifiable patterns.

5

The Psychological Game of Trading

Why Some Traders Win and Others Lose

About a year ago, I was browsing through a local bookstore one Sunday afternoon and a book on trading caught my eye. I'm not a big reader of market books, but this one was written by one of those market legends whose name is familiar to anyone who has ever spent any time around the Chicago trading pits. I wanted to learn his story. So I purchased the book and went home and started reading.

As I breezed through the chapters, I learned more than I ever needed to know about this particular author, his background and family, likes and dislikes. But not a word about trading. I kept reading until I reached the end.

Later that week, I called my editor (I have the same editor as did the author of the book) and asked her, "What's with this guy? How come he doesn't discuss how he trades?"

"He doesn't believe you can teach trading," she replied. "He believes trading is all psychological."

I disagreed with him then and I still do, but she had a point. How can you teach someone to be a trader?

You probably cannot. But you can point out some of the pitfalls and give some suggestions on how best to cope with them. There are two components to successful trading—one is knowing what to do and the other is doing it. As for the first, I suspect there is a great deal you can learn. There are so many mistakes that novice traders make that one hardly knows where to begin listing them. In general, however, all the cliches are true. You don't want to overtrade. You want to keep commission costs reasonable. You want to cut your losses and let your profits ride. You want to become an expert in your market. You want to embrace uncertainty and take trades before the outcome is known. You want to embrace a disciplined approach. You want to use a reasonable and intelligent trading methodology. Understanding that losses are a part of trading, you want to begin your trading career with sufficient cash to withstand any drawdowns, so that they don't come as a surprise when you start trading. And on and on and on.

These rules can be taught. When it comes to the second component, however, we are talking about deeply rooted psychological traits that may be hard to overcome. I don't think these concerns should be treated lightly, since success in trading is probably 70 percent psychological and only 30 percent based on what trading approach you use. Put another way, it doesn't matter so much what approach you take as it does who you are. I think I've mentioned that if you have a dozen different people trading a system that is 100 percent mechanical, you will have a dozen different results. Why? One would think the results would be similar, if not identical. Not even close. Here's the reason why. Trader A likes to swing for the fences. He's gotten into the market to make a killing and, as soon as he finds the right trading system, that's exactly what he intends to do. So he finds a system he likes and he begins to trade. The system makes money. Trader A is happy. But his personality is such that he isn't happy making just $1,000 a week. He wants to make ten times as much. As a result, he decides to start plunging in the market and the inevitable drawdowns practically clean him out. We are all caught between fear and greed. Trader A was a victim of his greed. Trader B, on the other hand, is a much more fearful type. She wants to be positive that she is correct before risking her money, so she watches the system on paper. Seeing the paper profits pile up, she is now convinced she has a winner. She takes her small position and promptly loses some money. She tries again the next day and loses again. She makes a final try on the third day. No luck. She quits trading. Why throw money down the drain? That's the day, of course, when the system begins a legitimate winning streak. Trader B's psychological profile is way over on the fearful side. I once knew a trader who managed to take only the losses of a winning trading system. He was always on the sidelines when the winners occurred and always in the market on losing days. Bad luck? Hardly.

THE WINNING ATTITUDE

In the late eighties, I made a weekend trip out to Las Vegas from Chicago with a group of friends. Two were LaSalle Street attorneys, two were novice traders in the S&P pit, the fifth person was a veteran S&P pit trader who was busy accumulating the fortune he was to make trading futures. I was the sixth person. Going out on the plane, I realized that I was the only one who had ever been to Las Vegas before. Having lived in California for eight years, this was no big thing for me. I went to Las Vegas practically every year, but I have to confess that up until that time, my success in generating profits in the gambling capital was less than stellar. Nevertheless, I understood most of the games and how they were played. So, sitting next to my friend the veteran S&P trader, I explained how I felt his chances were best at the craps tables. I told him how the game was played and how to get the best odds.

A quick study, he immediately seized on a few strategies.

"It seems that betting against the dice is like selling options," he said. "There will be times when the other side loses. But most of the time the seven will appear and you will win."

"Sort of," I explained. "But most of the time it will be a fifty-fifty affair. The casino has the edge regardless. But most people like to bet with the dice."

"Then I want to bet against them," he interjected.

"It depends on how the dice are running," I cautioned him. "You don't want to bet against the dice at a hot table."

"So there are trends," he replied. "The dice run hot and cold. Let's find the trend and clean them out."

That's exactly what he did. By the end of the weekend, this first-time player, whose business was to undertake risk, had nearly doubled his bankroll. He understood that you had to take intelligent risks when the odds favored a given outcome.

His success was far from beginner's luck. Standing at the craps table, he explained to me that even with the black $100 chips piled high on the table, this was strictly small potatoes compared to the high-flying S&P market.

The prospect of losing money didn't bother him. Indeed, he had fifty one-hundred-dollar bills in an envelope in his pocket.

Whether it is trading futures or throwing dice in Las Vegas, you have to go in armed to the teeth. He knew this and he knew that the first rule of money management is that you must play a game that you can win. How many first-time visitors to Las Vegas make money? I don't know. But in all my years of trying to beat the odds, the only consistent pattern has been this: When I needed the money I always lost. It was only once I became relaxed enough not to need to win, that I could do so.

Can you see the paradox at work here? Here's a guy who never played this game before, yet he knows how to win. Perhaps I should correct the statement slightly. He may never have played this particular game before, but he made his living taking on substantial risks—and winning. He had the psychological qualities needed to win.

How do you cultivate these qualities? How do you summon up the courage to do the right thing?

There are a lot of ways one might answer these questions. First and foremost, you must be rigorous in your analysis of how you trade and what you may be doing right or wrong. The best traders can look at their mistakes with an element of detachment. They can take satisfaction in their judgment when they are right and they can forgive themselves when they are wrong. I suspect that relatively few people are natural-born traders. The ability to remain calm and cool, when the natural thing would be just to panic, is a virtue found only in the minority. Nevertheless, I believe you can work at separating yourself from your emotions when you trade. And I believe this simple strategy will pay dividends far in excess of any trading system.

KNOWING WHAT DOESN'T WORK

I get a lot of calls that begin like this: "George, I know the market is open. Are you trading?"

"No," I always explain. "If I were trading, I wouldn't be talking to you."

Trading requires so much concentration that I couldn't conceive of trying to do anything else at the same time, especially something as distracting as answer telephone calls. You don't find surgeons in the operating room taking calls, you don't find attorneys arguing cases in court answering the phone you don't find airplane pilots talking to anyone during takeoff and landing other than co-pilots and air traffic controllers. Why should professional traders be any different?

I suspect this notion of the market being a no-brainer comes from a sort of casino mentality. People drink and gamble. People smoke and gamble. Why not treat trading as just another diversion?

You know the answer. The more distracted and less disciplined you are, the easier it is to lose your money. Creating a chaotic environment may work for the casino, but not for you. Indeed, it militates against your ability to think clearly and make sound decisions.

Over the years, I've learned the hard way about allowing distractions into my trading. If someone wants to stop by, I've learned to always say no. I just cannot afford the downside risk of letting even the most well-meaning question break my concentration when I'm trading. You'd be surprised how even a moment's loss of concentration can cost you money.

Some people function better, of course, amid a climate of chaos; witness the typical trading pit. You need to design a style of trading that is custom-fit for you. While I prefer a quiet environment, you may do just fine standing in a crowd. My point is, you must decide what works for you both in a practical and psychological sense.

We are all different. There is no right way to trade. I am not here to say you must do one thing or another. Because trading is ultimately a bottom-line enterprise, you must be the arbiter of whether your trading style is satisfactory or not. I can say that most new traders are too focused on the money. They want immediate success. The real success usually comes, however, long after the novice has served a challenging apprenticeship, just as it does in any profession.

While there are indeed many truisms in the market, nothing seems to work better than good, old-fashioned work. That means getting up day after day and doing your best. This is especially true after you have experienced one of the many setbacks that are so inevitable in the market.

I'm reminded of the Microsoft advertisement that asks, "Where do you want to go today?" You need to decide this before you begin trading. Unless you have a realistic idea of your own personal goals, you are unlikely to achieve them. I must add that these goals need to be realistic. I once met a man who had designed a simple trading program which he paper-traded using the prices in the newspaper. He assumed that if he could make profits on one contract (assuming, of course, that he could buy and sell at the prices shown in the newspaper), it would be a simple matter to trade ten or fifty or more contracts at the same prices. This was totally unrealistic for a variety of reasons. For one, large orders would move the market. In a thin market, you would never get anyone to take the other side. For another, one's psychology changes when you risk more money. Depending upon your personal circumstances, one contract might be just fine. But do ten contracts and you won't be able to think straight. If you don't believe me, try increasing your size and you'll see what I mean. So you must have realistic, achievable goals.

There seems to be an inverse relationship between how new a trader is and how difficult he senses beating the market will be. For the new guy, beating the market is a virtual sure-thing. This means, without substantial experience, he will step into the market and take money from a seasoned professional. Can it happen? Of course. Is it likely? Not on a consistent basis. This is a little like a guy who likes to play pickup games of touch football on weekends saying he thinks he could beat the players of the Green Bay Packers. Cultivate a little humility and you'll be way ahead of those who think it is easy.

Trading is mostly about behavior, especially behavior while under intense pressure. Once you get started, you'll find out things about yourself that perhaps you never knew existed. For instance, if your personality tends toward the fear side of the fear-greed equation, you might find yourself getting stopped out on small moves. If this is the case, you need to analyze how your fear is harming you in the market—and stop doing it! If you are given to reckless behavior, such as not taking perfectly legitimate profits, you may be a victim of your own greed. You simply want too much. These are all understandable emotions. Don't beat yourself up when you find yourself doing something stupid in the market. Everyone makes these mistakes. Rather, capitalize on the experience by making a mental note of how you sabotaged yourself and vow not to make the same mistake next time.

One particularly good way to keep yourself honest in this respect is to keep a written diary of your trading activities. You don't have to spend more than a couple of minutes writing in this diary, but you must stay with it. Just a couple of lines will do. For instance, "Sold the open today and sold more ten minutes late. Market started to break. Then they rallied in a stop-running exercise and I panicked and bought back position at the top. Must recognize this pattern and sell more next time. Market broke. I missed move."

It is important that you date each entry. Over time, you can look back and see whether you are still making the same mistakes. You also want to list your victories.

Along with a diary, you might want to chart your equity. This is a simple line, drawn on chart paper, that links your equity level as you move through time. I don't need to tell you in what direction you want the line to go. But be particularly sensitive to the overall trend of this line. If it is just down, you are probably too fearful and losing consistently. You need to analyze what you are doing wrong. If the line is quite volatile, up one day and down the next, you are probably too reckless. The line suggests you are taking too many chances. When you win, the line skyrockets, but when you lose, you are giving back all your hard-won profits, and then some. You can never win all the time, but you want the equity line to suggest steady growth. When you are new, this may not be possible, so strive just to keep the equity line moving sideways. With time, your hard work should change the shape of the graph.

We would all like to think that we have excellent insight into our own shortcomings, whether they be in business or our personal lives. Sometimes, though, we lack the very insightfulness that is required to do this job well. For this reason, you might want to consider professional help in the form of a therapist. This doesn't have to be a years-long engagement, but rather several weeks or months in duration, long enough to find out what might be holding you back from success in the market.

Years ago, when I first started trading, I remember consulting with a therapist when I was holding on to a long position in the metals market. At the time, I was determined to hold this position regardless of the consequences. The therapist explained to me one day that I had excellent intuition about the market, but unconsciously I was telling him only one thing—get out! I didn't listen to him. The market crashed. I lost all my hard-won profits while learning a valuable lesson about listening to my inner voice of reason.

I understand that something as insubstantial as intuition is a difficult, if not impossible, trait to quantify, but almost any knowledge you can gain in this area can place you in good stead. I clearly remember watching *Wall Street Week* back in the fall of 1987 when one of the panelists struggled to explain that, while he couldn't point to a legitimate reason for this feeling, he had a hunch that something wasn't right about the market. Days later, the market crashed. This was intuition talking.

Can you cultivate such an intangible as intuition? I think you can, but only f you are willing to put in the time observing everything you can about the market. How does this intuition begin to manifest itself? When you begin to see the move emerging before it does. You know when a move is over. How do you know? That's harder to explain. But once you realize what's going on, you will be much less apt to make what I call stupid mistakes. For instance, I once knew a trader who loved to buy breakouts. As a strategy, you can get away with this if you are selective and buy the right ones. But if you willy-nilly buy just any old breakout, here's what is going to happen. You are going to buy the top. Think about it. When the market breaks out, it hits a ton of buy orders. This pushes the market higher. Your broker must then bid your order alongside hundreds of other buy orders. So you become part of the problem. Your buying helps to drive the market higher. Then, by the time a willing seller is found (undoubtedly someone who bought in anticipation of the rally), the move is usually over.

This trader I knew would always react the same way when he placed his breakout trade. He would rant and curse his broker and brokerage firm, talking about the lousy fills. Meanwhile, the market would be soaring and he wouldn't be filled. Finally, the phone would ring and the fill would set him off.

"How can they fill me there?" he would scream. "I placed the order when it was 200 lower."

He grabbed the phone and dialed the broker and started screaming at him. Then he abruptly hung up.

"What did he say?" I asked.

"That I should get another broker."

I agreed with the broker. I pointed out that the breakout rally was only nine minutes long. The first three minutes were still in the consolidation and he didn't even pick up the phone until the fourth minute. Placing the order killed another minute and then the broker had to call down to the trading pit. The market was soaring. There probably weren't any sellers. By the time the order was filled, there weren't more than two or three minutes remaining to the top. At that point, panic selling sent it lower.

By the way, the market rarely accommodates foolish behavior such as this by returning to the highs, but that's precisely the kind of unrealistic expectations that such traders want. They then compound one problem by creating another. They become stubborn.

If you ever need a prescription for disaster, this is it: not knowing what you are doing, blaming others, becoming stubborn. This is a trinity of mistakes that you can live without!

An intuitive trader would have approached this set of circumstances in an entirely different fashion. She would have perhaps anticipated the move by buying early—what I call buying when the smoke is coming under the door. Once the whole world knows where the market is going, it is too late. Witness the March 2000 stock market buyers and dot-com mania. Plenty of people jumped aboard once they knew they had a sure-thing.

The same applies to getting out. Once the bullishness becomes overwhelming, it is over. Wherever there's a crowd, you want to be against them. In the same scenario, if you do make a mistake, you get out immediately. The intuitive trader does not dwell on his mistakes. He simply moves on.

WHAT'S HOLDING YOU BACK?

I've often said that there are a million ways to lose when trading, but only a few ways to win. When you screw up, it's normal to assume that you are fatally flawed and naturally incompetent. It just goes with the territory. My earliest memories of trading were based on thinking that everyone else was winning—and I alone was losing. I told you my fantasy about expecting the security guards to throw me out in the street. Is my experience so different from the typical trader's? I don't think so. Who hasn't thrown up his hands in frustration, convinced that virtually no one can survive in the dog-eat-dog world of trading? Such perceptions tend to be not only untrue, but also self-defeating.

The first thing you must do is stop beating yourself up. One of the most successful traders I ever met once said to me, "You have no idea how often I fail. If the average guy had losses like mine, he'd be out the window." This from a guy who occasionally made more than $100,000 in a day.

To put this in perspective, we need to categorize the types of errors that most traders make.

1. *Undercapitalized.* This is a common mistake made by new traders. Beating the market is difficult enough without having to worry about the money. Undercapitalized traders invariably think about the money to the exclusion of just about everything else. If you are trading a system, you need to know the maximum drawdown, and then expect to lose that amount right at the outset. With any luck, this won't happen, but it could. Being undercapitalized is probably the single most significant reason for traders busting out than any other cause. Just as you think you are about to master the learning curve, you run out of money. Be wary of brokers who will allow you to

trade on minimum margin; This is just giving you additional rope to hang yourself. By overfunding your account, you'll be better able to withstand the strains of losing streaks. In so doing, you won't have to add margin to your account. If being properly capitalized means you may have to work another six months at your present job, do so. You'll find that not being undercapitalized allows a freedom to act in the market that you won't have otherwise.

2. *Overtrading,* another fatal error of the novice trader. The idea is to make the money and keep it, not give it all back because you were reckless. If you can make even a small amount of money each day, a difficult task, your account will grow. Overtrading generally just helps the broker. New traders want to ride every trend (as if getting on the right side at the right time were easy), but this is the wrong goal. You want to make money, not be perfect.

3. *Listening to brokers.* If your broker were a hotshot at trading, she'd be risking her own money, not yours. No one is going to be as interested in your money as you. That's why you need to make the key decisions about how to trade. When your broker gives you a bad tip, she becomes a convenient scapegoat; now you have someone to blame. When you lose your own money, however, you have to internalize the loss and think about what you did wrong. This can become a valuable learning experience.

4. *Giving trading discretion to your broker.* Once you sign away your sovereignty over your own account, you open yourself up to all sorts of problems. The greatest single complaint that I hear from new traders is that "my broker lost my money." Even the best of brokers will have a conflict between his interests and yours. The dishonest ones, of course, will simply churn the account, leaving you with nothing but high commission expenses. Your legal recourse in this situation is minimal. Even if the final outcome is the same, it is somehow more satisfying to know that you made some honest mistakes in trying to learn how to trade as opposed to just being ripped off. I've even seen unscrupulous brokers steal winning trades from clients and leave losing trades in the clients' accounts. Unfortunately, the regulatory agencies do a very poor job of monitoring this type of activity.

5. *Trading too many markets.* Learn to be a specialist and trade no more than two or three markets at the same time. It is okay to switch markets if the volatility and liquidity pick up in one and lessen in another. You want to be where the action is, but market diversification definitely doesn't work when you are trying to aggressively trade. Better to put all your eggs in one basket

and watch that basket very closely. In addition, there are only a handful of good trading markets. Don't waste your time trying to jump from market to market.

6. *Believing you are invincible.* Few activities teach you humility as well as trading does. Seasoned traders respect the risk. Novice traders, no matter how lucky, treat success as their birthright. If you are given to a manic-depressive personality—too up when you win and too down when you lose—you are probably better off not trading. The best traders understand that trading is a process. For them, a winning day is the same as a losing day. Over time, they understand that their effort will pay off and they will win. Having this confidence, however, is a far cry from being a braggart.

7. *Failure to embrace the risk.* There are a few sure-fire ways to lose. One of them is insisting on certainty. Once you are certain, you are almost always wrong. There is no way to eliminate the risk without eliminating the potential profit. Seasoned traders know this. They also know that they must take reasonable chances in order to win.

8. *Thinking about the money.* The market doesn't know about your position, nor does it care. The market moves according to its own internal pattern. When you are focused on the money, you cannot think about the market and what it is likely to do. This problem almost always results from being undercapitalized, so teach yourself not to think about the money and, paradoxically, you'll begin to make money. The harder you try, the more you will lose. The people who win in the market are those who are relaxed and enjoy what they are doing.

9. *Lack of discipline.* You have to approach the market with a game plan. This need not be a system, but it should offer a roadmap as to how you will handle getting in and out, taking profits or losses, the size of your commitment, and so on. You don't want to try to make up your plan as you go along. When you take this approach, you become indecisive and let opportunities pass, which creates other problems. Having missed one opportunity, you may then try to force the market. Pretty soon, you are looking at losses and are unable to accept defeat. Then the downside spiral begins to snowball. To avoid this, you must have it out with yourself before the situation presents itself. "When I see what I'm looking for," tell yourself, "I'm going to take the trades regardless of how I feel." Those are the trades that result in winners.

10. *Looking for easy answers.* The only thing easy about the market is how easy it is to lose your money when you don't know what you are doing. No matter how easy a strategy appears, chances are the probabilities will eat up the profits if you persist in making the mistake of thinking you can always rely on strategy A or strategy B. If there were truly an easy way to beat the market, don't you think it would have been widely publicized years ago? There are techniques that may work well for periods of time, but no matter how good a given technique, there will always be exceptions. New traders tend to grow enchanted with market formulas. These are fine if they are used in the proper way—as a guideline, perhaps. But to suggest that the market always rallies or declines on a given move in an indicator is a mistake. If any broad statement could be made about this phenomenon, it would probably be that a variety of indicators all pointing in a given direction could be taken as a positive or negative signal. Regardless of how you interpret this, indicators and formulas are never an easy solution to a difficult question—namely, "What will the market do?"

11. *Not concentrating.* My greatest regrets in the market have come from letting people distract me when I was trading. The insidious nature of being distracted, moreover, takes a variety of forms—taking phone calls, socializing, listening to CNBC, and so on. Once you are focused on the market, you'll find that there are subtle clues when a market is getting ready to move. If you are not paying attention, you will surely miss them.

12. *An inability to pick up the phone.* If your fear of losing money is so great that you cannot pick up the phone, you need to have it out with yourself. Tomorrow, when the opportunity comes, you must take the trade, regardless of how you feel about it. Otherwise, you will be on the sidelines forever. This is really a matter of discipline. At the opposite side of the spectrum is the gunslinger who cannot put down the phone. In either instance, analyze your situation and push yourself to the middle. Trading may not be for you, but you won't give yourself a fair chance unless you can solve the fear-greed syndrome and put yourself alongside winning traders.

13. *An overreliance on mechanical indicators.* Many people believe that one way to take the emotion out of trading is to rely on mechanical indicators. This is a favorite approach among left-brained people, such as engineers, airline pilots, architects, and doctors, who are attracted to trading. Indicators provide black-and-white numbers. These are often translated into

percentages and answers that are so welcome among the numbers crunchers. Unfortunately, these numbers must often be interpreted since they don't always mean the same thing. For instance, take the notion of the premium. A high premium can mean the market is bullish, but do you buy it or sell it? A soaring premium can signal a reversal in a down market, but it can also mean you are nearing a top. The same is true of a high stochastics reading. When the market is soaring, the stochastics number will be high—and will stay high. At other times, a high reading suggests a top is nearing and you can sell. When you try to categorize a market with a number, you invite the possibility of serious market mistakes. By the way, regardless of what your indicator tells you, you are still going to get emotional when your money is at risk. I like the phrase *confirming indicator* since that is what I'm looking for when I utilize an indicator to make a trading decision, a confirmation of what I already sense on an intuitive level.

14. *Listening to the pundits.* One of the problems in listening to others for trading advice is that the advice is outdated by the time you hear it. I told you about my friend who couldn't turn around his clients fast enough—and he was standing in the middle of the S&P pit! Think of the difficulty in getting good, timely advice in your hands by mail, and we're assuming that the information is accurate. The fact is, the market changes so rapidly that you virtually have to be right on top of the situation to capitalize on a change in sentiment. The floor traders change their minds in a heartbeat. How are you going to benefit without being there with them? One solution has been to subscribe to a service that brings you the sounds of the pit, complete with market commentary, but this, too, is problematic. How do you interpret what the commentator has to say? When you read a market analysis in a publication such as *The Wall Street Journal* or *Investor's Business Daily,* the writer has to find a reason for the market rising or falling. So he or she will attribute it to falling interest rates, or fear of inflation, or profit-taking, or whatever. This information is worse than useless because it provides a false sense of security. A pundit speaking on CNBC, for instance, is expected to play the role of all-knowing expert; people want to hear his opinion. The fact is, the market will march to its own drummer, regardless of what the experts think.

Do you see yourself falling victim to one of the preceding fourteen pitfalls? You are not alone. Most traders make one or more of these mistakes as beginners. The challenge is to identify what might be holding you back and then proceed ahead, determined to change your style of trading.

DOING WHAT WORKS FOR YOU

No matter what mistakes you may have made in the past, there is always an opportunity to start over. Your particular set of strengths in the market will, no doubt, be highly individualistic. What works for you might not be suitable for another person. Nevertheless, you want to begin by listing your strengths. Are you able to see your mistakes, for instance, and put them aside? Or are you just stubborn? If thinking about the money is short-circuiting your trading, can you find a way to increase the size of your account? Are you willing to change? What many people see as serious setbacks, I often see as mere bumps in the road. I suppose all things are relative, but most people simply are not prepared for the normal course of trading, the normal cycles of wins and losses. By going back to basics, by identifying your strengths, you will begin your journey with an element of self-confidence, which is perhaps the most vital inner strength that any trader needs. You will inevitably discover that you have a whole host of qualities that will put you in good stead. From there, it is simply a matter of building on these strengths.

Let me give you an example. Let's say you recently fell victim to one of the pitfalls listed. You might have become a trading animal, buying and selling in six or seven markets at a time, with hardly an opportunity to watch any of them closely. Now you have paid the price. Your margin equity has been decreased by 40 percent and your broker is all smiles since she's the one who has been collecting the commissions off this reckless binge. It is time to clean up your act. The party is over and there's only one person to blame for your predicament. You need to get started on a new way of life.

I recently had a friend give up a lifelong addiction to alcohol. I cannot tell you how this single decision has transformed his life for the better. Where he found the strength to take such a drastic step, I'll never know. I just know that a lot of other people would be unable to do what he did. His ability to simply walk away from this addiction is an obvious strength.

Something akin to this strength is needed when you want to get back to basics in the market. You simply resolve not to do it anymore—and then keep your resolution. Then you focus on what will work for you. You carve out a plan of action and then go about implementing the plan.

I have a rule that says that I never take a trade unless I know where it is going and when it will get there. This may sound like an ambitious undertaking, but it works for me. I have another rule that says I don't want to miss good opportunities. This means that when I see the opportunity developing

I must seize the moment. I know well from experience that once it is gone—assuming I didn't act when I should have—I will be left empty-handed, saying, "I shoulda, woulda, coulda." Accordingly, I've trained myself to act amid the uncertainty of the moment, given the guidelines I've set for myself. The upside of this decision is that I've gained a tremendous sense of self-confidence by following my plan. The downside, of course, is that I'll occasionally be wrong, but I knew this all along. The point is, I have a game plan. I know exactly what I'm looking for and I know how to execute my plan. Please note that this is different from saying it is easy. Indeed, implementing the strategy is sometimes extraordinarily difficult.

But what's the alternative? You need to find an approach that works and then stay with that plan. When you lose the discipline, when you let down your guard, you open yourself to self-recriminations that have no place in the disciplined trader's lifestyle. This is akin to the alcoholic's falling off the wagon. You need to get back to basics and build on your strengths.

Sometimes you have to go through a transitional stage when you change from one style of trading to another. You may want to take some time off, or you may want to get started the very next day. There are two schools of thought on this matter. One is that losses have an eroding impact on your psychological ability to function. After a series of losses, you may be so defeated that you expect to lose, thus continuing the pattern. The other point of view suggests that you must get back in the market as soon as possible following a market defeat. I once met a trader who had 24 losses in a row before he started to win big. I admired his ability to stay with his game plan despite the losses. There's something to be said for both viewpoints. I'm not suggesting that one is right and the other is wrong. You have to do what works for you.

Your frame of mind is vitally important when you trade. You must avoid at all costs the obvious psychological pitfalls—fatigue, hangovers, anger and hostility, and grief. You have no business trading when you are under the sway of these powerful emotions. I'm a firm believer that you want to feel your best when you trade—and I mean both physically and mentally. Ideally, you want a confident state of mind, but this confidence cannot extend to unbridled optimism; it must be grounded in reality. As for the downside, you must be open to the possibility that the trade won't work. Losing trades are a part of the trading process. Here, again, you are the best judge of the state of your own psychological and physical well-being.

Identify your own energy cycle and try to implement your trades when you are feeling your best. (This is not always a possibility.) I've often noticed that the best trades come late in the day, after you have put in five or six hours in front of the computer screen. Do what you can to be prepared for these opportunities. I make it a point to take time off during the lunch hour when I know I don't want to trade. You can use this time to recharge your energies. It has been my experience that "tick hounds," who are glued to the screen all day, rarely do as well as traders who take time away from the market. The same applies to traders who stay up all night studying charts—or, worse, drinking. The well-rested and relaxed win the game.

Are you a solitary trader or do you enjoy collaboration? While I protect my privacy at all costs when I trade, other people enjoy sharing ideas and insights during the trading process. I've tried giving trading seminars with live trading. The results have been mixed. While it is always instructive for the class—whether I win or lose—I know that I could have done better had I been alone.

While there are a lot of amusing stories that come out of collaborative trading ventures (e.g., "He talked me into that trade"), you are probably better off keeping your own counsel. Even if you trade alone, you still have to contend with your broker. Most brokers cannot resist trying to get their two cents worth into the mix, usually with disastrous results. My brokers know that I'm not interested in their opinions. They are entirely professional and never mention whether I've been winning or losing. When I do lose, I try never to blame them for the results; this is how the client-broker relationship should be.

The best traders always train their family members how to answer the phone. I'm always pleased if I call a trader during market hours and am told, "He'll call you back." It means he has his priorities straight. You don't want to be bothered when the market is open.

We hear a lot about treating trading as a business. Unless you live in a place like I do, where a lot of people close up shop and go fishing, you want to keep regular hours. The best traders seem to have a sense of balance in their lives. They understand the notion of moderation in all things. Among the ranks of floor traders, there were always those who would populate the bars far into the night and come into the exchange in the morning all bleary-eyed. But a larger segment went home to family and friends and had an iron discipline over their personal lives. One necessary regimen to offset the incredible stress of trading is to maintain an ongoing exercise program. One trader I knew spent his afternoons at the gym, lifting weights. Another thought nothing of taking a

50-mile bike ride to rid himself of stress. Swimming and jogging are two other popular activities among traders.

While these observations may seem obvious, they are the subtle components that need to be tailored to the specific individual. You need to do what helps you maintain a positive psychological frame of mind. This will help you stay balanced and energized.

No matter how well prepared you are, there will always be those days when you are simply blindsided. On average, I'd say this typically occurs about once a month, usually in the form of what I call a search-and-destroy day, a day that is characterized by extreme volatility. On such a day, you'll see both the intraday highs and lows violated repeatedly. For the trader trying to find a trend, the situation is truly hopeless. I've experienced days like this when, trying to recoup a small $500 loss, I managed to lose over $10,000 by day's end. This results from jumping from side to side and increasing one's size. I cannot tell you the psychological devastation that days like this can create.

Following one of these search-and-destroy days, a trader turned to me and said, "You just have to accept it. The market is always right."

I agree with him. But there comes a time when you need to step back and observe what's going on. One rule I now use to cope with the possibility of a disaster such as this is to quit trading after three consecutive losses in a trading session. I divide the day into two parts, morning and afternoon. If the morning session results in three consecutive losses, I simply quit trading, walk away, and start over again in the afternoon session.

Failure to observe this rule results in the occasional situation where a small loss rapidly grows into a larger loss. Remember my story about doubling the number of contracts in the bond market? If you grow stubborn and insist on profits, sooner or later you will run into a truly bad losing streak, and increasing your size will only hasten your demise. It doesn't make sense to let one bad day take a substantial amount of your equity.

If you don't believe this will happen to you, you haven't traded long enough. It happens to everyone. I know the textbooks tell you to risk no more than five to ten percent of your equity. This is fine in theory. But in the real world you will occasionally be caught unawares. I know of many instances where unsuspecting novice traders got in over their heads and simply lost most of their equity in a single trading session. Need I repeat that the best loss is typically the first loss? Be prepared for the worst and you won't be surprised.

Over the years, I've been roundly criticized for opinions like these. "You are too pessimistic," one would-be trader told me. "Why do you always dwell on the possibility of losses?" On the contrary, I consider myself a realist. This particular trader ended up losing approximately $70,000 because he believed in fighting the trend. Far from being hurt from such criticism, I'm often amused. Why would someone with no experience be so quick to dismiss the voice of someone who knows what he is talking about? My only answer is because he or she wants to believe that winning profits in the market is easy.

Several years ago I spent a week trading with a client who displayed similar traits. She wanted to believe that beating the market was easy.

"Why are we just sitting here?" she complained. "Why aren't we trading?"

Actually, I was trying to concentrate at the time, looking for a good trade. But she didn't see that as a worthwhile activity.

"I have three lines," I said, pointing to the phone. "Be my guest."

I wasn't going to risk my money on a questionable trade.

"Go ahead," I urged. She wouldn't do it.

When I did find the trade I liked, she traded against me.

By the end of the week, after carefully selecting my trades, I had profits in excess of $10,000. She went home with losses. Some people are just bent on self-destruction.

There is a virtual army of desperate people out there looking for a quick fix in the market. I recently received a call from someone I'd never talked to before. His question: "Can I do this and make money?"

How should I know? I asked him what he'd been doing in the market.

"I've been selling puts on stocks," he replied.

"Selling puts?" I said. "The market's been breaking like a rock. Put prices have grown more valuable. You've been undoubtedly losing."

"I've been wiped out," he said.

He was looking for a quick fix to his problems. A tip sheet perhaps? There's no end to how much damage you can do to yourself in the market if you are truly determined. I'm sure he'll find someone with the easy answer.

As you can see, the only thing that works for some people is to get as far away from the market as they can. For a variety of reasons, many people simply aren't suited to the trading life. If you find that what works for you is to abstain from trading, then you have just saved yourself a great deal of money

LEARNING TO DO WHAT'S RIGHT

Perhaps you have reached the point where you can identify your shortcomings. Now you want to learn what you can do about overcoming them. For many people, this is a critical fork in the road. Unless you take the correct path, chances are you won't be able to continue trading much longer. There are a number of myths concerning successful trading. The sooner you learn to overcome the inevitable obstacles, the better off you will be.

These obstacles are what lie between where you are now and your stated goals. You may already be well on the road to success, but chances are you will encounter one of the following obstacles.

Obstacle #1: You Want to Trade for a Living

This is a worthy aspiration, but as an apprentice trader do you really think you can start off making a living at your chosen task? Some can, but most cannot. Each new trader has to master a learning curve. When you must win profits simply to pay living expenses, you put an unnecessary burden on yourself. Trading is difficult enough without the pressure of having to win. Indeed, one might view this approach as a prescription for failure, since you may find yourself taking unnecessary risks to meet your trading goals.

Risk capital means just that—money you can afford to lose. If you cannot afford to lose, you cannot afford to trade. The day that you cannot risk losing margin money is the day that you must close your account.

As a new trader, you should not remove money from your trading account to pay the mortgage or rent, day-to-day living expenses, or credit card bills. These expenses need to be taken care of first before you risk money in the market.

Down the road, when you have been able to create some consistency in winning profits, you can pull out money as you see fit. To anticipate profits, however, especially when you are new to trading, is unrealistic. As a new trader, your goal should be to learn everything you can about the market without losing your equity. Indeed, if you can keep your equity at a break-even level the first six months, you are probably well on your way to profitability with all your hard-won experience.

Obstacle #2: You Want to Buy Options Because of Their Limited Risk

When you purchase puts or calls, the risk is limited to the one-time cost of the put or call. This is the most you can lose. The problem is, you can lose 100 percent of the purchase price and, probabilities being what they are, this is a very real possibility. For some strange reason, this appeals to people who have heard that futures trading involves unlimited risk, since you can lose far more than your margin money.

Purchasing options is a little bit like buying a lottery ticket. In the lottery, the cost of entry is low and there is always the chance that the ticket will pay off big-time. The problem rests with the odds of winning. The same is true with an option. To make money by purchasing a put or a call, the underlying security must move a sufficient distance above or below the strike price just to return the cost of the option. At that point, you are at breakeven. To profit, the underlying security must then move even further. While this often happens, most of the time the underlying security doesn't move sufficiently and you end up losing money. Worse yet, it must move within a specific time period—prior to the expiration of the option. So you may be right on the move, but wrong on the timing, in which case you still lose 100 percent of your money at expiration.

If you want to make options your game, you are probably better off selling or writing puts and calls. Just make sure you understand the risks. The writer can receive only the fixed premium, yet he risks an unlimited amount if his judgment is incorrect.

Obstacle #3: You Have a Hard Time Identifying the Trend

A good trader can make money by fading, or trading against, the trend, but this is the hard way to do it. In a choppy market, finding the trend is not always the easiest thing to do, but you put yourself in the best position to win if you can line up the probabilities on your side.

The LSS 5-day oscillator and 1-day strength index are both designed to give you a quick percentage number to gauge underlying market strength. You are better off buying when the percentages exceed 50 percent, and selling when the percentages are in the lower 50 percent range. When you combine these numbers with the correct days of the week, Mondays being best for buying and Thursday best for selling, you have an even better chance of getting on the right side of the market.

The formulas are as follows:

One-Day Strength Index:

$$\frac{(\text{previous close} - \text{previous low}) \times 100}{(\text{previous high} - \text{previous low})}$$

Five-Day Oscillator:

$$\text{Highest price in last 5 days} - \text{Open 5 days ago} = X$$

$$\text{Last close} - \text{Lowest price in last 5 days} = Y$$

$$\frac{(X + Y) \times 100}{(\text{highest price in last 5 days} - \text{lowest price in last 5 days}) \times 2}$$

Obstacle #4: You Can Only Take Trades That Appear in Your Favorite Newsletter

While I have nothing against advisory firms and advisory letters, I think a reliance on them is a mistake. For a short-term trader, there's the problem of timing; there must be an immediacy in the information or it is useless. Moreover, no matter how well intentioned the letter writer, events change rather rapidly in the market. Most people use these letters as a crutch. They want someone to lean on, someone to blame. Typically, the subscriber to a letter will switch from one advisor to another. The search for the real answer goes on and on.

It is far better to learn to trade the market on your own. Spend the time to learn everything you can about the market you trade. After awhile, you won't need to look outward for your answers. Whether you are relying on a broker, advisor, television pundit, or letter writer, the answer you are looking for rests within you. The so-called experts provide definite answers because that is what their public demands.

Obstacle #5: You Cannot Pick Up the Phone

I think this is a much more common problem than overtrading. Most people would prefer to avoid uncertainty if at all possible. In the market, this can be accomplished by freezing at the switch and not getting into the market, although all your signals suggest this would be a wise course of action. By doing nothing, you create a certain outcome: You will neither lose nor gain money.

How do you deal with this dilemma? You embrace the risk. You force yourself to trade, despite your fears of taking a trade and losing; then you do the same thing the next day. After awhile, picking up the phone is no longer an issue; you just train yourself to do it. One trick to help you accomplish this goal is to refuse to think about the money, meaning you don't count your wins or losses when you are in a trade. You wait until after you have closed out the trade to see exactly how much you have won or lost. This is not easy to do, but it is necessary if you are fearful of losing money and cannot pick up the phone.

Obstacle #6: You Always Overstay the Market

Lacking an exit strategy, you wait until the market turns against you. This means, by definition, you are giving back a portion of your hard-won profits. This tendency comes from wanting too much from the market, from trying to capture the whole move as opposed to what the market will give you. I know this pattern well; oftentimes I've been its victim. It simply doesn't pay to overstay the market since you are always getting out at the wrong time.

How to deal with this? With time and price trading, you are always identifying the exit point well in advance of getting out. Once you are in the trade, you do a couple of quick calculations, and you know the downside risk as well as where the move should end. That's where you get out.

You need to have discipline to execute this strategy. The reason is, as soon as the market approaches your exit point, you will begin to think about holding on. The market is still going your way, why not hold on? This is greed speaking. Don't listen to it. Moreover, with a clearly defined exit point, you are usually selling into a crowd of buyers or, conversely, buying into a crowd of sellers. This translates into a good fill.

The exit point has to be realistic in terms of recent market action. Fearful traders tend to have one foot out the door almost as soon as they are in. This is also a mistake. You don't want to base your exit point on the amount of money you have made or lost, but on the reality of the market situation. Is it ready to reach its peak, or is it about to violate an important support area? The money has no bearing on this judgment. It is not enough to know when to get into a trade. You also need to know when to get out.

Overstaying the market is also a mistake because of its demoralizing nature. You are never quite satisfied because you know, if only you'd gotten out at the right time, you would be better off. Once you decide on a legitimate profit-taking point, take the profit and move on to the next trade.

Obstacle #7: You Always Get Caught on the Wrong Side at the Market Turns

This is an emotional mistake that causes many traders to lose money. The tendency is to get too enthusiastic when you are winning and too pessimistic when you are losing. Most people are extremely bullish at the top; witness the dot-com mania of early 2000. Likewise, most people are too bearish at the bottom, which translates into a devil-may-care attitude when you are winning. This is precisely the time when you need to take control of yourself and plan a strategic retreat. The reason? Tops and bottoms are made quickly, with all of the winners rushing to the exit at the same time. This translates into quick moves in the opposite direction, taking your profits with it.

I believe that most traders are cautious when they should be bold, and vice versa. The time to be bold in buying a market is when no one else is interested in it. That's when you can get a bargain. The time to be cautious is when the market has made a rapid rise. That's when it is vulnerable. Selling begets selling and you'll have panicked offers if you aren't careful. This, by the way, is why you always want to trade liquid markets. An abundance of buyers and sellers means there is always someone to provide you with a profit.

Another thing about market turns: They are always made quickly. The market rarely spends a lot of time at the highs or lows. Look on any price chart and you'll see what I mean. The extremes are always made quickly. Therefore, you cannot hesitate if you are going to buy or sell near an extreme.

Leading indicators can help you pinpoint an impending reversal move. In the S&P 500 market, the premium is an excellent leading indicator at the turning points. For example, if the market is breaking like a rock, you'll see all the corresponding indices—cash price, TICK, TICKI, Dow Jones—all knocking on the lows along with the futures price. Given this scenario, if you see the premium starting to rise, you know that someone is buying the market; this is the advanced signal that a reversal is imminent. The reverse, of course, is true at a market top. This is why you need to pay attention.

Obstacle #8: You Always Trade Just One Contract

Money management is critical for success in the markets. You need to know when to take on more contracts and when to hold back. As a general rule, regardless of what trading system you may be using, you can expect to make all of your profits on just 20 percent of your trades. This doesn't mean you will lose on four out of five trades, just that the net profits will be earned on just one-fifth of all your trades. Let's see how this might work. What you earn on Monday, you lose on Tuesday. You now have a fifty-fifty, win-to-loss ratio. Then you win on Wednesday. But you lose this profit on Thursday. You still have 50 percent winners, but, significantly, your net profit is zero. On Friday, you win big. This is your net profit on the week. Over the course of a month's time, therefore, your net profit is the sum of the four or five Friday profits.

I'm talking averages here, so it doesn't have to be Friday when you make the winning trades. It could be Monday or Tuesday or Thursday. The point is, you earn the bulk of your profits on a minority of your trades.

Can you see how risking the same amount of money on every trade could be a mistake? What if you could win more on the winners and lose less on the losers? How do you isolate the best trades?

There are a variety of approaches to the dilemma of finding the best trades. For one, you want to strive for a high net profit per trade. This is the net amount of money you earn on every trade. Let's say you earn $2,000 on four trades. The net amount is $500 per trade. Now, you might have made, let's say, $2,000 on one trade and $2,000 on another, but then lost $1,000 per trade on two consecutive trades. It doesn't matter how you reached the $2,000 figure. Once you factor in the four trades, it averages out to $500 a trade. As long as you have a good net amount of winnings on each trade over time, you are on your way to being a winning trader.

The problem comes, of course, when the net number is close to zero—or, worse, a negative number. Now you are losing money on every trade. If you make the valid assumption that, no matter how good your trading skills, you are going to have a certain percentage that are losers, then you can begin to concentrate on how best to increase your net-profit-per-trade number.

One approach is to be ruthless with the losers. Cut the losses to a minimum. Believe it or not, most new traders do the very opposite of the market truism "cut your losses and let your profits ride": They let their losses ride. This can happen for a variety of reasons. Perhaps you think the market will return your position to profitability. Once you find yourself beginning to hope that the market goes your way, you can pretty well write off your position as a loss. Perhaps you think you cannot afford to take a loss. One disastrous variation of this is to let a trade turn into an overnight trade because you don't want to take a loss, as if the situation might get better tomorrow. It rarely does. Perhaps you move your stop away from the market because you don't want it to be hit—or perhaps you simply don't have a stop. Perhaps you aren't paying attention. Perhaps you think a losing trade cannot happen to you. As you can see, there are many reasons why a small loss might turn into a larger loss. These are all mental errors, of course, created by a lack of discipline.

Another approach is to increase the profitability on the winners. When the profits are large enough, and you are carefully monitoring the size of the losses, it becomes almost impossible for the market to take back the profits. For example, let's say you are able to run up $7,000 in profits on seven trades. This averages out to approximately $1,000 a trade. Now a losing streak sets in. If you can limit the losses to just $500 per trade and you have the bad fortune to lose seven times in a row, you still have half of your winnings—$3,500. Chances are, you are not going to hit such a bad losing streak. The point is, if the profits are large enough, the losses aren't going to hurt you.

How do you get the large profits? For one, never limit the size of the profit based on a predetermined profit goal. Rather, always take what the market is willing to give. You need the big winning days to offset the inevitable losses, so don't artificially limit your profits. You can go broke taking a profit. Another thing, never let the market get away from you in terms of losses. Always pull the plug on a trade gone awry; otherwise, that one lapse in judgment could ruin a well-executed trading plan.

The general rule for money management is that you should bet more when you are winning and less when you are losing. This is good as far as it goes, but it requires some judgment. Both market winnings and losses tend to accumulate in cycles. As you enter into a winning cycle, you must be willing to take on more contracts. The losing cycles, of course, require that you pull back and go down to a minimal commitment.

The one mistake that most new traders make is to insist on certainty, so they watch a market until it becomes profitable, and then they jump aboard after observing what would have been three or four winning trades. This is the worst possible time to get into the market. Chances are, the losing cycle is about to begin. It's better to wait, while your system loses three or four trades, and then enter on the next signal, hoping the winning cycle is about to begin.

Just as traders can grow hot and cold, markets likewise have winning streaks and losing streaks. A market that is trending will return excellent profits to the trend followers, but as soon as the market enters into a trendless consolidation mode, the trend followers will encounter losses. You need to know where the market is in its cycle when you begin to trade.

The serious money is made when the market begins to run. That's when you want to step up your commitment. You'll know soon enough should your judgment prove wrong. The problem comes following a loss. What do you do then? If you are trading three contracts when you lose, you cannot very well go down to one contract and get the entire loss back, so you have to make a judgment. You can cut back the number of contracts and nurse the account back to health, or you can go in with the same number—or even double the number—in a high-risk attempt to recoup immediately. I would like to point out that you need only half the move to recoup what you initially lost, if you double the number of contracts. The problem is, you must be right.

Part of your decision in this regard depends on your attitude toward risk and your trading approach. If you are trading at your personal upper psychological limit, it won't help to increase the number of contracts; you won't be able to think correctly. If you are comfortable with the risk, you can undo the damage quickly and move on. By the way, when chasing losses in this fashion, consider it a victory when you get even. Then start over.

I know what you're thinking. What's wrong with trading just one contract? Nothing, except that you are never going to make any serious money that way. Between the cost of giving up the edge on the fills and the commissions, you are playing a marginal game. If you want to point to limited resources as holding you back, I'd point to the countless well-financed professionals you are betting against. They are not constrained by a limited bankroll—and you are competing against them. One strategy that works in this regard is to trade as if you are well financed even if you are not. This means occasionally being aggressive and not giving up too easily.

Obstacle #9: You Become Too Opinionated

I knew a Chicago soybean trader in the early 1980s who lost so much money that his clearing firm gave him a job—as a clerk. It took him years to work off his debt. His downfall was that he was one of the most opinionated people I'd ever met. He made pronouncements about the direction of various markets as if he truly knew where the market was going. Apparently, he believed what he was saying. Unfortunately, the market didn't cooperate. I knew another soybean trader who froze one day. He'd lost so much money he handed his trading cards to a friend and told him to get him out of the market. He couldn't take the losses. The worst offender of his own pronouncements was a twenty-six-year-old, millionaire metals trader. He borrowed his clients' money to plunge in the gold market. He ended up in prison.

While many new traders are understandably shy about their trading talents, a whole other segment take their initial success to mean they are invincible. One trader told me on this score, "I know enough to be dangerous." So many new traders fall victim to this shortcoming of believing their own opinions that it has become practically a rite of passage. Rarely does a week go by when I am not asked what I think about the market. I try to be relentlessly noncommittal. Despite the booming employment opportunities for pundits, I suspect that most traders would do well to steer clear of their pronouncements.

If you find yourself a candidate for the title of "Most Opinionated Trader," you need to step back and gain a little humility. The market is exceptionally good at bringing highfliers back to earth. You are only as good as your last trade.

Obstacle #10: You Are Trading the Wrong Markets

A trader lives in Texas, so he decides on trading live cattle. An Iowa farmer decides she'll be best at trading hogs. A Southerner finds cotton trading to his liking. Where you live or what you like to consume are hardly good reasons for deciding what futures or commodity you should trade. For one, if you are a grower, chances are that won't help you win on the futures exchange. For another, most commodities, due to volatility and liquidity constraints, simply aren't good trading candidates, although you can occasionally find a good opportunity for a long-term move. When it comes to short-term trading, there are two key requirements—liquidity and volatility. Unless you have both, you aren't going to enjoy the results. Their absence limits the available markets considerably.

Some people select markets for the wrong reasons. They learn that you can margin a contract of corn or oats for just several hundred dollars, and they select the market based on what they can afford. The reason the margin is low in these markets is because the opportunity for profit and loss is also low. Other markets, such as heating oil or unleaded gasoline, are often touted in radio campaigns during the winter months. Typically, the appeal is with shortages and rising prices, but seasonal studies have shown that these markets decline on average in the winter. The reason is that major producers and processors do their hedging in advance of the winter season. That's why they call it a futures market.

Realize that markets come and go. When inflation is high, both metals and grain markets will typically soar, but we haven't had a booming metals or grain market in years. This doesn't mean, of course, they cannot boom again.

In recent years, the action has been in the stock index futures and the interest rate markets because the stock market, at least until the early Spring of 2000, was soaring, often on the news of lowered interest rates. The opportunity for big profits existed, so these markets attracted a lot of participation. The rise of prices, of course, resulted in the rise of margins, as well as a host of new products being offered on the exchanges.

If we ever get the word *inflation* back in our vocabulary, you can bet that other markets will become popular again.

What's a new trader to do? Just remember the two words—*liquidity* and *volatility*. You need a lot of players both to give you a profit when you want one and to ensure that the fills are not out of line. Remember, for a price to be established, both buyer and sell must agree. You need the volatility—especially as a short-term trader—to earn a reasonable profit in the first place. Frankly, apart from stock index futures and U.S. Treasury bonds in the futures market, there are few short-term trading opportunities.

Obstacle #11: You Are Afraid to Sell Short

Most new traders have a difficult time with short-selling. "How can you sell something you don't own?" is the popular question. Moreover, the stock exchanges make short-selling difficult for investors by insisting on an uptick and substantial margin. The fact is, for futures traders, selling short is as easy as buying; you simply sell first and buy, or *cover,* later. The profit or loss is determined solely by the difference between the two prices and whether you were able to sell higher than you purchased. So what's the problem with short-selling?

We know that there is both a buyer and a seller for every contract that is traded. This doesn't mean, however, that if 100 contracts are traded, you have 100 buyers and 100 sellers. There might be 100 buyers and only one seller. Indeed, since most novice traders prefer buying, you probably have many more buyers than sellers. So what happens when the market starts to go lower? You suddenly have a lot of sellers (the former buyers) and prices tend to break. These sudden breaks generate lots of money for the relatively few short-sellers who are now covering their positions. Can you see how short-selling can be very profitable?

If most people are buying, who are these sellers? They tend to be sophisticated floor traders and other professionals. They understand that the public traders have a bullish bias and that most people in the market are usually wrong. One floor trader once described a bull market as trying to push a huge boulder up a mountain range. He characterized a bear market as what happens once you push the boulder off a cliff. Doesn't it make sense to trade both sides of the market as opposed to just the upside?

Obstacle #12: Your Timing Is Always Off

If you are fearful of losing money, you will always wait too long to take a position. If you are reckless, you won't pay attention to when the market wants to run. In either instance, your timing will be off. The best time to enter the market is when the most uncertainty exists—just before a move begins. The market will typically churn sideways prior to a substantial move as buyers and sellers try to size up the market.

In terms of time, there are three good opportunities. One is right at the open. Prices might have been driven lower, providing a good buying opportunity, or prices might have been driven higher, providing a selling opportunity. The second opportunity usually occurs sometime during the mid-morning when the market decides to make its first trend of the day. The final oppportunity occurs late in the afternoon, usually in the last hour of trading.

You want to avoid taking new positions during the noon hour, noon to 2:00 P.M. East Coast time. This is the time of day when the market churns. If you do take a position and the market dies on you, simply get out and look for a more opportune time. The best trades go your way immediately. If your timing if off, you are probably waiting for proof before committing yourself. This, of course, means you are too late, since the move is already well under way.

Obstacle #13: The Fills Are Killing You

If you find that you are always complaining about the fills you are receiving, perhaps you are doing something wrong in the market. Bad fills are typically a problem of timing. If you are selling into a crowd of sellers, guess what is going to happen to your order? That's right, your broker will have to offer the market lower to draw out a buyer. The reverse occurs when you decide to buy amid a crowd of buyers. Now your broker will have to outbid the next guy, taking the market higher.

The public buyers typically buy at the last offer. The public sellers typically sell at the last bid. One way to avoid bad fills is to do your buying and selling when the market is relatively stable, before a huge trend begins.

I once traded two different accounts with two different brokerage firms. To rate one against the other in terms of the fills, I realized it wasn't appropriate to put in one buy order with one and then another with the other brokerage firm. In the minute or so between orders, the market might have changed, so I decided to test them by putting in competing *market on close* (MOC) orders. Over a period of several months, I noticed that the best that brokerage B could do was to equal brokerage A. Otherwise, the fill was always a tick or two worse. By comparing them in this fashion, I realized that one firm was a little better in filling orders, at least this particular type of order.

So, apart from changing brokers, you can also try putting in limit order as opposed to market orders. This will limit the broker to filling the order a your price or better, but there will be times when you won't have the luxury of selecting the price you want to exit or enter the market. Let's say your position is losing and you want out. By placing a limit order, you may not get any fill at all.

Before you place a trade, you might want to ask your broker what the current bid and asked price are. She might say, "seventy at eighty," which means seventy bid, eighty asked. Remember that a market spread can widen out to, say, "seventy at even." Now you are looking at a seventy bid versus an even-asked market. Using this information, you might want to raise the bid or lower the offer in hopes that your order might be filled.

"Then sell me one at ninety, or better," you might tell your broker. You could also just say, "Sell me one at ninety" (the "or better" is understood). Or you might say, "Sell me one at ninety fill-or-kill," meaning it must be executed immediately or it becomes void. There are times when you might want to be very selective in entering the market, but when you just want in—or, more likely, out—you have to go market and hope for the best.

Spreads between the bid and the ask tend to widen in slow markets or when liquidity dries up. Even in a thriving market, there will be times when the spreads will widen, so be careful when you throw in a market order. The worst time, of course, is when you join a crowd going in the same direction. Then you are asking for trouble. Most floor brokers do an excellent job in filling orders, and, while there are exceptions, the bulk of all orders are filled in a responsible manner. The problem arises when a customer thinks he is entitled to a price he sees on a screen. In addition to the built-in time lag, there is the problem of finding someone to take the other side of the trade. This opposing trader, no doubt, thinks you are wrong. Why else would he buy when you are selling? If the future were so certain, the fills would be even worse.

Poor fills can also mean you are simply trading the wrong market. Several years ago, my LSS system was making good money in the coffee market, a market not known for its good fills. One of the features of the system was to sell "market on close." As word of its success got out, more and more orders became bunched up to sell MOC. After awhile, some brokers I know were getting their clients out a half hour to an hour before the close. Why? Because the pit couldn't stand up to the weight of these selling orders. The LSS traders were taking the market lower against themselves. That's why you don't want to trade thin markets, and that's why many floor traders say "MOC" stands for "murder on close."

Obstacle #14: Excessive Commission Costs

I've saved this one for last because it is one of the most common errors made by new traders. The cost of the commission may seem small in comparison to the size of the contract, but, over time, brokers count on capturing a certain percentage of your equity. If you open an account for $5,000, the broker sees this as an opportunity to capture at least half that amount in commissions in the first year—assuming you last that long.

Commissions are a cost of doing business, but why make those costs any higher than they need to be? One often hears the argument that one gets what one pays for. Did you know, however, that the same guys filling orders for customers paying $50 a round-turn are filling orders for customers paying half that amount, and less? In fact, the guy filling the order doesn't have a clue what you are paying in commissions. All he knows is that he is being paid approximately $2 a trade. The rest goes for overhead and for the broker and brokerage house. If there were ever a case where you don't get what you pay for, it is probably in the brokerage business.

There's the story of the trading guru who suggested that all his clients do business with the XYZ brokerage house. The round-turn commission fee was $100. In my floor trading days, I paid just one dollar per round-turn. Once I left the floor, I traded upstairs for just $8 per round-turn. Even today, I pay only $12 per round-turn. Granted, there may be reasons why I pay these relatively low fees, but what is the justification for any trader paying above $40 per round-turn? It makes no sense to me.

I know all the arguments: The service is better, the fills are excellent, the broker holds your hand. Once you give discretion to your broker (a mistake in the first instance), she will typically charge you a higher fee because now she is calling the shots. Or you join a fund or other managed account program and, in the small print, it outlines the fee arrangement the manager has with the brokerage house. Because there are fees associated with clearing trades, a certain minimal level can be expected. Lately, I've been hearing from people who trade the E-mini S&P paying "just $20 per round-turn." Well, do the math. The E-mini is just one-fifth the size of the larger S&P, so you are really paying $100 per round-turn in terms of the large contract, the one on which I pay just $12 per round-turn. Another ploy of the brokerage community is to quote the commission in terms of just one side, as if you could buy and not sell. So a $25 commission is really a $50 commission when you take into account the notion that you are going to be taking round-turn. When it comes to commissions, you want fast executions and that's it. Shop around and you will be able to find a reasonably low commission.

You may have fallen victim to some of these pitfalls. Becoming aware of what has been holding you back can make a big difference in how you will trade in the future. I know that until you recognize and act on overcoming these common obstacles, you won't be ready to tackle the truly difficult art of trading.

PUTTING WHAT YOU KNOW INTO PRACTICE

This is the difficult part: How do you take the raw material of wanting to be a trader and turn it into a reality? I wish there were one path and one easy answer. Unfortunately, it is not quite that easy, so I'll tell you some of the things I've observed over the years and perhaps they will resonate with you.

One of the most successful traders I ever knew grew up dirt-poor in a single-parent home. He married young and started a family. One day, his wife bounced a check at the local convenience store for an inconsequential amount of money. The store owner taped the check to the cash register in his small Illinois town for everyone to see. The trader decided right then what he had to do. He called his uncle and arranged to borrow several thousand dollars, then took the train to Chicago and arranged to get on a futures exchange. He made money from the very first day. Speaking later about how he got started, he told me there was never any doubt in his mind that he would be a success.

In the early 1970s, when I lived in Los Angeles, I met someone who later became a friend. The first day I met him he told me his name and that he was a television writer. At the time, he was only a couple of years out of college and didn't have any credits as a television writer. When he wasn't writing, he would sneak into the studios and throw scripts into producers' cars. The security guards were always throwing him off the studio lots. He spent a lot of time calling up television executives and promising to messenger over a script, then he would drive his own car to the studio and drop off the script. He would then race home and call the studio executive: Did the messenger drop off the script?

Several years passed. He kept up his routine of writing and hustling. He never took no for an answer. When he finally sold his first script and it was made into a television movie, he held a big party. There was never any question in his mind that he was a television writer.

During this same period of time, a number of new faces would show up poolside at our little garden apartment complex in Los Angeles. They had all come out there with one goal in mind—to get started in a glamous career in Hollywood. After a month or two, just about all of them would leave town. Meanwhile, my friend the television writer kept writing and calling. Never once did he consider going back home. You know who became a success at his chosen career? Today, he is a producer of a number of well-known television shows.

I have another friend who lost money for years, trying to learn how to trade. His ambition was to become a floor trader. So I invited him to my annual outdoor Fourth of July party that I hold in Chicago every year. There, surrounded by floor traders, ex–floor traders, brokers, and floor-traders-turned-real-estate-brokers, he was grilled (no pun intended) by the crowd: How old are you? What's makes you think you can do this? It's a tough life, and so on. Most tried to dissuade him from doing what they had done, or had tried to do. He didn't listen to them. Today, he is one of those guys you see jumping up and down in the high-flying S&P 500 pit at the Chicago Mercantile Exchange. Not only does he love it, he makes great money. I don't think there was ever any doubt in his mind that he would be a success.

If you can see a common theme here, you would not be mistaken. Perseverance can overcome a number of shortcomings in the skills department. As Woody Allen likes to say, "Seventy percent of success is just showing up." Assuming you can muster the requisite amount of perseverance, you'll want to set up a trading plan. Here's what you'll need:

1. A brokerage account

2. Funding for brokerage account

3. Data service

4. Method of trading

These are all relatively straightforward, with the possible exception of selecting a method of trading. Nevertheless, you must think about each. You want to make certain that your funds are safe by dealing with a clearing firm of a major exchange or an IB, which stands for "introducing broker," who clears its trades with a clearing firm. In most instances, you will be asked to open your account by writing a check directly to the clearing firm. This is a good sign since it suggests your money will be held by a firm with major safeguards against financial insolvency.

We've already covered the notion of commission costs. You want to keep them low. By the way, even if you live in New York or California, you are better off dealing directly with a firm based in Chicago, assuming, of course, that you plan to trade the Chicago markets. All these firms have toll-free numbers. By dealing directly with a clearing firm, you are cutting out the middleman and paying one less layer of commission. I think I've already explained that the same broker in the trading pit will probably fill the order anyway, regardless of its origin.

The size of your account, of course, will depend on your financial circumstances. While having a relatively large account definitely has its advantages, don't think for a minute that a poorly traded, large account will do better than a well-traded, small account. If you don't know what you are doing, having more money only means you will lose a lot more. Where do you think the quip, "To make a small fortune in the futures market, start with a large fortune," comes from? Throwing money at the market is not the answer. On the other hand, having a cushion of safety certainly helps if you are going to withstand the normal rigors of trading.

I'm no expert on data services, but I would suggest that you need equipment that is suitable to your particular style of trading. If you need to look at the market only once or twice a day, you can probably get by without live data. Delayed data is readily available at a lower price than live data. Moreover, in recent years, even the exchanges have started providing free live data on the Internet. Buy what you need and what you can afford. I've met many traders who have felt that the answer to their success is in the technology. I've even known traders who have had as many as seven or eight computer monitors. Do you need all that stuff? I don't think so.

That leaves us with the selection of a method of trading. You want this decision to be tailored to your particular psychological temperament. Are you a hands-on or hands-off type of individual? If you are going to track the market only two or three times a day, then you need an approach that will try to capture the day's overall trend. It also means that you are going to have to place your stop well out of the line of fire. One benefit of this approach is that you will indeed be able to capture an entire day's trend if you are successful in picking the right direction. The downside, of course, is that this approach lacks a certain flexibility. You want to know the pluses and minuses of a style of trading before you begin. Otherwise, you will find yourself jumping from one style to another without the benefit of really capitalizing on any one approach.

As an alternative to the hands-off approach, you may want to fine-tune each trade with precision. With this approach, you will undoubtedly be capturing small profits, but with significantly much less risk. This appeals to a certain type of individual, and will require closer attention to the market. You'll want to have live data and a sophisticated software package for tracking the market. With more in-and-out trading, you'll also want to establish excellent, low-cost brokerage services with speed of execution as a main priority.

Between these extremes there are no doubt many variations. The tendency among new traders is to jump from one approach to another. I would caution against this. The best traders become experts at doing one thing well, and doing it over and over. Successful trading is very much a matter of finding a good fit between who you are and your style of trading. You want to be comfortable with what you are doing.

People often ask me if I feel they are suited to the high-stress game of trading. I know in a general sense that most people are not, but I've learned that there are some clues that suggest one person may be better suited than another. Let's begin with something we have no control over, our age. While younger people tend to have less money than people nearing retirement age, they do have time on their side, so I'll tell a young, would-be trader this: "You have a lot to gain, but relatively little to lose. The worst thing that is going to happen is you will lose a little money and you will go on to something else."

The situation, however, is quite different for someone who is nearing retirement age and wants to risk her hard-won pension money. Is this really risk capital? Can she afford to lose the money? What are her alternative sources of income?

Perhaps the best candidate is someone who had already made a substantial amount of money in another enterprise. Typically, this individual is a self-made man who has made his money in some type of entrepreneurial venture. Such an individual understands that there is no guarantee. He understands risk. Moreover, he is willing to take intelligent chances in order to reap the rewards.

The least likely good candidate, however, is the mirror opposite. She has one thing on her mind—the money. She could care less about the hard work and long hours that are required to succeed. She wants the easy solution. I once referred a would-be client of mine to a former client (I'll call him Bob) who was able to make good money in the market. When the would-be client called me back after speaking to Bob about his experience, the first thing he said was, "How long did it take Bob to start making $7,000 a week?" Now, this guy had none of Bob's qualities, including the bankroll. He thought he could make this kind of money on a virtual shoestring. I immediately told him I didn't think I could help him.

I didn't say this out of altruism. Rather, it was pure selfishness. I well knew that I would be the first one blamed when he drove into a ditch on his road to riches. Bob, who had been trading for years, had paid his dues. This wanna-be, new guy had not.

I'm reminded of an excellent movie that came out in the early eighties starring Jerry Lewis and Robert DeNiro, "The King of Comedy." Although this movie is painful to watch (which probably explains its lack of success when it first appeared), it is a brilliant portrayal of our culture's obsession with fame. DeNiro plays this untalented, cheap, stand-up comedian who fashions himself a star like Jerry Lewis, who plays a successful talk show host. DeNiro lives at home with his mother in New Jersey and pretends he is Jerry down in his basement with cutout figures of big stars. One night after Jerry Lewis finishes a show, DeNiro's character, Rupert Pumpkin, strong-arms himself into Jerry's limousine. Jerry trys to be polite and tells him he has to start in the clubs and work his way up. Finally, to get rid of him, Jerry tells Rupert to send him a tape of his monologue. This sends Pumpkin on a desperate journey to insert himself into Jerry's life at all costs, culminating in a scene where Rupert takes Jerry hostage, and the ransom is an appearance on Jerry's show. DeNiro's character has his 15 minutes of fame and is sent to prison. But later he gets a big-dollar book deal and appears on the cover of *Time* magazine, an instant celebrity who, despite being sent to prison, "stills considers Jerry a friend." Since the appearance of this fictional black comedy, we've had a host of real-life examples of fame-at-all-cost types front-paged across our newspapers. This movie's problem? It was much too real.

When Jerry starts to explain in the limousine how you have to start with the basics, Rupert dismisses him immediately. He doesn't want to hear about the hard work. He wants the brass ring, the celebrity status. There must be a gimmick that he could learn in a half hour that would make him a success. Unbelievably, the quick fix actually works and becomes, in fact, emblematic of our present culture.

What does this have to do with trading? Plenty. You are not going to become the next George Soros without hard work. The market rarely rewards inexperience. It takes time to fashion yourself a market operator, even on a small scale. There are plenty of people who would like to short-circuit the learning process. Ross Perot had a colorful phase for this type: "Big hat, no cattle!"

Throughout these pages, I've discussed the difference between the theory and the practice. It is one thing to have an intellectual appreciation of something and quite another to have a deeply felt, emotional knowledge. The most graphic illustration of this dichotomy occurred in the 1988 presidential election when CNN newsman Bernard Shaw asked Democratic candidate Michael Dukakis what he would do if his wife was raped and murdered. Instead of saying the honest thing ("I'd want to kill the sonofabitch!"), Dukakis opted for some mealymouthed, politically correct answer. That, among other things, killed his chances of winning the election.

Likewise, in the market, the theoretical answer won't do. You are going to be putting your money on the line. You must have a gut feeling that what you are doing will win the game, or you won't be able to do it. This is why hot-line services and black-box systems don't work for investors. Without an emotional connection to why they are taking a signal, investors are understandably loathe to risk their money. When a contractor builds a house, he creates a framework around which the walls will be built. Without the framework there is no house. It is the same when you trade the market. Certain events occur within the concept of a framework of how the market works. For example, today is Tuesday. The market opened strong and sold off during the day. Yesterday, which was Monday, was a very bullish day. What happened today is what should happen on a Tuesday following a strong Monday: People take profits. I know this on an emotional level. That's why I rarely want to buy on a Tuesday morning following a strong close on Monday.

Can you see why paper trading is no substitute for the real thing? I can tell you to cut short your losses until I'm blue in the face. You probably won't pay any attention until you forget to place a stop someday and go to the dentist. The pain from the drilling in your teeth that day will be the least of your pain.

When I tell you to do your buying or selling inside the consolidation, this information didn't come from a theoretical understanding of the market. I learned this from being on the wrong side of the market and trying to sell into a crowd of sellers. It is a frightening experience to be standing in the middle of the trading pit trying to sell along with a hundred other people. Where do you think the buyers are in such a situation? They are waiting for the market to bottom out so they can buy at bargain prices. There are no buyers on the way down. This is the type of experience that hits home. It is deeply felt. It is a lesson that you don't forget.

Can you see why new traders do stupid things? They think you can simply enter a sell order and get filled at the last price on the screen. The market doesn't work that way. That's why the floor traders do so well in managing risk; they understand on an emotional level what the market can do to them.

I told you about my $1,200 cup of coffee. Do you think I will ever forget that mistake of stepping out for a few moments when I should have been watching the market?

Years ago, I worked for a very successful guy who used to say, "We are doing all the right things." He knew that in time his efforts would pay off. They did. In the meantime, he kept doing the right things. You won't always be rewarded right away.

Two years ago, I had lunch with a friend who is a professional stock investor. His previous five stock selections had all made money for me. So when he told me about an African, copper-mining stock, I took notice and went out and bought 50,000 shares. I am not indifferent to my friend or to his extraordinary success. He has earned my respect. He doesn't select these stocks on a whim. He researches the financials, the background, the management, the industry. I'm certain he did his homework, not to mention his almost two-million-share commitment to this stock. Was I starting to get emotional? You bet.

Not long ago, I discovered a story in the business pages of *The New York Times*. It mentioned that the country clubs and golf courses in the copper-mining region of Africa were booming. It develops that when these industries in Africa were nationalized years ago, most of the trained management left Africa. Now that they were returning again, there'd been a boom in golfing. The caddies and other workers who profit from the country club business were very optimistic. Guess what that means for the prospects of my mining stock?

Sometimes a truly esoteric event on one side of the world can register shock waves across continents. Some twenty years ago, there was a little-noted "crop failure" off the coast of Chile. The anchovy crop had suddenly disappeared, which caused the so-called "beans in the teens" syndrome to kick off in Chicago, since soybeans were a substitute source of protein. As soybeans skyrocketed, some traders grew rich.

I know there's a lot of talk about not being emotional about the market, but I have to be emotional or I cannot pick up the phone. Do you think I'd sink all that money into mining shares if I didn't see an excellent payoff down the road? Do you think I'd load the boat on Monday morning if I didn't think the market was poised for a good rise? One needs a certain degree of confidence and enthusiasm, but this, as I've said, must be grounded in reality.

GETTING IT TOGETHER

There's a well-known saying on Wall Street that if you don't know who you are, the market is an extremely expensive place to find out. If your life up until now has been like a cork floating on a rough sea, I frankly don't think you are cut out for this activity. You have to be well-grounded. Again, I know what you are thinking: If only I could make some serious money in the market, everything would be fine. Money, ironically, won't solve a money problem.

The market is a metaphor for life. All your weaknesses, all your strengths will be magnified a hundredfold in the rough-and-tumble world of trading. If I were young and just starting out, I know that I would find a way to keep knocking on the door of a trading exchange. I wouldn't care about the pay. I'd just want to learn everything I could.

Trading teaches you that there is no downside to life. No matter what happens, you can always bounce back. After a while, it gets in your blood. You know that you can deal with whatever comes. There are countless stories of winning traders who came back from serious losses, but there are also countless stories of traders who kept throwing away money until they were ultimately ruined. Hopefully, you are someone who can learn from your experiences.

I've often asked myself why the best trades are the ones that are hardest to take. I'm not sure I have a good answer. What seems to work best is to simply enjoy the process—as opposed to trying to make things happen—and let go. We've all known people who thought the answer was in learning everything there was to know. This, however, creates only a sort of academic knowledge. How do you acquire the ineffable street smarts that enable you to outmaneuver the crowd?

Learning to trade is a cumulative process. It takes a long, long time to successfully integrate market knowledge with the need for action. Thinking too hard only makes a challenging task more difficult. How many times can you allow good opportunities to pass you by without becoming demoralized? How many times can you allow reckless behavior to sabotage your trading without wanting to give up? Far too many people are forever caught between the proverbial rock and a hard place. Given profits, they are fearful of losing them; given losses, they see an impending disaster that they are powerless to do anything about.

I have a friend who is forever letting his broker talk him out of good trades and into bad ones.

"Why do you listen to him?" I asked him one day.

"Because I don't have the experience," he replied. "I haven't been around long enough to know what I'm doing."

"Neither has he," I said.

My friend has good instincts. He is learning to identify patterns and trust his own judgment. The losses are teaching him that you don't touch a hot stove with bare hands. In a small way, he is learning to get it together as a budding trader.

Despite the chaos and confusion that often reigns in the market, the best traders have an inner Rock of Gibraltar in their personality. I've seen this quality countless times in the best of them. It is manifested in the ability not to panic, to try and size things up amid the often ongoing confusion, and to make sensible decisions.

On a cold, wintry day in January, 1986, I was scheduled to have lunch with a friend at the Merc Club, a private dining establishment at the Chicago Mercantile Exchange. As I walked over to the exchange, I wondered how he was doing because it was the day that the *Challenger* exploded off the coast of Florida. The market had broken like a rock on the news. His clerk quickly informed me that he couldn't leave the pit. I understood immediately.

Here's what happened. He had loaded the boat that morning in S&P futures when the news hit. There wasn't time to get out. The paper losses were in excess of $50,000. He didn't panic. He simply stood there and watched the market slowly gain ground. By the end of the day, he was even. Talk about not panicking. How many people would have had the fortitude to hold on?

He later told me what had happened. "There wasn't time to act. The market imply broke. I knew the news was purely emotional. So I decided to wait."

But how did he know?

With experience, one gains an inner awareness. Did you ever notice that young children never have to struggle to learn their native language? I have a friend who speaks fluent Spanish, French, and Italian—in addition to English, of course. He is so conversant in these languages that his doorman in New York thought he was from South America and restaurant owners in France think he is Italian. As someone who has struggled through high school and college Spanish, I am in awe of this ability.

"How did you learn all these languages?" I asked him one day.

"I seem to know it before I know it," he replied.

This is the same ability that seasoned traders have about the market. They know it before they know it—and that includes sensing trouble.

I suspect that you don't see this inner awareness as an important quality, but I can tell you that having the right psychological fit for trading is far more important than learning any single formula or strategy. If you feel that you are the round peg in a square hole, you need to start to observe patterns. In time, like my friend who learned to stop listening to his broker, you will begin to trust your instincts.

In my Chicago years, I knew a guy named Brian who was one of the best analysts in the bond market I'd ever seen. He could tell you where the high and the low would come in within a tick almost every day. He would spend hours waiting for the right opportunity. If he couldn't jump aboard a move just seconds before it made a fast break or rally, he didn't want the trade. Indeed, most of the time he spent scratching trades, which means he would end up selling it where he bought it, paying just the marginal exchange commission of a dollar or two. He was the ultimate scared-money player. The problem was there were precious few perfect opportunities where the risk could be eliminated entirely, so he often spent his days without taking any trades.

Brian had one other shortcoming. He hated to spend money. If you went to a restaurant, he always insisted on ordering the house wine to save a few dollars, even if he wasn't picking up the bill. He used to tell me how he always managed to get a free *Wall Street Journal* every day by waiting until someone getting off the train left one on the seat.

"Did you were wonder why," I asked him one day, "after ten years, you are still doing one-lots?"

"I've often wondered about that myself."

Money was like blood with him. You couldn't get him to entertain the thought that there was a lot more available if only he'd loosen up his tight-fisted approach to the market. Indeed, with what he knew, he could have made millions on his analytical techniques. He really could pick the highs and lows.

At the time, I would invite clients down to the exchange and take them out to lunch. This was a slow time in the market anyway and I hit upon a perfect opportunity to use Brian's knowledge.

"Look," I told him. "I have these people coming for lunch. Why don't you join us and they can profit from your insights into the market." When he realized I was also buying, he jumped at the chance. I believe it worked well for everyone.

If you see a little bit of yourself here, you know in which area you have to start working. At the other side of the risk-averse spectrum was my friend Alex, whom I knew in Los Angeles in the late seventies. Alex, who, believe it or not, was also a futures trader, loved to take his friends out to dinner and order up a storm. I used to meet him at this little Mexican place named Pancho's under the San Diego freeway overpass. In the shape of a giant sombrero, Pancho's was the ultimate Mexican dive, complete with loud jukebox music, ice-cold Mexican beer, and giant steaks. We would have these raucous dinners with the music blaring in the background and Alex would summon the waiter.

"I'll tell you what we want to do," Alex would tell him. "These steaks were so good, get us all another one." We would eat two dinners and go home stuffed.

Alex was both expansive and utterly charming. There was never a shortage of good-looking women when he was around. And, of course, he always insisted on picking up the check. He once lent me hundreds of dollars when I was desperately short of cash. I paid him back and never forgot his generosity.

When it came to his market activities, guess what kind of trader Alex was. That's right. He would swing for the fences. He never had a problem in placing his money on the line. His optimism never faded despite whatever setback he'd encountered. Moreover, he was richly rewarded when the market went his way. The good times at Pancho's were just a prelude of better times to come. He managed to acquire fast automobiles and houses overlooking the sea. It wasn't until years later that I learned the party had come to an end.

It's an old story. Leveraged to the hilt, his lifestyle collapsed like a house of cards once the money dried up. What particular event did him in, I don't really know. I just know that I was never able to experience this life in the fast lane because I was so busy just trying to survive.

Remember what I said about the Rock of Gibraltar? I don't care what your external circumstances are, inside you have to be solid. You cannot be flying high, you cannot be down in the dumps. The Greeks had it right: In all things, moderation. Not surprisingly, the Greeks also coined the word *hubris,* which means excessive pride or self-confidence. Though some people undoubtedly acquire this sin when they win in the market, the more appropriate sentiment is gratitude and humility.

By the way, the middle course, whether in trading or in life, is always the best one to choose. The reason the Greeks chose moderation as a goal to strive for is because that's what maximized happiness. That's why a leisurely candlelit dinner of shrimp and linguine, washed down by two or three glasses of a crisp, cold, dry chardonnay, is preferable to a case of Thunderbird red consumed on a sidewalk in the Bowery. More is not always better.

There's a philosophical element here, of course, that must be considered alongside the psychological. There's the medieval notion of life as a wheel; you may be down today, but tomorrow the wheel may turn and you may be on top. This is also biblical: "The first shall be last and the last shall be first." If you think these are just casual statements, you've never spent much time around the markets.

We are all very much products—and perhaps victims—of who we are and where we came from. This may be the final arbiter of exactly who wins and who loses in the market. Our circumstances are very much an accident of birth. Nevertheless, there are always those survivors who overcome whatever obstacles are placed in their path. Above all, you must not attribute market success to luck. Luck is what comes to those who persist in their chosen activity. Several years ago, I had the good "luck" to win $25,000 on a $5 ticket I purchased in the Florida lottery. Over the years, I don't think I ever met anyone who won this much money in the lottery. Here's how I did it: I played the same four-digit "Play Four" number once a month for ten years. Was I lucky? You bet. The probabilities against that number appearing were 10,000-to-1. But I put myself in the position to win by persisting. I'm not suggesting you go out and invest in lottery tickets; on the contrary, this is a notorious bad bet. I'm only suggesting that you have to make your own luck.

The lucky people are those who do what they love and have a capacity to do it well. Take any champion athlete, such as Michael Jordan or Tiger Woods, and look at their commitment to their profession. They may have been well-rewarded for what they do, but they have been concentrating on the job—not the money—since their youth. In virtually any field of endeavor, this is always the case. The genuine superstars never get there by accident. I don't know about you, but I find that I'm the luckiest when I work the hardest.

I get special satisfaction from winning profits on trades that I've been able to find in the market. I believe that winning is a combination of hard work and perseverance. There will always be those who will pretend that anyone can tame the trading challenge, that successful trading is about little more than learning three or four simple formulas. These people don't understand what trading is about. I enjoy trading because of the precise intellectual and moral challenge that it presents to me. Do I have what it takes? Do I have the market savvy? Do I have the fortitude? When I said the market is a metaphor for life, I meant it. The rewards are far more than monetary.

Index

Printed in the United States
by Baker & Taylor Publisher Services